ONCE UPON A TIME
in Great Britain

St. Martin's

Griffin

New York

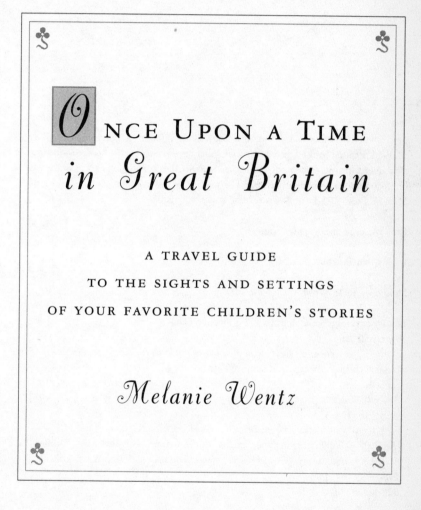

ONCE UPON A TIME
in *Great Britain*

A TRAVEL GUIDE
TO THE SIGHTS AND SETTINGS
OF YOUR FAVORITE CHILDREN'S STORIES

Melanie Wentz

For a list of permissions see page 265.

www.stmartins.com

Design by Susan Walsh

Library of Congress Cataloging-in-Publication Data
Wentz, Melanie
    Once upon a time in Great Britain : a travel guide to the sights and settings of your favorite children's stories / Melanie Wentz. — 1st ed.
        p. cm.
    Includes index.
    ISBN 0-312-28338-5
    1. Literary landmarks—Great Britain—Guidebooks. 2. Children's stories, English—Handbooks, manuals, etc. 3. Great Britain—In literature—Guidebooks. 4. Setting (Literature)—Guidebooks. 5. Great Britain—Guidebooks. I. Title.
PR109 .W46 2002
820.9'9282'0941—dc21

First Edition: August 2002

10 9 8 7 6 5 4 3 2 1

To Tom and Hannah,
for enduring the U-turns and enjoying the scones

CONTENTS

ACKNOWLEDGMENTS   xi

INTRODUCTION   xiii

Part I: *Much-Loved Classic Stories*   1

Peter Pan by James Barrie
(London, Scotland)   3

The Secret Garden by Frances Hodgson Burnett
(Kent)   15

Alice's Adventures in Wonderland and *Through the Looking-Glass*
by Lewis Carroll
(Oxford, Wales)   23

The Wind in the Willows by Kenneth Grahame
(Berkshire, London, Scotland)   35

The Chronicles of Narnia by C. S. Lewis and
The Hobbit by J. R. R. Tolkien
(Oxford)   49

The Dr. Dolittle Books by Hugh Lofting
(Wiltshire)   63

The Winnie-the-Pooh and Christopher Robin Books
by A. A. Milne
(London, East Sussex)   71

The Borrowers and *Bed-knob and Broomstick* by Mary Norton
(Bedfordshire, London)   87

The Tale of Peter Rabbit and Other Stories by Beatrix Potter
(The Lake District, London, Scotland)   95

The Legend of Robin Hood
(Nottinghamshire)   109

Robert Louis Stevenson's Writings for Children
(Scotland)   117

Mary Poppins by P. L. Travers
(London)   133

Part II: *More-Recent Favorites*   143

Watership Down by Richard Adams
(Hampshire, Berkshire)   145

Thomas the Tank Engine and Other Stories
by the Reverend Awdry
(Wales, Yorkshire, London)   153

The Paddington Bear Stories by Michael Bond
(London, Brighton)   163

Charlie and the Chocolate Factory and Other Stories
by Roald Dahl
(Birmingham, Wales, Buckinghamshire)   171

Ring of Bright Water/The Otter's Tale by Gavin Maxwell
(Scotland)   181

The Harry Potter Stories by J. K. Rowling
(London, Oxford, Gloucester, Edinburgh, and other locations)   189

The 101 Dalmations by Dodie Smith
(London, Kent)   203

Part III: *British Favorites for Americans to Enjoy*   211

Greyfriars Bobby by Eleanor Atkinson
(Scotland)   213

The Children of Green Knowe Stories by Lucy Boston
(Cambridge, London)   219

The Postman Pat Stories by John Cunliffe
(Lake District, London, Bath)   227

Cider with Rosie or *The Edge of Day* by Laurie Lee
(The Cotswolds)   233

The Railway Children and Other Stories by E. Nesbit
(Kent, South Yorkshire)   241

Swallows and Amazons and Other Stories by Arthur Ransome
(The Lake District)   251

BIBLIOGRAPHY   263
PERMISSIONS   265
INDEX   267

$\mathcal{A}$CKNOWLEDGMENTS

I AM EXTREMELY GRATEFUL TO THE PEOPLE WHO ENCOURAGED me in the beginning when this idea was just a tiny seedling taking root, especially Isabel Bradburn and Bonnie Ross. My sister, Lisa Wentz, was a terrific resource and a cheerleader the whole way through. I am also so grateful to friends in the UK who contributed ideas and enthusiasm, especially Catherine Grant and Huw Davies, Heather McMillan, David Goldberg, Charlotte Villiers, and Tony Prosser. William Plowden and the 1998–99 Atlantic Fellows in Public Policy and their families contributed ideas and interest when they were needed most. And special thanks to Bob Day for all his hospitality and good cheer.

For ongoing advice, help, and encouragement, I want to thank Kate Stacy, Sara Glaser, Marc Freedman, Dave and Amy Rowe, Marty Fleisher, Alice Fishman, and Anne Cheng. Andrew Feldman, Gabriel Rowe, and the Davies brothers were very generous with materials from their collections.

Joanna Jacobs at St. Martin's Press, Paige Wheeler at the Creative Media Agency, and Amy Kossow deserve special thanks for their expertise and enthusiasm. Thanks also to Christopher and Diana Awdry and Diana Boston for their time and input. The Glasgow Public Library, the Mitchell Library, the Oakland Public Library, and California Lawyers for the Arts were wonderful resources.

I also want to thank my father and mother, Fred and Mani Wentz, for introducing me to all these stories when I was young. They've been such good lifelong companions!

Finally and most importantly, huge thanks to my husband, Tom Long, for his patience, understanding, and help all the way through and to my daughter, Hannah Long, for bringing me back to these wonderful books and for her generous offer to illustrate this entire book for me.

Introduction

As our family prepared for a trip to Britain, I searched through travel book sections in local bookstores hoping to find a guide that would help me locate the Britain that was alive in my imagination: Mary Poppins's London, Pooh Bear's Hundred Akre Wood, or Charlie's chocolate factory. The best I could come up with was fairly limited information about Beatrix Potter and Robert Louis Stevenson that focused on their lives not their stories. There were excellent literary guides, but they were firmly focused on adult books and authors.

We were embarking on a year-long stay in Britain, so it seemed a good opportunity to research and write the book I'd hoped to find. And many miles and rolls of film later, here it is. *Once Upon a Time in Great Britain: A Travel Guide to Favorite Children's Stories* explores classic British stories, such as *Alice's Adventures in Wonderland, The Tale of Peter Rabbit,* and *Winnie-the-Pooh,* as well as more-modern favorites like *The 101 Dalmations* and *Charlie and the Chocolate Factory.* It also includes books that are much-loved in Britain but not as well-known in the United States, such as *The Children of Green Knowe* stories by Lucy Boston (set in a Norman mansion outside Cambridge that is open to visitors) and Arthur Ransome's *Swallows and Amazons* (set in the Lake District of Cumbria). This book's primary focus is on visiting places and activities connected to well-loved stories and their characters, but it also includes information about visiting interesting places associated with the authors' lives. There is a brief biographical sketch of each author and, where possible, information about where the original artwork and manuscripts can be seen. Most chapters include a section of related activities that will appeal especially to children. I've also tried to pro-vide interesting options for anyone who wants to travel a bit off the beaten path, from the Western Highlands of Scotland to a small village in the Midlands to a forest south of London. For parents trying to find activities that will be engaging and fun for their children and closely linked with the rich literary history of Britain, this book will be a great resource. For adults who grew up on *The 101 Dalmatians, The Wind in the Willows,* and *Mary Poppins,* this book hopes to provide a new dimension to their travel plans in Britain.

Our year in Britain involved a lot of travel from our home base in Glasgow. Visiting places connected with great children's stories turned out to be a great way to see parts of Britain off the main tourist trail. When we had a couple of hours waiting between trains in Gloucester, we sought out the house Beatrix Potter used for her illustrations of *The Tailor of Gloucester.* A trip to Oxford found us meandering out of town to the tiny village of Binsey for a picnic beside an ancient well that inspired Lewis Carroll to create the "treacle well" in Alice's adventures. Two weeks in the Western Highlands of Scotland were highlighted by a visit to a nature reserve for otters and a hike down to the isolated beach where Gavin Maxwell lived and wrote *Ring of Bright Water.* The visits were delightful and memorable, and although visiting with a child meant we moved at a slower pace, we got to take everything in through her eyes as well.

For adults and children alike, the joys of traveling are linked to the imagination. Often the excitement of going to a given place is built on images from stories and movies we have loved. The challenge, especially when traveling with children, is to connect the place they are visiting with those imagined scenes in a way that is fun and meaningful. My hope is that *Once Upon a Time in Great Britain* will provide an enjoyable way to do just that for adults who have loved these stories since childhood and for children who love them as part of their growing world.

Much-Loved Classic Stories

I

Peter Pan
by J. M. Barrie

Mrs. Darling first heard of Peter Pan when she was tidying up her children's minds. It is the nightly custom of every good mother after her children are asleep to rummage in their minds and put things straight for next morning. . . . Occasionally in her travels through her children's minds Mrs. Darling found things she could not understand, and of these quite the most perplexing was the word Peter. She knew of no Peter, and yet he was here and there in John and Michael's minds, while Wendy's began to be scrawled all over with him. The name stood out in bolder letters than any of the other words, and as Mrs. Darling gazed she felt that it had an oddly cocky appearance. . . .

—*Peter Pan*, 1928

A SPRINKLING OF FAIRY DUST AND OFF THEY FLY OVER THE rooftops of London to Neverland. Wendy, Michael, and John Darling slip away with Peter Pan and Tinker Bell to an enchanted place where children never grow up. They play with mermaids, make friends with Indians, and live in a cozy underground home that can only be reached by a secret passage through a tree trunk. The menacing Captain Hook and his band of pirates lurk about and provide excellent enemies to overcome.

Alas, there is no way to visit Neverland, but it is possible to enjoy the place that inspired J. M. Barrie as he was writing the original play, Hyde Park and Kensington Gardens. Barrie himself paid to have a statue of Peter Pan placed in Hyde Park, and it makes a wonderful excuse to wander around one of the world's great urban parks. A new playground dedicated to the late Princess Diana features fanciful play areas inspired by *Peter Pan*.

Barrie's birthplace, the charming village of Kirriemuir, is nestled into the hillside in a picturesque area north of Edinburgh, right down the road from one of Scotland's most famous castles. The modest house in which Barrie was born has been restored to its original state and houses a display about Barrie's life and the early stage productions of *Peter Pan*.

A Brief Biography of J. M. Barrie

Nothing that happens after we are twelve
matters very much.—*J. M. Barrie*

James M. Barrie was born in **Kirriemuir, Fife, Scotland,*** in 1860, the ninth of ten children. His father was a handloom weaver, his mother the daughter of a stonemason. When James was

*NOTE: Items in boldface are described in detail in the following pages.

six, his thirteen-year-old brother, David, died in a skating accident. David had been his mother's great favorite, and she never fully recovered from her grief. Barrie later wrote that he never was able to make his mother forget that pain for "when I became a man, he was still a boy of 13." From *Peter Pan* to the title of Barrie's final play, *The Boy David,* the boy who never grew up surfaces repeatedly in Barrie's work.

The large family lived in a tiny row house that also housed his father's loom and yarn shop. Barrie's earliest success as a writer came from stories about his childhood in the town of "Thrums," a thinly disguised Kirriemuir. ("Thrums" are short strands of thread that are left over in the weaving process.)

From the age of eight, Barrie was sent away to school, first to **Glasgow** and then to Dumfriesshire in southern Scotland. He lived with his older brother Alexander, who taught at both schools. Barrie attended the University of Edinburgh from 1878 to 1882, but he had a lonely time of it. At barely five feet tall, he found himself feeling isolated from the social life of his peers. Later in life, after his literary success, Barrie returned to the University of Edinburgh in 1909 to receive an honorary doctorate and in 1930 to be given the honorary position of chancellor of the university.

Upon finishing his university degree, Barrie spent a short stint as a journalist in Nottingham and then moved on to London to pursue work as a novelist and playwright. He had his first play produced in 1891, and several successful plays followed, including *Mary Rose* and *The Admirable Crichton.* At one point three plays by Barrie were running in London at the same time.

Barrie married an actress, Mary Ansell, in 1894 in Kirriemuir. Their marriage was not a happy one. It ended in divorce in 1909 after Barrie became aware that Mary was having an affair. They had no children.

Barrie's success afforded him a pleasant life in London living near **Kensington Gardens,** where he walked each day with his Saint Bernard dog, Porthos. On one of these walks he made friends with three young brothers, George, Jack, and Peter, the children of Sir Arthur and Sylvia Llewelyn Davies. Barrie often walked with the boys in the park or visited them at their home. Eventually Barrie became almost a member of their family, spending summer vacations with them, taking them to plays, and seeing them on almost a daily basis. The stories and games they made up together on these occasions grew into a series of stories about a boy named Peter Pan. Porthos found a place in the stories as the children's nanny. These stories evolved into a play, *Peter Pan or the Boy Who Would Not Grow Up*, which was first produced in 1904. It was an instant success. Peter Pan eventually found his way into several books, including *Peter Pan in Kensington Gardens* (1906), *Peter and Wendy* (1911), and *Peter Pan or the Boy Who Would Not Grow Up* (1928).

In 1912, Barrie commissioned a **Peter Pan statue** to be placed in **Kensington Gardens, London,** where it still stands today.

When Arthur and Sylvia Davies died of cancer within three years of each other, Barrie adopted their five sons (two of whom, Nico and Michael, had been born since Barrie first befriended the boys), thereby gaining a family. A great deal of tragedy touched their lives. One of the boys, George, was killed in 1915, a casualty of World War I. Michael, Barrie's favorite, drowned in the Thames near Oxford a few weeks before his twenty-first birthday. He drowned in still water with a close friend in what may have been a double suicide. Barrie wrote: "All the world is different to me now. Michael was pretty much my world." And in 1960, long after Barrie's death, Peter Llewellyn Davies killed himself by jumping in front of one of London's subway trains. A headline read: "The Boy Who Never Grew Up Is Dead."

Barrie continued to write successful plays on into the 1920s. At the age of seventy-seven, he wrote his last play, *The Boy David.* He was too ill to attend any of the performances of the work, which turned out to be his least successful play.

Barrie died in June 1937. He is buried in the cemetery overlooking the town of **Kirriemuir,** his birthplace. Shortly before his death, he signed over all the royalties for *Peter Pan* to the **Great Ormond Street Hospital for Children** in London. A special Act of Parliament continued this arrangement after the copyright expired in 1988. The hospital received over half a million dollars alone from the Steven Spielberg movie *Hook.*

A Brief Biography of Arthur Rackham

Born in London in 1867, Arthur Rackham studied art in evening courses at Lambeth School of Art for seven years, from age seventeen to twenty-four, while working in an insurance office. In 1892, he found work as a staff artist for a newspaper, and he began to illustrate books. His reputation for imaginative and fantastical artwork began to build with the publication of his illustrations for *Grimm's Fairy Tales* in 1900. His illustrations accompanied James Barrie's *Peter Pan in Kensington Gardens* (1906) and a 1907 version of Lewis Carroll's *Alice's Adventures in Wonderland.* He continued to illustrate classic works and children's books throughout the rest of his career until his death in 1939. His final work, illustrations for *The Wind in the Willows,* by Kenneth Grahame, was published posthumously. Rackham's first-edition books and original artwork continue to be popular with collectors internationally.

Places Connected with the Story of Peter Pan

HYDE PARK/KENSINGTON GARDENS, LONDON

Hyde Park and Kensington Gardens form one continuous expanse of parkland in the heart of London to the northwest of the Buckingham Palace area. The western half of the park, between Kensington Palace and a lake called the Serpentine, is known as Kensington Gardens. Kensington Palace was the birthplace and childhood home of Queen Victoria and the residence of Princess Diana before her death.

Barrie spent his many years in London living close by Kensington Gardens at various addresses (see below). Strolls through the park were part of his daily routine, and as mentioned earlier, he began several significant friendships with children there. In 1906, James Barrie published a book titled *Peter Pan in Kensington Gardens.* It was a reworking of an earlier book, *The Little White Bird,* and included an early version of the Peter Pan story. In that version Peter is a baby who flies away from his mother when he is just seven days old and goes to live in

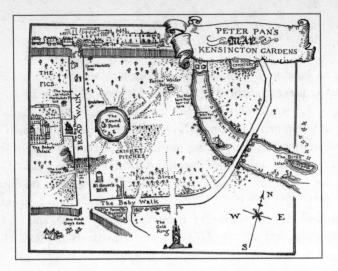

Kensington Gardens. He lives on an island in the Serpentine and sails across the water each evening in a boat made from a thrush's nest to play in the park once the gates are closed. Arthur Rackham did the gorgeous illustrations. The first chapter of the book is a charming tour of the gardens, which gives a flavor of how it might have been to stroll around them as a child with James Barrie.

> . . . I shall pass on hurriedly to the Round Pond, which is the wheel that keeps all the Gardens going. It is round because it is in the very middle of the Gardens, and when you are come to it you never want to go any farther. You can't be good all the time at the Round Pond, however much you try. You can be good in the Broad Walk all the time, but not at the Round Pond, and the reason is that you forget, and, when you remember, you are so wet that you may as well be wetter.
>
> —James Barrie, *Peter Pan in Kensington Gardens*, 1906

In addition to the Llewellyn Davies boys, Barrie had another child friend, a little girl aged four named Margaret. She called Barrie her "friendy," but her childish pronunciation turned it into "wendy." Barrie used this as the name for his heroine in the stage version of *Peter Pan,* a name he invented. Sadly, little Margaret died at age six.

In 1912, James Barrie commissioned a statue of Peter Pan by Sir George Frampton. It was based on photos that Barrie had taken of Michael Llewellyn Davies dressed in a Peter Pan costume. Barrie had it erected in secret one night in Kensington Gardens so it would seem to have appeared by magic. It is located at the spot where the baby Peter Pan landed each evening on the shore of the Serpentine (see map, page 8). The base of the statue is a clamor of fairies and animals. It's a good spot for feeding the ducks or having a picnic and reading Barrie's story about Peter Pan's babyhood.

London is a fascinating city, but its crowds and noise can be overwhelming for travelers of any age. A walk through the park to the areas that inspired James Barrie and his young friends to invent Peter Pan can be a relaxing break for adults and an opportunity for children to run around and be "mad-dog," as Barrie terms it. Toy boats, formal or informal, can be sailed on the Round Pond. The newly restored, gold-covered Albert Memorial, Queen Victoria's tribute to her husband, is a stunning sight at the edge of the park across the road from the Royal Albert Hall. The Household Cavalry ride out from the Hyde Park Barracks every morning at 10:30 A.M. on their way to Whitehall.

The closest tube stop is Lancaster Gate on the north side of the park, but there are several other stops on other tube lines that will get you quite close.

Elsewhere in the United Kingdom

KIRRIEMUIR, FIFE, SCOTLAND

James Barrie was born in the village of Kirriemuir. It's worth a visit in its own right as a lovely Scottish village with its red-stone houses and winding lanes; but it also offers Barrie's birthplace/museum, grave, and the unusual gift Barrie bestowed upon the town. Kirriemuir is also just five miles down the road from Glamis Castle, the setting for *Macbeth* and the childhood home of the Queen Mother. It is pictured on some Scottish banknotes (pound notes issued by Scottish banks as opposed to English ones).

Barrie lived the first twelve years of his life in a tiny four-room house at 9 Brechin Road, also known as Lilybank, in Kirriemuir. Today the home is refurnished as it would have been when Barrie was a child. An adjoining house has been set up as an exhibit on Barrie's life, complete with the original Peter Pan costume from the 1904 play. One unexpected but compelling momento on display is a letter from Barrie's friend, the explorer Capt. Robert Scott. As he and his expedition party lay dying in the heart of Antarctica, Scott asked Barrie to take care of his widow and child. (Barrie made good on his friend's request.) The washhouse in back, which was used by all the tenants on the street in Barrie's day, served as a stage for plays Barrie created as a child. It is said to be the inspiration for the house the lost boys built for Wendy in Neverland.

In 1929, Barrie gave an unusual gift to the town of Kirriemuir: a camera obscura. This device displays a panoramic view of an external scene inside a darkened room, using only mirrors and lenses. Barrie's camera obscura provides a perfect 360-degree view of the Vale of Strathmore. The scene is reflected onto a saucer-shaped viewing table through a mirror and lens located on the roof. Housed in a cricket club at the very top of the hill behind Kirriemuir, the camera obscura is still in operation today and open to the public. On a clear day, mountains as far as fifty miles away can be seen.

Barrie is buried in the cemetery on the hill above his birthplace, and his grave site affords a lovely view of the valley. He was offered a spot in Westminster Abbey in London, but he chose to come back to Kirriemuir to be buried with his parents and siblings.

Barrie's birthplace is run by the National Trust and is open to the public. There is a small gift shop and a quaint tearoom. It is open Easter weekend and from May through the beginning of October, Monday to Saturday, 11:00 A.M.–5:30 P.M.; and Sundays, 1:30–5:30 P.M. There is a modest admission fee. For more information, call (01575) 572646.

The camera obscura is open for Easter weekend and from May through September daily from 1:30 to 4:30 P.M. Demonstrations are held every twenty minutes. There is free parking, a picnic area, and a good playground. Admission is £1.50. During open hours, call (0374) 737036 for information. At other times, call (01307) 460461.

To reach Kirriemuir by car, drive north from Edinburgh to Dundee on the M90 via Perth. From Dundee, follow the A90 to the A926. Follow the signs to Glamis Castle and continue down the road for five miles past the castle.

Other Places Connected with J. M. Barrie's Life

CORNER OF LEINSTER TERRACE AND BAYSWATER ROAD, LONDON

James Barrie lived in the modest house on the corner from 1901 to 1909 during the years he was writing the play and early versions of *Peter Pan*. It sits across Bayswater Road from the Porchester Terrace Gate to the park, and it's easy to picture the little man walking the big Saint Bernard across the road each afternoon.

The closest tube stop is Queensway. Walk up Bayswater Road toward the Marble Arch for four blocks to reach Leinster Terrace.

GREAT ORMOND STREET HOSPITAL FOR CHILDREN, LONDON

Although James Barrie had no particular connection to the hospital, he left the copyright for *Peter Pan* to it in his will. The copyright was then extended into perpetuity by an Act of Parliament, making it the copyright that never grows up. Over the years the proceeds from the sales of the book, play, and movies have funded a substantial amount of the good work done by this institution, including a Barrie Wing. Their benefactor is remembered by a playful statue of Peter Pan at the front entrance and a Peter Pan Café inside, with the whole cast of characters on big banners on the walls.

Visiting a hospital isn't on most people's list of what to do in London, but if you find yourself in Bloomsbury, there is one feature that makes this hospital worth a stop. The Chapel of St. Christopher was built in 1875 and moved en bloc to the new hospital, which was contructed in the 1980s. It's a stunning little Byzantine jewel box designed by Edward Middleton Barry. Oscar Wilde called it "the most delightful private chapel in London." There is a plaque on the wall commemorating James Barrie's gift to the hospital as well.

The hospital archives across the street at 55 Great Ormond Street are open to the public. They have a small display of Peter Pan items, including items from the original stage production. The archives have nothing for sale, however. Ring the bell for entrance. Telephone: (207) 405-9200, X5920. Open Monday to Friday, 10:30–4:00 P.M.

GLASGOW ACADEMY, GLASGOW, SCOTLAND

Barrie studied at the academy from the age of eight until he transferred to Dumfries Academy in Dumfriesshire. His brother Alexander was the classics master at Glasgow Academy. They lived at 5 Burnbank Terrace nearby. The academy continues to be a private school for primary and secondary students. It is located on the Great Western Road on the banks of the river Kelvin in Glasgow, just across the bridge from the Kelvinbridge underground station.

Places to See Original Artwork/Manuscripts

SCOTTISH NATIONAL PORTRAIT GALLERY, EDINBURGH

Barrie's portrait hangs on the second floor of the museum. He was a man of almost elfen stature. George Bernard Shaw said of Barrie after they both attended their good friend Thomas Hardy's funeral, "I looked very well myself, but Barrie, blast him, looked far the most effective. He made himself look especially small." In this rather eerie portrait, Barrie looks very small and alone.

Admission to the gallery is free. Open Monday to Saturday,

10:00–5:00; Sunday, 2:00–5:00. Address: Corner of Queen Street and St. Andrew Street in New Town, Edinburgh.

THE BEINECKE RARE BOOK AND MANUSCRIPT LIBRARY, YALE UNIVERSITY, NEW HAVEN, CONNECTICUT

The Beinecke Rare Book and Manuscript Library at Yale houses the largest collection of Barrie's papers and original manuscripts, including the original manuscript for *Peter Pan,* several of the original Arthur Rackham illustrations for *Peter Pan in Kensington Gardens,* and costume drawings for the original stage production of *Peter Pan.* The materials are available for research purposes only and are not on display. Telephone: (203) 432-2972.

Other Activities for Children Who Love Peter Pan

DIANA, PRINCESS OF WALES MEMORIAL PLAYGROUND, KENSINGTON GARDENS, LONDON

Any *Peter Pan* fan under the age of ten will not want to miss this playground. Built as a memorial to the late Princess Diana, the playground has a full-scale pirate ship complete with rigging to climb, a mermaid cove with water spouting out of the rocks to keep the mermaids comfortable, and a teepee area to shelter the brave Tiger Lily. There is also a treehouse to explore and an area given over to making music featuring a large, hanging xylophone. A special area is provided for children under three. The café next door has a good, inexpensive lunch menu and outdoor seating.

The Royal Parks have put together the Diana, Princess of Wales Memorial Walk, which leads through four of central London's parks, highlighting areas connected to the princess's life. The playground is one stop on the walk, which will also lead you past the Peter Pan statue if you choose to follow it. Brochures entitled "A Walk for Diana" are available at park entrances.

The playground is located in the northwest corner of Kensington Gardens at the top of the Broad Walk just off Bayswater Road. The closest tube stop is Queensway. Notting Hill tube stop is also close by.

BRITISH AIRWAYS LONDON EYE NEAR WESTMINSTER BRIDGE, LONDON

You may not spot Neverland, but you will "fly" above the spires and rooftops of London by taking a spin on the London Eye. Built as part of the millennium celebration, the giant white wheel looms large on the south bank of the Thames. One circuit on the Eye lasts thirty minutes and rises to a height of 450 feet, providing great views without the need for fairy dust.

The London Eye web site (www.ba-londoneye.com) offers a webcam that gives a "real-time" picture from the Eye and changes positions every sixty seconds.

Tickets must be booked in advance, and you must arrive during the half hour before your "flight time." Make reservation more than three days in advance by calling (0870) 5000-600. You may also purchase tickets in advance or on the same day in the County Hall Building next door. Admission is £9.50/adults, £5/five–fifteen years old, £7.50/seniors; children under five ride free. The Eye is in operation from 9:00 A.M. to 10:00 P.M. from April 1 through September 10, and from 10:00 A.M. to 6:00 P.M. from September 11 through March 31. It is closed Christmas Day.

The closest tube stop is Westminster (a five-minute walk across the Thames) or Waterloo.

THE SECRET GARDEN

by Frances Hodgson Burnett

❧ It was the sweetest, most mysterious-looking place anyone could imagine. The high walls which shut it in were covered with the leafless stems of climbing roses, which were so thick that they were matted together. . . . There were other trees in the garden, and one of the things which made the place look strangest and loveliest was that climbing roses had run all over them and swung down long tendrils which made light swaying curtains, and here and there they had caught at each other . . . and had crept from one tree to another and made lovely bridges of themselves. . . . It was different from any other place she had ever seen in her life.

—*The Secret Garden*, 1911

WHEN MARY LENNOX TURNS THE KEY IN THE LOCK TO OPEN a hidden gate and enter a neglected garden, she begins a process that unlocks her own heart and plants the seeds of growth and reconciliation in the gloomy world she inhabits. The magic power of nurturing living things and connecting with nature pulses through the story. *The Secret Garden*'s depiction of personal transformation through contact with nature seemed to strike a chord with readers at the beginning of the twenty-first century, and its popularity shows no signs of abating.

The garden that inspired the story has lost its wildness, but it remains a charming English walled garden. It is attached to an historic estate in a beautiful area of Kent, about an hour south of London by car. Frances Hodgson Burnett discovered the garden thanks to the help of a robin who befriended her and who eventually made his way into her book. The little hut where Burnett wrote remains intact in a corner of the restored garden.

A Brief Biography of Frances Hodgson Burnett

I love to dig. I love to kneel down on the grass at the edge of a flower bed and pull out the weeds fiercely and throw them into a heap by my side. I love to fight with those who can spring up again almost in a night and taunt me. I tear them up by the roots again and again, and when at last after many days, perhaps, it seems as if I had beaten them for a time at least, I go away feeling like an army with banners.

—Frances Hodgson Burnett

Frances Hodgson was born in Cheetham, Manchester, in 1849, the third of five children. She loved stories above all else and claimed to have begun reading on her own by age three. Her father, who owned and ran a furniture store, died of apoplexy when Frances was four. Her mother struggled to keep the store going while raising five children. By the time Frances was fifteen, Manchester's economy was falling apart due to the lack of cotton imports caused by the Civil War in America. Mrs. Hodgson sold the store, and the family sailed from Liverpool to Quebec. They traveled by train to Knoxville, Tennessee, where Frances's uncle owned a dry goods store. The family moved into a log cabin in the town of New Market, Tennessee, which Frances described as "a curious little village—one unpaved street of wooden houses, some painted white and some made of logs, but with trees everywhere, and forests and hills shutting it in from the world."

Frances gloried in being part of what seemed to her a real-life adventure into the exotic wilds of America. She submitted her first story to a publisher in 1867, at age seventeen, but it was sent back to her because the editors thought it seemed too British to be original. Frances promptly submitted another, purely American, story, and the publisher ended up buying both stories for thirty-five dollars. Thus began an extremely prolific writing career that allowed Frances to earn her own living and eventually to become a very wealthy woman.

In 1873, Frances married Swan Burnett, a neighbor who was just beginning his career as an eye doctor. Their first son, Lionel, was born in 1874. The following spring they moved to Paris and lived in a small apartment near the Champs Elysees. A second son, Vivian, was born in 1876. Struggling financially, the family moved back to the United States to Washington, D.C., where they settled in at 1215 "I" Street. Frances began to write the first of several mildly successful adult novels. Two of these were adapted as plays in New York.

However, her first real success came in 1886 with the publication of her first book for children, *Little Lord Fauntleroy*. The rags-to-riches story of a working-class American boy who suddenly inherits a British lordship remained popular well into the next century. It became a hit play in 1888 in both New York and London, and mothers began dressing their sons in "Little Lord Fauntleroy" suits. Movies of the story were made in 1914, 1921, 1936, and 1980. Burnett eventually earned over one hundred thousand dollars from the story, which made her a wealthy woman for her time. In 1936, movie producer David O. Selznick funded a plaque for the wall of the Burnetts' house in Washington, D.C., which reads: "On this site fifty years ago, the deathless classic *Little Lord Fauntleroy* was written."

Two years later, in 1888, Frances published her second children's book, which has also remained a favorite, *Sara Crewe, or, What Happened at Miss Minchin's.* The book was revised in 1905 and renamed *A Little Princess.* This was more of a riches-to-rags-to-riches story about a little rich girl sent to a London boarding school. Her father dies, the family money appears to be gone, and suddenly Sara Crewe is demoted to being a mistreated servant at the same school. In the end a mysterious neighbor befriends Sara and helps her regain her fortune.

After many years of unhappy marriage, Frances and Swan Burnett filed for divorce in 1895. She married Stephen Townsend, an actor who was ten years her junior, in 1899. This marriage also turned sour rather quickly. This second marriage and subsequent divorce gave Frances a reputation for scandal and independent thinking that she shared with another popular children's writer of the day, Edith Nesbit. Both women, as it turned out, also shared a love of the same area of Kent, where they lived within twenty miles of each other. (See chapter on *The Railway Children* by E. Nesbit, page 241.)

Frances periodically returned to England for extended stays. Between 1893 and 1913, she crossed the Atlantic twenty times. Her longest British residence was at **Great Maytham Hall** in Kent, which she rented from 1898 to 1907. During her stay, she discovered and restored an old walled garden that had fallen into disuse. This became the inspiration for *The Secret Garden,* published in 1911. (Oddly enough, Edith Nesbit wrote a book titled *The Wonderful Garden,* which also came out in 1911.) Burnett's story tells of a lonely, unpleasant little girl who finds a forgotten garden with the help of a robin. She and an older local boy bring the garden back to life and, in the process, heal both her loneliness and her sickly cousin. This book was a success but not on the scale of *Little Lord Fauntleroy.* However, over the years it has come to be considered Burnett's best work. It was made into a movie in 1949 and again in 1993, was filmed twice for television in 1975 and 1987, and became a Tony Award–winning musical on Broadway and in London in the 1990s.

After leaving Great Maytham Hall, Frances bought land at Plandome, Long Island, New York, overlooking Manhasset Bay. She built a large estate, where she remained for the rest of her life. She continued writing and gardening until her death in 1924. She is buried at God's Acre, Roslyn, Long Island.

Places Connected with The Secret Garden

There had been snow even in Kent and the park and garden were white. I threw on my red frieze garden cloak and went down the flagged terrace and the Long Walk through the walled gardens to the beloved place. (My robin came.) We have been too near to each other—nearer than human beings are. "I love you and love you and love you—little soul." Then I went out of the Rose Garden. I shall never go into it again.

—Frances Hodgson Burnett describing her last visit to Great Maytham Hall, 1907

GREAT MAYTHAM HALL, ROLVENDEN, KENT

The current Great Maytham Hall was rebuilt in 1909 just after Frances Hodgson Burnett had left it for good. It's an impressive building of red brick but altogether too warm and welcoming to capture the feeling of *The Secret Garden*'s Misselthwaite

Manor. The hall is surrounded by lovely green lawns and grand old trees, far too gracious and gentle to remind anyone of the desolate Yorkshire moors that Mary Lennox and Dickon explored. It's really only in the walled Secret Garden itself that the connection is made. The old door that Frances Hodgson Burnett discovered under the ivy, perhaps with the help of her robin friend, has been bricked up but can still be seen. After the garden was restored, Burnett came here often to write in a small gazebo that still stands in one corner. It is a civilized garden now with an arbor and paved paths and, alas, very few roses.

The eighteen acres of grounds at Great Maytham Hall offer a sweeping view out over the Kent countryside. One old, multitrunked lime tree on the front lawn was a particular favorite of Burnett, who believed it had a magical effect if you kept one of its leaves in your pocket.

Great Maytham Hall is now owned by the Country Houses Association, which restored the building after it had been abandoned in the 1950s. It has been renovated to serve as apartments for active senior citizens. The house itself is occasionally open to visitors in the summer. Call for exact dates (telephone number below). The grounds and gardens are open Wednesday and Thursday afternoons from 2:00 to 5:00 P.M. from May through September. There is a small admission fee.

Rolvenden is about thirty-five miles south of London. Take the M25 (London Ring Road) to the M20 toward Dover. At junction 9 (Ashford), follow the A28 toward Tenterden. Rolvenden is six miles beyond Tenterden. Alternately, follow the A21 south from the M25, passing Royal Tunbridge Wells. Take the A268 east until it intersects the A28. Follow the A28 east to Rolvenden.

Maytham Road turns off from the A28 in the middle of Rolvenden just by the church. Follow Maytham Road for one-half mile. Great Maytham Hall is on the right. There is parking at the hall. Telephone: (01580) 241346.

Other Activities for Children Who Love The Secret Garden

THE MANOR HOUSE, HEMINGFORD GREY, CAMBRIDGESHIRE

The gardens surrounding the Manor House at Hemingford Grey have the magical feeling that they are a special haven for children, just as Lucy Boston described them in her series of books about "Green Knowe." Although not a walled garden as described in *The Secret Gar-*

den, it has many of the same qualities as Burnett's fictional retreat. At the Manor House, topiary figures are hidden in different corners of the garden, with a section of giant chess figure topiaries between the house and the River Great Ouse. The garden fans off in every direction from the ancient Manor House, creating areas that feel private and perfect for pretend games. Hemingford Grey is located near the town of Huntingdon, which is sixteen miles northwest of Cambridge. If you are traveling by car, it takes about an hour and a quarter from London or twenty minutes from Cambridge. Follow the signs for Hemingford Grey off the A14. Once in the village, follow the small signs to the Manor House. Park on High Street near The Cock Freehouse and take the peaceful walk along the river to the garden gate. There is limited parking for the disabled at the house. By train, travel from Kings Cross station in London to Huntingdon and then take a taxi for the four-mile trip to Hemingford Grey. The No. 5 bus from Cambridge stops in Hemingford Grey.

See the Lucy Boston chapter, page 221, for more-detailed information about the Manor House at Hemingford Grey. Diana Boston, Lucy's daughter-in-law, continues to live in the house and schedules and guides the tours. It is necessary to make an appointment to visit. Telephone: 01480-463-134. Fax: 10480-465-026. Admission: £4.00 per person.

THE FAIRYLAND TRUST

Mary Lennox's secret garden had a special magic to it when she discovered it wild and overgrown after many years of neglect. The Fairyland Trust is a new organization that intends to identify and protect untouched areas in the British countryside that retain a similar magical feeling. The trust was launched in 2001 by three conservation-minded mothers who were tired of seeing the countryside gobbled up by developers and who wanted to preserve places to stimulate children's imaginations. In addition to protecting natural areas, their organization aims to buy land that has been damaged and replant it with wild trees and plants to create new "Fairylands." Their hope is that children can come to these and older, more established sites to observe the flowers and trees, make wings and wands for themselves, and connect with an older, wilder world that is disappearing. They are currently soliciting suggestions of places people identify as "magical" in the British countryside. They've posted a map on their web site of "special fairy places" all around Britain. Although they will not be actively publicizing these places, their hope is that people will enjoy them quietly.

To contact the Fairyland Trust, write to P.O. Box 21, Holt, Norfolk NR25 7XR. Telephone: (01263) 741-537. Web site: http://freespace. virgin.net/sarahj.wise/home.html.

Kent & East Sussex Railway, Tenterden, Kent

If you are planning to visit the setting that inspired Frances Hodgson Burnett's *The Secret Garden* in Kent, you may also want to enjoy a ride on the Kent & East Sussex Railway, a steam railway that originates in nearby Tenterden. Take the A28 northeast from Rolvenden about six miles to Tenterden. Follow the signs from the High Street in Tenterden. Trains run every weekend from April through October, every day in July and August. The line passes through seven miles of beautiful, rolling countryside. Parking is free. Telephone: (01580) 765155.

ALICE'S ADVENTURES IN WONDERLAND *and* THROUGH THE LOOKING-GLASS

by Lewis Carroll

❧ . . . Alice started to her feet, for it flashed across her mind that she had never before seen a rabbit with either a waistcoat-pocket, or a watch to take out of it, and burning with curiosity, she ran across the field after it, and fortunately was just in time to see it pop down a large rabbit-hole under the hedge. In another moment, down went Alice after it, never once considering how in the world she was to get out again.

—*Alice's Adventures in Wonderland,* 1865

ALICE NO SOONER GETS TO THE BOTTOM OF THE RABBIT HOLE than she is nibbling and drinking her way into alternately giant and tiny sizes, chatting with a cat that keeps disappearing right before her eyes, baby-sitting a baby pig, taking tea at a mad tea party, seeking help from a hookah-smoking caterpillar, and playing croquet using flamingos and hedgehogs as mallets and balls. It's a wild and witty story that has remained a favorite of children and adults for over 135 years. What kind of a person and what kind of a setting could have produced such a story in the heart of Victorian England?

The surprising answer is a shy, stuttering math professor in Oxford, the graceful, sedate intellectual center of England. On a warm July afternoon in 1862, Lewis Carroll (whose real name was Charles Dodgson) composed a story for the entertainment of three little girls as they took a leisurely boat ride down the River Isis, to a favorite picnic spot. A trip to modern Oxford offers the possibility of taking that same trip by boat or on foot along a beautiful stretch of river on the outskirts of town. The lucky visitor may even see a white rabbit hurry across the Port Meadow on the way. The center of town is rather congested and noisy, but a stroll around the gardens and campuses of some of the thirty-six colleges that make up Oxford University can be an idyllic step into the world of the educated elite of Britain. A visit to Christ Church College, where Carroll lived his entire adult life and where the real Alice spent her childhood, provides a fascinating look at the extent to which Carroll wove specific features of everyday life in Oxford into his stories.

A Brief Biography of Lewis Carroll

> I'd give all the wealth that years have piled,
>   the slow result of life's decay,
> To be once more a little child,
>   for one bright summer day.
> —Lewis Carroll, introductory poem to
> Alice's Adventures in Wonderland, 1865

Charles Lutwidge Dodgson, a shy Oxford mathematician, created a pen name for himself by translating his first two names into Latin (*Carolus Ludovicus*) and then translating them back into English and inverting them, and so became Lewis Carroll. In much the same way he took the social conventions of the day and the rules of linguistics and logic and turned them inside out to create two stories that continue to intrigue adults and charm children 140 years later: *Alice's Adventures in Wonderland* and *Through the Looking-Glass*.

Born in 1832 in **Daresbury** near Liverpool, Carroll was the son of the village vicar. He entertained his ten brothers and sisters with puppet shows, homemade puzzles, and games. When Carroll was eleven, his father moved to a better position at Croft-on-Tees in Yorkshire. Carroll attended **Rugby School** in Warwickshire from the age of fourteen, but the rough-and-tumble atmosphere of the private school proved to be a difficult experience for the shy boy with a stutter.

However, Carroll found his niche when he entered **Christ Church College, Oxford University,** at the age of eighteen. It became both his home and his workplace for the next forty-seven years until his death. He led the quiet life of a bachelor don, tutoring and instructing students in mathematics. He was an accomplished amateur photographer, and it was while he was taking pictures that he met Alice.

Alice Liddell was four years old when her father became dean at Christ Church and the family moved into the Deanery on campus. She and her two sisters met Carroll one day when he was taking photographs of the cathedral from their garden. Carroll was awkward and shy around adults, but he delighted in the company of children. His apartment was full of toys and costumes, which the children often wore while he photographed them. In later life Alice remembered enjoying the photo sessions because Carroll told them entertaining stories as they posed. An undergraduate once asked Carroll if children ever bored him, and he replied, "Little children are three-fourths of my life; I don't see how they could bore anyone."

The shy don often took the three sisters on outings to the Botanic

Garden or the deer park at nearby Magdalen College. One of their favorite treats was a boat ride on the river Isis (as the Thames is called in Oxford). Carroll and a friend, Robinson Duckworth, took the girls on just such an outing on July 4, 1862, traveling a few miles up the river from the **Folly Bridge** to **Godstow** for a picnic. The girls begged for a story, and the one that Carroll made up along the way became the basis for *Alice's Adventures in Wonderland.* In the story when Alice finally gets out of the pool of her own tears, she is accompanied by a Duck and a Dodo, a Lory and an Eaglet. This is a reference to everyone in the picnic party: the Lory and the Eaglet are Alice's sisters, Lorina and Edith, the Duck is Duckworth, and the Dodo is Dodgson (Carroll), who had a slight stutter that sometimes made his name come out "Do-Do-Dodgson." Alice begged Carroll to write the story down, and he sat up all night trying to remember what he'd made up that afternoon. Alice didn't receive the final version with Carroll's hand-drawn illustrations (now in the **British Library**) until Christmas 1864. It was inscribed "A Christmas Gift to a Dear Child in Memory of a Summer Day."

The story was first published in 1865 with illustrations by John Tenniel (see below). Alice received her copy of the published book on July 4, 1865, on the third anniversary of their "golden afternoon." It was immediately a huge popular success. Alice, meanwhile, was growing up and did not spend much time with Carroll after 1864. She married Reginald Hargreaves in 1880 and lived out her life in Lyndhurst near Southampton. She is buried in St. Michael and All Angels Church in Lyndhurst.

In 1871, Carroll published *Through the Looking-Glass,* which was also a big success. The book was inspired by stories that Carroll told the Liddell girls while visiting them at their grandmother's house at Hetton Lawn near Cheltenham in 1863. The large mirror that hung over the mantelpiece there may have sparked the idea. A walk up nearby Leckhampton Hill during Carroll's visit offered a view out over the tree-bordered fields of the surrounding countryside. Alice and Carroll were reminded of a chessboard, thus inspiring the many chess references in *Through the Looking-Glass.*

Carroll lived out his life in Oxford. He died in 1898, at the age of sixty-six, while visiting his sisters in Guildford, just southwest of London. He is buried on the Mount just west of Guildford.

A Brief Biography of John Tenniel

Born in 1820 in Kensington, London, John Tenniel was the son of a fencing master. Tenniel's artistic talents were encouraged at a young age, and by age seventeen his painting was displayed at the Royal Academy. While he was fencing with his father at age twenty, one of Tenniel's eyes was grazed by his father's sword. He permanently lost his sight in that eye but managed to hide the fact from his father to spare his feelings.

Tenniel participated in the decoration of the then-new Houses of Parliament with frescoes and paintings. He collaborated on the illustrations for a book by Charles Dickens, *The Haunted Man,* in 1850. His acquaintance with Dickens led to a role in Dickens's amateur theatrical group, which toured the country to raise money for good causes. Tenniel was offered a position on the staff of *Punch,* the magazine of political commentary and cartoons, in 1851. He stayed at *Punch* for fifty years, where he served as chief cartoonist from 1864 until 1901. He was knighted in 1893 for his political cartoon work. His time at the magazine coincided almost exactly with the reign of Queen Victoria, his retirement occurring just before her death.

In addition to his cartoons, Tenniel was much sought after as a book illustrator, and he illustrated many books during the 1860s and '70s. His illustrations for the two Alice books in 1865 and 1871 are by far his most famous work. He had a turbulent relationship with Lewis Carroll after Carroll objected to the quality of the reproduction of Tenniel's prints in the first edition of *Alice's Adventures in Wonderland* and had the books withdrawn from circulation. Tenniel illustrated *Through the Looking-Glass* with great reluctance, and it was the last time he illustrated a book.

After his retirement from *Punch,* Tenniel lost the sight in his good eye and became totally blind. Sir John Tenniel died three days before his ninety-fourth birthday in 1914.

Places Connected with the Alice Stories
in or Around Oxford

A BOAT RIDE OR WALK ALONG THE THAMES (CALLED THE RIVER ISIS IN OXFORD) TO GODSTOW

If you are lucky enough to be in Oxford when the weather is fine, a trip along the river to Godstow for a picnic or pub lunch is as much a treat in the twenty-first century as it was in July 1862 for Lewis Carroll, Alice Liddell, and her sisters. Between May and September, you can rent a boat near the Folly Bridge, which is just below Christ Church Meadow along St. Aldate's Street. There is also a lovely pathway along the Thames from the Folly Bridge, which continues for approximately three miles up the river to Godstow. There are interesting sights all along the way, including lots of people "mucking about in boats" in various ways. The river and path pass by Port Meadow, a gift from William the Conqueror to Oxford. The meadow has been undeveloped "common land" for grazing livestock and frolicking children for almost a thousand years. There is a short connecting path that leads from the main pathway to the village of Binsey, another delightful spot for a picnic with *Alice* connections (see below). Eventually, the river meanders on to Godstow and the ruins of an old Benedictine abbey. No one knows exactly where Carroll and the Liddell sisters picnicked at Godstow while composing Alice's adventure, but on a warm, sunny day, the whole area has a quiet, lazy feel to it that would definitely be conducive to letting the imagination meander along like the river. If you don't fancy a picnic, the venerable and very popular Trout Inn has tables by the river that will serve you well.

♣ [Alice's sister] sat on, with closed eyes, and half believed herself in Wonderland, though she knew she had but to open them again and all would change to dull reality . . . the rattling teacups would change to tinkling sheep-bells, and the Queen's shrill cries to the voice of the shepherd boy—and the sneeze of the baby, the shriek of the Gryphon, and all the other queer noises, would change (she knew) to the confused clamor of the busy farm-yard—while the lowing of the cattle in the distance would take the place of the Mock Turtle's heavy sobs.

—*Alice's Adventures in Wonderland*, 1865

BINSEY

The charming, tiny village of Binsey makes a great detour from a riverside walk or an excellent destination for a picnic or a pint. There is yet another wonderful old pub here, the Perch, which even has a play area for small children. A walk past the village away from the river and down a quiet country lane brings you to St. Margaret's Church. The church dates from the eleventh century. Legend has it that St. Frideswide, Oxford's patron saint, fled to this church when she was pursued by an unwanted suitor. He was struck blind for being so insistent, but Frideswide was able to call forth healing waters from the well beside the church that cured his blindness. In gratitude, he left her alone, and she went on to found a convent. The medieval word for healing remedy was "treacle," which in modern British English means molasses. The well has always been known as the Treacle Well, and Carroll played on this when he had the Dormouse tell the story of a well full of molasses (treacle) at the Mad Tea Party. At first Alice insists there can't really be such a well, but then she recollects that indeed there might be just one. Alice's nanny lived nearby the church, and there are graves bearing her family name, Prickett, in the churchyard.

ALICE'S SHOP, 83 ALDATE'S, ACROSS FROM THE ENTRANCE TO CHRIST CHURCH COLLEGE

When Alice Liddell bought candy at this five-hundred-year-old shop as a child, the clerk's voice reminded her of a sheep. Carroll used that private joke in *Through the Looking-Glass* (chapter 5) where Alice enters the shop and finds a sheep behind the counter knitting with fourteen pairs of needles. Sir John Tenniel visited the shop when working on his illustrations for the book and drew the shop in reverse, creating a "looking-glass" image. Today the shop is dedicated to Alice gifts and memorabilia. It makes an easy stop when entering or leaving Christ Church College. There is a pleasant tearoom and gallery next door that features Alice paraphernalia and displays prints and originals of Lisbeth Zwerger's eye-catching illustrations for a recent version of *Alice's Adventures in Wonderland*. Telephone: (01865) 723793.

Other Places Connected with Lewis Carroll and Alice Liddell's Lives in Oxford

CHRIST CHURCH COLLEGE

Christ Church College was Carroll's home for forty-seven years, from his entrance as an undergraduate until his death. The self-guided tour of the college leads through Tom Quad, named for the grand tower designed by Sir Christopher Wren in 1681. Lewis Carroll's living quarters were located in the corner of the quad to the right of the tower. They are not open to the public. Alice Liddell's family lived in the Deanery, which is located along the east side of the quad. After visiting the Hall (see below), you may want to explore the cathedral. At the front of the Military Chapel, there is a window depicting St. Catherine, modeled on Edith Liddell, Alice's sister. The garden area between the cathedral and the college library is where Carroll first met Alice and her sisters while taking photographs.

A tour of Christ Church College will include a visit to the Hall, the college dining room. The undergraduates still dine here daily in their robes, with the dons and dean sitting at the raised head table. Scriptures are read each evening before dinner. The walls of the enormous room are crowded with pictures of many of the influential graduates of the college, including thirteen prime ministers. To an American it feels quintessentially British. Considering all the great deeds accomplished by all those venerable men hanging on the walls, it is interesting that the guard noted that the vast majority of visitors are mainly interested in finding Charles Dodgson's portrait! It hangs near the entrance. In addition, there is a stained-glass window dedicated to Carroll and Alice Liddell and several characters from the Alice stories.

Christ Church College is open 10:00–11:30 A.M. and 2:00–4:00 P.M., Monday through Saturday, and 2:00–5:00 on Sunday. There is an admission charge of £3. The visitor's entrance is through the Memorial Gardens off St. Aldate's Street. Telephone: (01865) 276150.

Elsewhere in the UK

DARESBURY, CHESHIRE

Lewis Carroll was born in Daresbury in 1832. His father was the vicar of All Saints' Church at the time. The vicarage burned down in the 1880s, but the church is still very much intact and in use. For the centenary of Carroll's birth, the church  organized an international "subscription" to collect money for a stained-glass window honoring Carroll. The window was completed in 1934 and remains in excellent condition. The central portion of the window features a scene of the birth of Jesus with Carroll and Alice in attendance. Carroll's life is depicted in the upper portion while the lower portion features several characters from *Alice's Adventures in Wonderland* as drawn by Sir John Tenniel. All Saints' Church is open to visitors on Friday afternoons from 2:00 to 5:00 P.M. Visitors can purchase everything from postcards to dish towels of the window, with the proceeds going toward its upkeep.

Daresbury is located halfway between Liverpool and Manchester. The tiny village is easily accessible by car, taking the M6 to the M56 (west). Exit at junction 12 off the M56 and drive a quarter mile to the Daresbury turnoff. Pass the Ring o' Bells pub (an old coach station) and turn left to reach the church car park. The truly dedicated will want to see the Alice in Wonderland weathervane on top of the village school nearby.

RUGBY SCHOOL, RUGBY, WARWICKSHIRE

Rugby School's principal claim to fame is as the place where the sport of rugby originated back in 1823 when a student had the audacity to pick up the ball and run with it. Lewis Carroll attended Rugby for four years from 1846 to 1850 as a teenager, living in what is now called School House. Coincidentally, Arthur Ransome lived in Carroll's rooms fifty years later when he attended Rugby (see the *Swallows and Amazons* chapter, page 251). The rough and rowdy atmosphere at Rugby didn't suit the shy Carroll, and it may have heightened his appreciation for the more subdued world of Oxford, which he attended upon finishing at Rugby.

Although mostly devoted to the history of rugby football, the Rugby School Museum does pay tribute to Carroll in a case about Rugby's distinguished alumni. Guided tours of the school grounds leave from the museum daily at 2:30 P.M. The museum is located at 10 Little Church Street in the town of Rugby, immediately next to the school campus. Fee parking is available across the lane. The museum is open from 10:30 A.M. to 12:30 P.M. and from 1:30 to 4:30 P.M., Monday through

Saturdays; 1:30–4:30 P.M. only on Sundays. Telephone: (01788) 556109. Web site: www.rugby-school.warsks.sch.uk.

The town of Rugby lies close to the meeting of the M1, M6, and M45, just east of Birmingham. Take junction 18 from the M1 or junction 1 from the M6 and follow the signs to the center of town.

Places to See Original Artwork/Manuscripts

THE BRITISH LIBRARY, LONDON

The John Ritblat Gallery: Treasures of the British Library at the British Library is an amazing place to visit for the whole family. It showcases the richness of British culture from the original Magna Carta to the original score for "Yesterday" by Paul McCartney. One of the highlights is the original manuscript of *Alice's Adventures Underground* that Lewis Carroll wrote by hand and illustrated for Alice Liddell between 1862 and 1864.

There is also a delightful exhibit about the history of children's literature in Britain in the Pearson Gallery of Living Words. On display are early examples of "Alice" products, including a postage-stamp case from 1890. It is accompanied by a humorous pamphlet written by Carroll about how to write a letter.

The British Library is located next to St. Pancras station at 96 Euston Road. It is open on Monday, Wednesday, Thursday, and Friday, 9:30 A.M.–6:00 P.M.; Tuesday, 9:30 A.M.–8:00 P.M.; Saturday, 9:30 A.M.–5:00 P.M.; and Sundays/holidays, 11:00–5.00 P.M. There is no charge for admission to the exhibits. The closest tube station is Kings Cross/St. Pancras. Telephone: (0171) 412-7332.

Other Activities for Children Who Love Alice's Adventures in Wonderland

THE ALICE IN WONDERLAND CENTRE, LLANDUDNO, NORTH WALES

The Liddell family built a vacation home in the Victorian resort town of Llandudno, North Wales, in the early 1860s. That house has now become the Gogarth Abbey Hotel, complete with croquet and an indoor, heated swimming pool. There is some controversy over whether or not Lewis Carroll ever visited the Liddells at Llandudno, but there is no controversy over the way the town embraces its Alice connection. There is a statue of Carroll along the West Shore beach and one of the White Rabbit near the model yacht pond.

In the center of town, just off Mostyn Street, is the Alice in Wonderland Centre. With a walk-in rabbit hole and animated displays of scenes from Alice's adventures, this will charm younger children. The whole experience takes about twenty minutes, which suits young attention spans. There is also an "Alice Curio" gift shop.

The Alice in Wonderland Centre is open seven days a week from Easter through the end of October, and Monday to Saturday the rest of the year. Hours are 10:00 A.M.–5:00 P.M. Telephone: 01492-860082. Internet: www.wonderland.co.uk.

The Gogarth Abbey Hotel is located on the West Shore in Llandudno. Telephone: 01492-876-211 or 212. It has four rooms, all with private facilities. The Liddell Restaurant in the hotel has lovely views of the water.

THE WIND IN THE WILLOWS
by Kenneth Grahame

♣ "I beg your pardon," said the Mole, pulling himself together with an effort. "You must think me very rude; but all this is so new to me. So—this—is—a—River!"

"*The* River," corrected the Rat.

"And you really live by the river? What a jolly life!"

"By it and with it and on it and in it," said the Rat. "It's brother and sister to me, and aunts, and company, and food and drink, and (naturally) washing. It's my world, and I don't want any other. What it hasn't got is not worth having, and what it doesn't know is not worth knowing."

—The Wind in the Willows, 1908

$\mathcal{M}$ANY OF THE AUTHORS INCLUDED IN THIS BOOK, FROM A. A. Milne to J. K. Rowling, mention *The Wind in the Willows* as a childhood favorite and major influence. According to C. S. Lewis, "The child who has once met Mr. Badger has got ever afterwards, in its bones, a knowledge of humanity and English history." Kenneth Grahame's story of the animals who live along the River and in the Wild Wood captures the quiet beauty of the British countryside and something of the British character as well. The story alternates between gently poetic vignettes and a rollicking tale of the exploits of the pompous, but lovable, Mr. Toad. To this day there's a good chance of meeting someone in your travels through Britain who brings to mind Badger, Ratty, or Toad.

The Wind in the Willows may entice you into spending some time along a quiet portion of the Thames or one of the other rivers in the south of England. A day's boat trip from Reading will take you along a lovely, willow-lined section of the Thames, where you are sure to recognize scenes from E. H. Shepard's illustrations for the story, including a visit to the great house that bears a remarkable resemblance to Toad Hall. Younger readers will enjoy a "walk-through" replica of scenes from the book, located in the beautiful Peak District. And the truly dedicated can bundle up for an evening of "badger watching" in several locations throughout England and Scotland.

A Brief Biography of Kenneth Grahame

The part of my brain I used from age four to about seven can never have altered.
     —Kenneth Grahame, on his return to his childhood home at age forty-six

Kenneth Grahame was born in **Edinburgh, Scotland**, in 1859, into an established Edinburgh family that traced its roots back to the twelfth-century monarch Robert the Bruce. His mother, Bessie, grew up on the same street as

Robert Louis Stevenson. When Kenneth was very young, the family moved to Inverary, Scotland, in an attempt to help his father in his struggle with alcoholism. His mother died of scarlet fever shortly after Kenneth turned five. His father was completely unable to care for his four children so they were sent south to live with their maternal grandmother in Cookham Dene, Berkshire. Their grandmother lived in a large, run-down house along the Thames. Kenneth and his siblings were given great freedom to run wild outside, and Kenneth always remembered this as the best part of his childhood. The children were eventually sent back to Inverary to live with their father, but his alcoholism had only worsened. His parental responsibilities soon proved too heavy to bear, and Mr. Grahame Sr. went off to live the rest of his life in a more bohemian fashion in France. The children never saw him again, although Kenneth did travel to France for his funeral years later.

Kenneth and his brother were sent to St. Edward's School, Oxford. At age sixteen, to Kenneth's bitter disappointment, his uncles decided he should become a bank clerk rather than going on to university studies at Oxford. After working for one uncle for a short time, Kenneth became a clerk at the **Bank of England,** where he continued to work for the next thirty years. He eventually worked his way up to one of the three highest positions at the bank, becoming the youngest man ever to be appointed secretary of the bank at age thirty-nine.

Grahame's personal and social life away from the bank focused on the London literary scene. He began by writing poetry, but his focus soon shifted to essays about childhood. These were published regularly and were eventually collected into two very successful books, *Pagan Papers* (1893) and *The Golden Age* (1895). Both books include essays about a nine-year-old boy named Harold who thrives by living in an imaginary world. A third success, *Dream Days* (1898), features the story of "The Reluctant Dragon" as told to Harold and his siblings. Theodore Roosevelt was such a fan that he sent copies of all three books to England to be signed by Grahame. *The Golden Age* and *Dream Days* were reprinted after the turn of the century, with illustrations by Maxfield Parrish, the American artist and illustrator. Partly due to the success of those editions, Parrish went on to become one of the most sought-after illustrators of the early part of the twentieth century.

At age forty, Grahame was a literary success and a respected banker. He married a wealthy woman named Elspeth Thomson, and their only child, Alistair, was born in 1900.

Alistair, called "Mouse" by his parents, was blind in one eye, with impaired vision in the other. On Mouse's fourth birthday, Kenneth began telling him a story about a water rat, a mole, and a toad. These stories continued for years and were written down in letters from Grahame to Mouse, who at age seven was spending the summer at the beach with his nanny. The family moved back to Cookham Dene when Mouse was six, but the experience did not match up to Grahame's fond memories of his own childhood years spent playing along the Thames.

In 1907, at age forty-eight, Grahame published the stories he'd been telling to Mouse as *The Wind in the Willows*. After the book's success, Grahame decided to resign his position at the bank. He eventually moved to Church Cottage in **Pangbourne,** where he walked almost daily along his beloved Thames. He never wrote another substantial piece for publication.

His marriage was never a happy one, although both Kenneth and Elspeth doted on Alistair. Alistair, who was a very sensitive boy with considerable health problems, went through a difficult adolescence, which involved short stints at Rugby and Eton. He had private tutoring for a few years before taking his entrance exams for Oxford. After he passed the exams in 1919, the committee recommended that he be given a tutor as if he were totally blind. A few days later he was found late at night decapitated by an oncoming train on the tracks outside Oxford. It was never resolved whether the death was an accident or a suicide.

The Wind in the Willows has been published in over one hundred editions, with illustrations by E. H. Shepard (see page 76), and Arthur Rackham (see page 7) among others. A. A. Milne adapted it for the stage, and over the years it has been made into animated films and a TV musical.

Kenneth Grahame lived out his life quietly in his home on the Thames in Pangbourne. He died of a cerebral hemorrhage in 1932. He is buried in Saint Cross Churchyard, Holywell, Oxford.

Places Connected with The Wind in the Willows

"Nice? It's the *only* thing," said the Water Rat solemnly, as he leaned forward for his stroke. "Believe me, my young friend, there is *nothing*—absolutely nothing—half so much worth doing as simply messing about in boats."

—*The Wind in the Willows*

The River Thames from Marlow to Pangbourne

This is the stretch of river that Kenneth Grahame knew and loved. His younger years were spent near Marlow, and he retired to Pangbourne, where he lived out his final years. The river meanders and winds its way between the two boating towns, passing lovely villages, drooping willow trees, wealthy homes, and the city of Reading. Kenneth Grahame took E. H. Shepard on a tour around this area to help Shepard get the right feeling into his illustrations for *The Wind in the Willows*.

The best way to see the river, of course, is "by simply messing about in boats." One of the best options is to take the boat from Reading upriver to Mapledurham House, a dead ringer for Toad Hall (see details below). A boat from Reading to Mapledurham departs at 2:00 P.M. from Caversham Promenade behind the Holiday Inn in Reading. The trip takes forty minutes each way and runs on weekends only. Tickets are £4.10/adults, £3/children. Telephone: (01189)-481088.

There are several boat rental companies near the bridge in Henley-on-Thames, which is about halfway between Marlow and Pangbourne. Take the A404 from junction 8-9 of the M4. Exit at A4130 and follow it west to Henley-on-Thames. Both organized cruises and boats to rent are available.

Pangbourne, Berkshire

The small town of Pangbourne, where Kenneth Grahame spent the last years of his life, is located along the Thames just northwest of Reading. Take the A340 from junction 12 of the M4. If you pass through it on your way to Mapledurham House, you might want to have a bite to eat at the Ducks Ditty coffee shop in the town center. It has Ratty's "Up tails all" poem decorating its windows and a figure of Mr. Toad inviting you in for lunch or dinner.

As you head toward the Whitchurch Bridge, there is a riverside public park on the right with pay-and-display parking (purchase a ticket from the machine and stick it inside your windshield). This is a great place for kids to run off excess energy and play right at the water's edge.

There is no guardrail along the water so it may not be appropriate for very young children. The willow trees and old toll bridge provide a lovely backdrop to the passing boats.

Mapledurham House, Across the Thames from Pangbourne, near Reading

> Rounding a bend in the river, they came in sight of a handsome, dignified old house of mellowed red brick, with well-kept lawns reaching down to the water's edge. "There's Toad Hall," said the Rat. . . . "Toad is rather rich, you know, and this is really one of the nicest houses in these parts, though we never admit as much to Toad."
>
> —*The Wind in the Willows*

Was Mapledurham House the inspiration for Toad Hall? You'll get different answers to this question depending on whom you ask. The family that has lived in the house for over five hundred years doesn't think so. Quite understandably they emphasize the dignity and fascinating history of this impressive property. However, if you look at E. H. Shepard's drawing of Toad Hall and its location on his map of The River and The Wild Wood, you will probably come to a different conclusion. No matter where the truth lies, if you are looking for a Toad Hall to visit, you won't find a better one than Mapledurham House.

The house sits grandly along the Thames just across the river from Pangbourne (see above), where Kenneth Grahame lived out the last years of his life. It has been owned by descendants of the Blount family since 1491. When Henry VIII broke away from the Catholic Church and took England with him, the Blount family held on to their Catholic faith. The house retains many features of the persecution the family underwent as a result, including a secret chapel and cryptic oyster shell symbols on the exterior that signaled their sympathies to fellow Catholics. The village around the house has remained unchanged for 150 years and features the last working gristmill on the Thames. The grounds of the house along the Thames are perfect for picnicking beneath the (what else?) willows. There is a gift shop and tearoom in the fourteenth-century manor next to the main house.

Mapledurham House and grounds are open weekends only, 2:30–5:00, Easter through September. Admission is £4 for the house only, £3 for the watermill only, and £6 for a combined ticket. Children under five are free, five–fourteen half price.

For the full life-on-the-river experience, take the boat from Reading up the river to Mapledurham (see above). By car from Pangbourne, cross the Thames by the charming Whitchurch Bridge, 10 pence toll. The tollhouse dates back to 1792, although the bridge has been updated. Continue straight for about three miles until you reach a "T" junction. Turn right onto the B4526, toward Reading and Chazey Heath. You will pass the King Charles Head pub, where you can stop and have a pint in the heart of the Wild Wood. Continue on for another mile until you see a right turn for Mapledurham House. Follow this narrow country lane where Mr. Toad must have tried out his canary yellow caravan as well as his motorcar. You reach the end of the road at the Thames and Mapledurham House.

From Reading, take the A4074 toward Oxford and follow the HIS-TORIC HOUSE signs, which will put you onto the B4526. Take a left turn onto the signposted country lane mentioned above.

Other Places Connected with Kenneth Grahame's Life

32 CASTLE STREET, EDINBURGH, SCOTLAND

Kenneth Grahame was born in this imposing house in 1859. Robert Louis Stevenson was only nine years old at the time and living just a couple of blocks away on Heriot Row (see Stevenson chapter for details). Castle Street is in the New Town section of Edinburgh, at the end of Princes Street closer to the castle. No. 32 has been converted to business use and is not open to the public.

16 PHILLIMORE PLACE, LONDON

A blue plaque marks the house where Grahame lived during the years when he was secretary of the Bank of England. However, as the plaque reflects, the accomplishment for which he is remembered is writing *The Wind in the Willows* during those same years. Phillimore Place is just a few short blocks off of Kensington High Street, near the Kensington High Street tube stop. Walk up Argyll Road, past Phillimore Walk to Phillimore Place and turn left. The house is on the left. It is a private residence and not open to the public.

BANK OF ENGLAND MUSEUM, BARTHOLOMEW LANE, LONDON

This museum has done an excellent job of making the history of banking in Britain lively and interactive. Although there's not much to appeal to children under the age of ten or so, older kids and adults may find the videos and interactive exhibits about how modern money systems and banking have developed interesting. It will be a sure hit with anyone who collects coins or banknotes. As secretary of the bank in the early years of the twentieth century, Kenneth Grahame is highlighted in the exhibit about the Victorian Era in the Rotunda Room. A first edition of *The Wind in the Willows* is on display next to a letter from the four royal children of the time to Mr. Grahame thanking him for having them to tea.

The museum is just a block from the Bank tube station. Take exit 2 and walk a block up Threadneedle Street, then turn left on Bartholomew Lane. Admission is free. Open Monday to Friday, 10:00–5:00 P.M.; closed weekends and holidays. Telephone: (207) 601-5545.

Places to See Original Artwork/Manuscripts

THE BRITISH LIBRARY, LONDON

The Pearson Gallery of Living Words at the impressive new British Library (which used to be housed in the British Museum) features a wonderful exhibit on British children's literature. An early edition of *The Wind in the Willows,* with illustrations by Arthur Rackham, is included in the exhibit.

The British Library is located next to St. Pancras station at 96 Euston Road. It is open on Monday, Wednesday, Thursday, and Friday, 9:30–6:00 P.M.; Tuesday, 9:30–8:00 P.M.; Saturday, 9:30–5:00 P.M.; and Sundays/holidays, 11:00–5:00 P.M. There is no charge for admission to the exhibits. The closest tube station is Kings Cross/St. Pancras. Telephone: (0171) 412-7332.

GREENBANK HOTEL, FALMOUTH, CORNWALL

In 1907, Kenneth Grahame stayed at the historic Greenbank Hotel while on holiday. He wrote letters to his son, Alistair, filled with their ongoing saga of Toad, Rat, Mole, and Badger, which eventually became the published story. The Greenbank Hotel owns and displays some of these letters in its lobby. The hotel is located along the harbor in Falmouth. Telephone: (01326) 312440.

Other Activities for Children Who Love The Wind in the Willows

THE WIND IN THE WILLOWS ATTRACTION, PEAK DISTRICT, ROWSLEY, DERBYSHIRE

There are lots of good reasons to visit the Peak District, Britain's first national park. The scenery is beautiful, the villages are charming, and there are grand old houses to visit. However, a connection with Kenneth Grahame or his stories is not one of them! Yet this is where the Wind in the Willows Attraction is located. Even more inappropriately, it is part of an outlet store mall. If you are mentally prepared for all that, you can have a lovely time at the Wind in the Willows Attraction, especially if you are traveling with young children.

The attraction is an indoor re-creation of E. H. Shepard's illustrations for *The Wind in the Willows.* Re-creating the natural world indoors may seem to be missing the point a bit; but given the amount of rainy weather one can encounter in Britain, it can be a practical convenience. Visitors first view a short slide show of the story itself, and then they are able to wander along a path through re-created three-dimensional scenes, both oversized and tiny, of Shepard's drawings. Children up to age eight or nine will be delighted with the sounds, movement, and even the scents that accompany each scene. One favorite was the chaotic battle scene at Toad Hall, where the tables spin, food is spilling everywhere, and stoats and weasels are falling topsy-turvy. The younger children will enjoy spying creatures in the miniature scenes that are interspersed throughout the exhibit.

Finally, a natural science exhibit about the real-life animals in the story includes coloring activities, games, and a movie on a large screen showing the creatures in their natural environment. The gift shop is brimming with *The Wind in the Willows,* Beatrix Potter, and Pooh Bear items, including some nice enlargements of E. H. Shepard's sketches.

The village of Rowsley is a lovely twenty-five-minute drive from Chesterfield. Take the A617 from junction 29 of the M1. Catch a glimpse of Chesterfield's crooked church steeple and then take the A619 toward Chatsworth. You can cut across the B6012 to Rowsley through the beautiful land surrounding stately Chatsworth, or you can continue to Bakewell and then head south on the A6 toward Matlock. In Rowsley, look for signs to Peak Village outlet stores. There is ample free parking.

The attraction is open every day except Christmas and New Year's Day from 10:00 until 4:30 or 5:30 P.M. in the summer. Admission is £3.25/adults and £2/children. Telephone: 01629-733433.

BADGER WATCHING

If you log onto www.badgers.org.uk, you'll find a list of twenty-four local groups throughout Britain who look after the interests of their local population of badgers. Many of these groups offer the opportunity to hike out at dusk to a "hide" near a badger sett. Observers sit quietly for an hour or more watching the resident badgers peacefully go about their badger business. It's a wonderful opportunity to see these secretive animals up close. Badgers have occupied some of the setts for hundreds of years, making them the wildlife equivalent of the great houses of British nobility. The admission fees for badger watching are generally used for ongoing conservation efforts. Due to the need for quiet and sitting still, this activity is not well suited to very young children. Three notable badger watches (although there are many more in other areas) are:

The New Forest Badger Watch: The New Forest is a lovely area on England's southern coast between Bournemouth and Southampton. This badger watch features a weatherproof "hide" with seats and the opportunity to view the badgers underground through a glass wall. It is offered every evening from March 1 through October 31. Tickets are £10/adults, £5/children seven–fifteen. Book on line at www.badgerwatch.co.uk. Telephone: 01425-403412.

Badger Watch Dorset: A bit farther west, in Thomas Hardy country, this watch is located just north of the town of Dorchester. The "hide" is a short walk from the car park, and the area around the sett is lighted for better viewing. Badger watching is offered from February through November; tickets are £8/adults and £6/children. Telephone: 01300-345293. Web site: www.badgerwatchdorset.co.uk.

Falls of Clyde Wildlife Reserve, New Lanark, Scotland: This badger-watching opportunity has the advantage of being next to a World Heritage Centre, the preserved village of New Lanark. Called the birthplace of Scotland's industrial revolution, the village was built by Robert Owen in the early 1800s as a social experiment in an attempt to create a humane environment for his cotton mill workers. It's well worth a day's sightseeing and includes shops, historic re-creations, and even a ride through history with a young girl who worked in the mills.

At the edge of the village, the old dye works have been transformed into a nature center. Here you can pick up a trail that follows the river to three separate waterfalls. The center also organizes badger watches during the summer, and visitors are often lucky enough to see otters, kingfishers, owls, and bats as well. The badger watches take place at dusk during the summer (6:30–8:30 P.M.). They are only offered twice each month, and it is necessary to reserve a ticket in advance. It's a thirty-minute walk to the badger sett, and the whole experience ususally lasts two and a half hours. The center also offers more active "bat walks" at dusk. Bring insect repellant.

To inquire about badger-watch dates and reserve tickets, telephone (01555)-665262. Tickets cost £5/adults, £1/children. More information is available at www.swt.org.uk. The nature center is open Monday to Friday, 11:00–5:00, weekends 1:00–5:00. It is closed in January. You may also contact the Scottish Wildlife Trust. Telephone (0141) 248-4647. Web site: www.swt.org.uk.

New Lanark is twenty-five miles southeast of Glasgow. From Glasgow, take the M74 south and exit at junction 9 for the B7086 toward Lanark. For a more scenic drive along the river Clyde, exit at junction 7 and follow the A72 south to Lanark. Follow the signs to New Lanark.

A Boat Trip on the Thames near Oxford

The boat trip on the Thames described in the *Alice's Adventures in Wonderland* chapter is also evocative of *The Wind in the Willows,* even if it is a bit farther up the river than Ratty or Mole might have ventured.

National Museum of the Performing Arts, London

Also known as the Theatre Museum, this colorful showcase for London's rich theatrical history includes a small exhibit about a production of *The Wind in the Willows* by the National Theatre. Titled "From Page to Stage," the exhibit includes a video about how the production developed and was put together.

The museum is located on Russell Street, which leads off of Covent Garden. It is open Tuesday to Saturday from 10:00 to 6:00 P.M. Admission is £4.50/adults; children under sixteen are admitted free. Telephone: 0207-943-4700.

THE CHRONICLES OF NARNIA
by C. S. Lewis
and THE HOBBIT
by J. R. R. Tolkien

♧ "This is the land of Narnia," said the Faun, "where we are now; all that lies between the lamppost and the great castle at Cair Paravel on the eastern sea. And you—you have come from the wild woods of the west?" "I—I got in through the wardrobe in the spare room," said Lucy. "Ah," said Mr. Tumnus in a rather melancholy voice, "if only I had worked harder at geography when I was a little Faun, I should no doubt know all about those strange countries. It is too late now."

—*The Lion, the Witch and the Wardrobe*, 1950

♧ [Hobbits] are (or were) a little people, about half our height, and smaller than the bearded Dwarves. Hobbits have no beards. There is little or no magic about them. . . . They are inclined to be fat in the stomach; they dress in bright colors (chiefly green and yellow); wear no shoes, because their feet grow natural leathery soles and thick warm brown hair like the stuff on their heads (which is curly); have long clever brown fingers, good-natured faces, and laugh deep fruity laughs (especially after dinner, which they have twice a day when they can get it).

—*The Hobbit*, 1937

$\mathcal{T}$WO CLOSE FRIENDS WHO SPENT THEIR LIVES LIVING QUIETLY in Oxford, teaching, writing scholarly works, and taking walks while arguing about religion, ended up creating two of the most enduring fantasy worlds in literature. *The Chronicles of Narnia* and *The Hobbit* continue to delight children on one level and intrigue adults on another. Each world stands on its own, complete with maps and a history/mythology. Each world so begged to be expanded that Lewis ended up writing seven Narnia books and Tolkien produced the monumental *Lord of the Rings.*

Although fantasy worlds by definition cannot be visited, a visit to Oxford does provide a chance to experience the special environment that nurtured the creation of these two imaginary worlds, including a hike through the land Lewis owned and often walked with Tolkien.

A Brief Biography of C. S. Lewis

Tolkien, there is too little of what we really like in stories. I am afraid we shall have to try and write some ourselves.
—C. S. Lewis in a letter to J. R. R. Tolkien, 1937

Clive Staples Lewis was born in Belfast, Ireland, in 1898, the son of a staunchly Protestant solicitor and his wife, an accomplished mathematician. He was called "Jack," a nickname that he carried for his entire life. Jack had one brother, Warren or "Warnie," who was three years older, and the two brothers were very close throughout their lives. The family moved to a spacious house called "Little Lea" when Jack was seven. Later in life Lewis described the long, empty hallways and intriguing rooms and attics of the new home. The brothers liked to sit inside a large wardrobe built by Lewis's grandfather and make up stories.

Childhood ended abruptly for Lewis when he was nine. His mother died of cancer, and, within a month, Jack was sent away to boarding school in England. This separation from his family at the time when he needed them most strained Jack's relationship with his father for the rest of their lives. Unfortunately, the boarding school was run by a man who eventually was taken to court for his cruelty toward his students. After a miserable eighteen months, Lewis was sent to a different school, Cherbourg House, in Malvern, near Worcester. Jack eventually joined Warren at Malvern College, where he excelled at Latin and Greek. However, Jack continued to loathe boarding school life. Eventually his father sent him to live with his own former tutor for private instruction in the aptly named town of Great Bookham, Surrey. This setup suited Jack's personality and academic talent perfectly, and he spent two happy years preparing for his Oxford entrance exams.

He entered Oxford in 1917 but was sent off to fight in France within a few months. He described his capture of sixty German prisoners as "discover[ing] to my great relief that the crowd of field gray figures who suddenly appeared from nowhere all had their hands up." He was wounded by an exploding shell in 1918 and sent home.

He returned to his studies at Oxford, where he was a stellar student, winning prizes and getting top marks as he earned his degree in English. In 1925, he became a fellow and tutor in English literature at Magdalen College, Oxford. He held that position for nearly thirty years until he was denied the position of professor of poetry at Oxford but was offered the position of professor of medieval and renaissance literature at Cambridge. (The man who was given the poetry position, Cecil Day-Lewis, later became poet laureate of Britain and the father of Daniel Day-Lewis, the actor.) Jack spent the final nine years of his career commuting from Oxford, where he continued to live, to his teaching duties at Cambridge.

Throughout Lewis's Oxford years, he supported and lived with Mrs. Janie Moore, the mother of a good friend who had been killed in the war. She was twenty-eight years older than Lewis, and there is a great deal of speculation about their relationship. It is definite that Lewis took complete responsibility for Janie Moore and her teenage daughter, even in his early student years when he was living on a minimal monthly allowance from his father. Jack, his brother, Warren, and Janie Moore bought a house together in 1930 called **The Kilns.** Janie Moore continued to live there with the brothers until her death in 1951. She was a lively, nurturing woman of little education who may have provided a good balance to Lewis's immersion in the academic world. In his autobiography, *Surprised by Joy,* Lewis writes, cryptically: "One huge and complex episode will be omitted. I have no choice about this reticence. All I can or need to say is that my earlier hostility to the emotions was very fully and variously avenged." Perhaps a mother figure, perhaps a more intimate companion, she was the only woman since his mother to play a role of any consequence in Lewis's life until his marriage at the age of sixty in 1956, five years after Moore's death.

Jack became close friends with J. R. R. Tolkien during the late twenties. Their ongoing discussions of Tolkien's strong faith contributed to Lewis's abandonment of atheism and return to Christianity in the early thirties. (See Tolkien biography for more detail.) Lewis went on to write several popular books on theology and literature, including *The Screwtape Letters* in 1942. In this same period, he wrote a trilogy of science fiction novels for adults. However, the seeds for his most famous work were planted in 1939 when a group of four children who had been evacuated from London during the Blitz came to live at The Kilns. Jack wrote to a friend, "I never appreciated children till the war brought them to me." One girl asked him if there was anything behind the old wardrobe he'd brought over from his Irish childhood home. This started an idea that was finally put down on paper nine years later as the first Narnia book, *The Lion, the Witch and the Wardrobe.* Six more books followed, and they were published between 1950 and 1956 to great critical and popular acclaim. At the same time, Lewis was writing his most respected scholarly work, *English Literature in the Sixteenth Century.*

Lewis was by now a famous author and Christian apologist who received many letters every week from fans around the world. One fan with whom Lewis struck up an ongoing correspondence was an American writer, Joy Gresham. She eventually moved to Britain with her two sons, David and Douglas. Eventually she obtained a divorce from her abusive husband. Lewis wrote the autobiographical *Surprised by Joy* during these years. In 1957, Joy was diagnosed with breast cancer. Jack and Joy were married at her hospital bedside expecting her remaining days to be few. However, Joy experienced a remarkable remission, and they enjoyed three unexpected years together before the cancer finally won in 1960. Jack and Joy's relationship was the basis for the 1993 movie *Shadowlands,* starring Anthony Hopkins and Debra Winger.

Lewis resigned from Cambridge in the summer of 1963 due to a heart and bladder condition. He died at The Kilns on November 22, 1963, the same day that John F. Kennedy and Aldous Huxley died. He is buried in the churchyard at Holy Trinity Church in Headington Quarry, Oxford.

Places Connected with The Chronicles of Narnia and The Hobbit

He was standing by the edge of a small pool—not more than ten feet from side to side—in a wood. . . . It was the quietest wood you could possibly imagine. There were no birds, no insects, no animals, and no wind. You could almost feel the trees growing. The pool he had just got out of was not the only pool. There were dozens of others—a pool every few yards as far as his eyes could reach. You could almost feel the trees drinking up the water with their roots. This wood was very much alive. When he tried to describe it afterward Digory always said, "It was a *rich* place: as rich as a plumcake."

—*The Magician's Nephew*

The nature reserve was once part of the eight acres belonging to the Lewis brothers and Mrs. Moore as owners of The Kilns. Henry Stephen was an Oxford don who bought the land after Lewis's death to preserve it from development. Lewis and Tolkien often walked here together. Although it is impossible to know the reserve's role in inspiring the imaginations of both Lewis and Tolkien, as one steps off the suburban street onto the quiet path leading around a still pond, it's not difficult to feel that you have entered "The Woods between the Worlds" or Middle-earth. The placard at the entrance describes the reserve as "a memorial to imagination," a fitting tribute to both authors.

The reserve is a lovely piece of preserved woodlands. It would make a great "car break" at any time, although it will be quite muddy during rainy weather. It is located at the dead end just past The Kilns, where an unmarked path enters the trees next to a tall hedge. If only there were a lamppost. Entrance is free.

To reach the reserve from the center of Oxford, follow the High Street across the river Cherwell where it forks. Take the left fork. Follow the A420 (E) to a rotary. The third road leaving the rotary is the 4142 (eastern bypass). Take the first, quick left onto Green Road and then an immediate right onto Kilns. The fourth right is Lewis Close. The Kilns is the redbrick building on the right. The reserve path begins at the very end of the street.

Other Places Connected with C. S. Lewis's Life

THE KILNS, LEWIS CLOSE, OXFORD

Lewis purchased The Kilns and eight surrounding acres with Warren and Mrs. Moore in 1930. All three lived out their adult lives here. At present, it is a private residence and not open to the public. However, you can get a good look at the outside from the street as you make your way to the nearby nature reserve (see above). In the spring, the close is very peaceful, with daffodils nodding under the birch trees. The C. S. Lewis Foundation, Redlands, California, owns the house and plans to convert it into a museum and residential Christian study center by spring 2003. Tours may be

available before then. Contact the foundation in the United States. Telephone: 909-793-0949. Web site: www.cslewis.org.

MAGDALEN COLLEGE, OXFORD UNIVERSITY

Lewis was an English professor at Magdalen College from 1925 until 1954, when he accepted a position at Magdalene College, Cambridge. His office or "rooms" were in the New Building with a view over the Deer Park and Magdalen Tower.

The hours during which the college is open to the public vary during the school year. The college is located on the High Street, across from the Botanic Gardens, next to the river Cherwell. (Magdalen is pronounced "maudlin," possibly to confuse American tourists.)

HOLY TRINITY CHURCH, HEADINGTON QUARRY, OXFORD

Lewis is buried in the churchyard. There is a commemorative stained-glass window in the church. Headington Quarry is on the east side of Oxford near the A40 bypass.

THE EAGLE AND CHILD PUB, OXFORD

(See "Other Places Connected with J. R. R. Tolkien's Life," page 58.)

A Brief Biography of J. R. R. Tolkien

John Ronald Reuel Tolkien was born in Bloemfontein, South Africa, in 1892, the first child of bank manager Arthur Tolkien and his young wife, Mabel. At the age of three, young Ronald, as the boy was called, and his baby brother, Hilary, returned to Birmingham, England, with their mother. Their father was expected to join them a few months later, but he contracted rheumatic fever and died in South Africa. Mabel and the two boys were left with very little money. They found inexpensive lodging in the hamlet of **Sarehole** on the outskirts of Birmingham. The family spent four years there living a rural life. Ronald later described this period as "the longest-seeming and most formative of my life."

In 1900, the Tolkiens' time in Sarehole came to an end. Ronald entered King Edward's Grammar School in the heart of Birmingham, and the family moved into the inner city to accommodate the change. In that same year, Ronald's mother converted to Catholicism to the dismay of both her family and her in-laws. Fr. Francis Xavier Morgan, a local priest, became a very close friend of the family. When Ronald's mother became ill with diabetes and died in 1904, Father Morgan was named her sons' guardian in her will. Ronald was eleven at the time.

The early death of his mother coupled with her devout Catholicism contributed to J. R. R. Tolkien's lifelong devotion to the Catholic faith. The brothers returned to the city to live with an elderly, unsympathetic aunt. Ronald continued at King Edward's Grammar School, developing a keen interest in Middle and Old English and the classical languages. He made up entire languages and alphabets just for his own amusement.

At age sixteen, Ronald and his brother moved to a boardinghouse in Birmingham, where they made the acquaintance of another lodger, a pretty nineteen-year-old named Edith Bratt. Edith and Ronald became close friends and eventually fell in love. Word got back to Father Francis, who felt that Ronald was far too young for such an attachment and forebade Ronald to see Edith again.

Ronald eventually went off to study at Oxford, and Edith moved to another town; but they vowed to stay true to each other. During his student years, Tolkien fell in love with **Oxford,** the city where he was to spend most of his adult life. He studied old Germanic, Gothic, Welsh, and Norse languages. His interest in Finnish eventually led to the development of yet another invented language that became High-Elven in his later writings.

Three years later, on the day Ronald turned twenty-one, he wrote Edith asking her to marry him, only to find that she was engaged to someone else. He rushed to see her and convinced her to marry him instead. Three years later, when Ronald was about to go off to fight in France, they were married by Father Morgan.

Ronald's war experiences included fighting in the horrific trenches of the Battle of the Somme. He contracted a bad fever and returned to England in December 1916. Many of his very closest friends had been killed in action. While convalescing, Tolkien wrote down the first piece of what eventually became the mythological world of *The Hobbit* and *The Lord of the Rings.* In November 1917, the Tolkiens' first son, John, was born. After a stint as a dictionary lexicographer and four years teaching at the University of Leeds, Tolkien was appointed professor of Anglo-Saxon at Oxford. He remained at Oxford until his retirement in the 1960s.

Tolkien first became friends with C. S. Lewis while reading Icelandic sagas with a group of Oxford dons. It became a long and true friend-ship, deepened by their lengthy and ongoing discussions of Christian-ity. Tolkien played a pivotal role in Lewis's eventual return to the Christian faith. Both men formed the nucleus of the Inklings, a group of friends who met informally each Tuesday morning at **The Eagle and Child** pub and on Thursday evenings at Lewis's office. They read each other stories and poems they were working on, and heated discussion often followed.

One day, as Tolkien was grading exams, he jotted this sentence down on an empty page: "In a hole in the ground there lived a hobbit." Tolkien later explained, "Names always generate a story in my mind. Eventually, I thought I'd better find out what hobbits were like. But that's only the beginning." The story developed over many years and was told to the Tolkien children in several forms. *The Hobbit* was published in 1937 with Tolkien's illustrations. It was an immediate success with both children and adults.

Tolkien spent the next twelve years working on a complete mythology connected to *The Hobbit* and written for adults. The long anticipated *Lord of the Rings* trilogy finally appeared, volume by volume, from 1954 to '55. It made Tolkien a famous and financially comfortable man at the age of sixty-four. He and Edith retired to the seaside community of Bournemouth, where Edith died in 1971. Tolkien moved back to Oxford, where he died in 1972 of a chest infection. He is buried beside Edith on the outskirts of Oxford at **Wovercote.**

> I am in fact a hobbit in all but size. I like gardens, trees, and unmechanized farmlands; I smoke a pipe, and like good plain food (unrefrigerated), but detest French cooking; I like, and even dare to wear in these dull days, ornamental waistcoats. I am fond of mushrooms (out of the field); have a very simple sense of humor . . . I go to bed late and get up late (when possible). I do not travel much.
> —J. R. R. Tolkien

Other Places Connected with
J. R. R. Tolkien's Life

GRACEWELL LANE, SAREHOLE, BIRMINGHAM

The Sarehole area is now very much a part of the city of Birmingham. All that remains of the rural area that Tolkien loved so well in his boyhood is the Sarehole Mill Recreation Ground with the river Cole running past a large playing field. Tolkien's family lived nearby on Gracewell Lane, a small, quiet little alley that somehow has managed to retain the feeling of a country lane as the city has surrounded it. I was unable to locate No. 5, so it may no longer exist.

Sarehole is located southeast of the center of Birmingham. Take the A435 from junction 3 of the M42, which is the major highway south of the city. Follow it through suburban Birmingham to the B4146, Cole Bank Road. Turn left and cross over the river Cole, passing the Sarehole Mill Recreation Ground on the right. At the next traffic circle, turn right onto Wake Green Road. Gracewell Lane veers off to the right in less than a quarter mile.

OXFORD UNIVERSITY, OXFORD

Oxford University is actually a collection of thirty-six colleges that together enroll over fourteen thousand students each year. Tolkien earned his undergraduate degree at Exeter College, which is on the south side of Broad Street at the corner of Turl, right in the center of town. There is a bust of Tolkien in the Exeter College chapel. From 1926 to 1945, Tolkien returned to Oxford as a professor of Anglo-Saxon to teach at Pembroke College. Pembroke is across St. Aldate's Road from Christ Church College (see the *Alice's Adventures in Wonderland* chapter, page 30). From 1945 until 1959, Tolkien was a professor of English language and literature at Merton College, which is on the other side of Christ Church College between Merton Street and the lovely Christ Church Meadow. Merton College provided a flat at 21

Merton Street for Tolkien in his final years. Each college has its own schedule of hours when it is open to the public, and the hours vary during the school year.

THE EAGLE & CHILD PUB, OXFORD

It's easy to understand why the Inklings found The Eagle & Child pub (nicknamed the Bird & Baby) to be so congenial. It's a cozy, quiet old pub with small rooms and alcoves and a fire burning in the grate. The room where the Inklings gathered and read their works-in-progress is called the Rabbit Room. There are photos of Tolkien, Lewis, and their comrades on the walls and excellent beers on tap. It's a great place for lunch or to wind down after a day in Oxford. Or go on your own with a copy of an Icelandic saga in the original medieval Icelandic and relax.

No. 20 Northmoor Road, Oxford

The Tolkien family lived at 22 Northmoor Road for four years and then moved next door to No. 20 in 1930. Tolkien wrote *The Hobbit* and *The Lord of the Rings* in this nondescript house, where his family remained until 1947. It is a private home and not open to the public. The Oxford Tourist Information Centre in Gloucester Green in the center of town distributes an excellent, detailed sheet about Tolkien in Oxford that includes the addresses of Tolkien's other residences over the years. The information is compiled by the Tolkien Society.

To reach Northmoor Road, follow St. Giles north from the town center. The road splits; stay right on Banbury Road. Turn right onto Bardwell Road and follow it to Northmoor.

Wolvercote Cemetery, Oxford

Tolkien and his wife, Edith, are buried on the western side of this cemetery. There is a map of the cemetery at the gate, and small markers point the way to the Tolkiens' graves.

Wolvercote Cemetery is on the Banbury Road just past the A40 bypass.

Places to See Original Artwork/Manuscripts

Memorial Library, Marquette University, Milwaukee, Wisconsin

The head librarian at Marquette University had the good sense to recognize the value of Tolkien's work a few years before the rest of the world. He bought Tolkien's original manuscripts of *The Hobbit* and *The Lord of the Rings* for under five thousand dollars in 1958. The library has a permanent display on *The Lord of the Rings* that is open to the public as well as an extensive collection of Tolkien-related materials. A display about *The Hobbit* may be added when the library moves into a new building in 2003. A picture ID is required to enter the library, which is open from 8:00 A.M. to 5:00 P.M., Monday through Friday. For more information, contact the library. Telephone: (414) 288-7556. Web site: www.marquette.edu.

BODLEIAN LIBRARY, OXFORD UNIVERSITY, OXFORD

The Bodleian Library houses most of the original manuscripts of Lewis's work that survive, although they are not on display to the public and are only available for scholarly research. The Bodleian Library quadrangle is located in Oxford, off of Broad Street, between the Sheldonian Theatre and the Radcliffe Camera. Telephone: (01865) 277188. Web site: www.bodley.ox.ac.uk.

MARION E. WADE CENTER, WHEATON COLLEGE, WHEATON, ILLINOIS

The center features a display on Lewis and the other Inklings, which includes the old wardrobe made by Lewis's grandfather. Some of Lewis's papers and correspondence are also here. The original map of Narnia drawn by illustrator Pauline Baynes is also on display. Admission is free. Telephone: 630-752-5908.

THE DOCTOR DOLITTLE BOOKS

by Hugh Lofting

♣ "What in the world is it?" asked John Dolittle, gazing at the strange creature.

"Lord save us!" cried the duck. "How does it make up its mind?"

"It doesn't look to me as though it had any," said Jip, the dog.

"This, Doctor," said Chee-chee, "is the pushmi-pullyu—the rarest animal of the African jungles, the only two-headed beast in the world! Take him home with you and your fortune's made. People will pay money to see him." . . .

"But does the er—what-do-you call-it really want to go abroad?"
"Yes, I'll go," said the pushmi-pullyu, who saw at once from the Doctor's face that he was a man to be trusted.

—*The Story of Doctor Dolittle*, 1920

$\mathcal{A}$N ECCENTRIC, PORTLY LITTLE MAN WEARING A TOP HAT and carrying a black bag—a nineteenth-century naturalist, linguist, and misanthrope—Doctor Dolittle is an unlikely children's hero. But this gentle, studious man has found a way to do the one thing that every child longs to do: He can talk to animals in their own language. In the course of the twelve books Hugh Lofting wrote about him, the good doctor voyages all over the globe and even to the moon in his quest to learn all he can from the animal kingdom. Assisted by his wise and faithful parrot, Polynesia, Jip the dog, Dab-Dab the duck, Gub-Gub the pig, and Chee-Chee the monkey, Doctor Dolittle helps a dog testify in court, aids the bulls in bringing an end to bullfighting, organizes the foxes to undermine foxhunting, and converts a gang of pirates into birdseed farmers, among many other adventures.

Doctor Dolittle's fictional village of Puddleby-on-the-Marsh is in some ways every small, charming English village, but the Wiltshire village that was used as the setting for the 1967 movie *Doctor Dolittle* is a picture-perfect example. Spend a day wandering the little lanes of this modern-day Puddleby. Enjoy a picnic by the stream that runs through the village, and, in the spirit of the good doctor, be sure to bring a little extra for any ducks or squirrels that might wander by.

A Brief Biography of Hugh Lofting

My children at home wanted letters from me—and they wanted them with illustrations rather than without. There seemed very little of interest to write to youngsters from the front; the news was either too horrible or dull. . . . One thing, however, that kept forcing itself more and more on my attention was the very considerable part the animals were playing in the world war. . . . If we made the animals take the same chances we did ourselves, why did we not give them similar attention when wounded? But obviously to develop a horse surgery as good as [ours] would necessitate a knowledge of horse language. . . .

—Hugh Lofting, on the beginning of the idea of Doctor Dolittle
The Junior Book of Authors, 1934

Hugh Lofting was born in Maidenhead, England, just west of London, in 1886. One of six children, he had a great fondness for animals and kept a small zoo in the linen closet until it was discovered. At age eight, he was sent to a Jesuit boarding school, Mount St. Mary's, in Chesterfield, Derbyshire. With only 120 students, the school was a little world unto itself, quite protected and close-knit. Upon gradua-tion at age eighteen, Lofting made the decision to learn a profession that would allow him to indulge his wanderlust. He headed to America to study civil engineering at the Massachusetts Institute of Technology in Boston, returning to London Polytechnic a year later to complete his degree. He then headed to Canada to work as a surveyor and prospector. This Canadian period was followed by stints in West Africa and Cuba working for railway companies.

By 1912, Lofting was convinced, not only that he hated engineering, but that he was a terrible engineer. He returned to the United States and married Flora Small. They settled in New York and promptly had two children, Elizabeth and Colin. Lofting began to pursue a career as an author, writing humorous articles and short stories for magazines. When World War I began, he went to work for the British Ministry of Information in New York. In 1916, he enlisted as a British soldier and was sent over to fight in France and Flanders. He returned home in 1917 after being wounded.

Lofting's experience in the trenches resulted in a lifelong aversion to war and the glorification of war. In 1923 and 1924, he wrote articles for the *Nation* magazine condemning the depiction of warfare in children's literature:

> [A] boy may not have heard his father boasting of the genius of a crack regiment, but he has read a whole heap of so-called children's classics in which highly painted heroes galloped, glorious and victorious, across bloody battlefields. That kind of battlefield has gone for good—it is still bloody, but you don't gallop. And since that kind of a battlefield has gone, that kind of book—for children—should go too. . . .

While posted at the front, Lofting found himself searching for an entertaining subject to write about in his letters to Colin and Elizabeth. Appalled by the mistreatment of animals during wartime, he came up with the idea of an eccentric doctor who gives up his human medical practice in favor of caring for animals by learning their languages. The children loved the letters, and Colin began calling himself Doctor Dolittle. Lofting's wife kept all the letters and convinced her husband that they should be a book. The family was sailing home to America from Britain in 1919 when they made the acquaintance of a well-known writer, Cecil Roberts. Roberts read the manuscript and enthusiastically promised to show it to his publisher.

The Story of Doctor Dolittle, with Lofting's illustrations, was published in 1920 to instant popularity. Lofting followed it up with *The Voyages of Doctor Dolittle* in 1922, which won the Newbery Medal that year. The books were quickly proclaimed classics. Lofting and his family settled in Madison, Connecticut, where he continued to write and illustrate a Doctor Dolittle book each year for the next six years. In 1927, Flora died. Lofting married Katherine Harrower-Peters, who died in an influenza epidemic before they had been married a year. Lofting's health was deteriorating, and his energy for writing yet another Dr. Dolittle book was waning. His son later said that Lofting tried to finish the series by sending the good doctor to the moon in the eighth book of the series, but public demand resulted in *Doctor Dolittle's Return* in 1933.

In 1935, Lofting married Josephine Fricker, a Canadian he had met on a lecture tour. They moved to Topanga, California, near Los Angeles, where their son, Christopher, was born in 1936. Lofting's health continued to fail as the world entered yet another widespread war. Hugh Lofting died in Santa Monica, California, in 1947, at age sixty-one. The final three of the thirteen Dr. Dolittle books were published posthumously.

Places Connected with the Doctor Dolittle Stories

CASTLE COMBE, WILTSHIRE

The literary Puddleby-on-the-Marsh, Doctor Dolittle's hometown, lies at some undetermined spot deep in Cornwall, but the cinematic Puddleby is Castle Combe (pronounced "coom"). The 1967 movie musical of *Doctor Dolittle,* starring Rex Harrison, was filmed using this entire village as a backdrop. It's easy to see why it was chosen. Castle Combe has been voted "the Prettiest Village in England" more than once, and it's a postcard scene everywhere you look. A lovely stream that passes through the lower end of the town was "enhanced" in the movie to look like a harbor. The movie company built the stone landing area near the little bridge as part of this illusion, and it's become a permanent feature of this historic town. Other lasting alterations included putting all the utility wires underground and replacing all the TV antennas with a community antenna.

Dolittle's Bar in the Castle Inn by the market plaza has photographs on the wall of the filming of *Doctor Dolittle.* It offers a good, reasonably priced lunch as well. The gift shop/newstand on the other side of the square sells an excellent guide to the town for 60 pence. Don't miss the ancient clock inside the old church, which has been striking the hour accurately since about the time Columbus sailed to the New World.

The town museum, a small building on the road between the parking area and the village, is open Sundays, 2:00–5:00 P.M., from Easter through October 1. Telephone: (01249) 782-250.

Castle Combe is located seventy miles west of London and fifteen miles east of Bristol. Although it is only a mile or two from the M4, it takes a bit of circling about to get there from the highway junction. Exit at junction 17 and head south on the A350 toward Chippenham. Take the A4 west toward Bristol, then follow the signs to the B4039 to Castle Combe. There is a free parking area about a quarter mile above the village. It's worth parking here and strolling into the village, which has very narrow roads and can become quite congested in the summertime. Occasionally there are llama sightings from this parking area—or was it a . . . no, couldn't be!

Places to See Original Artwork/Manuscripts

THE BRITISH LIBRARY, LONDON

There is a delightful exhibit about the history of children's literature in Britain in the Pearson Gallery of Living Words. A first edition of *The Story of Doctor Dolittle* from 1920 is part of the display.

The British Library is located next to St. Pancras station at 96 Euston Road. It is open on Monday, Wednesday, Thursday, and Friday, 9:30–6:00 P.M.; Tuesday, 9:30–8:00 P.M.; Saturday, 9:30–5:00 P.M.; and Sundays/holidays, 11:00–5:00 P.M. There is no charge for admission to the exhibits. The closest tube station is Kings Cross/St. Pancras. Telephone: (0171) 412-7332.

Other Activities for Children Who Love the Doctor Dolittle Stories

THE WALTER ROTHSCHILD ZOOLOGICAL MUSEUM, TRING, HERTFORDSHIRE

This museum may not have an actual pushmi-pullyu, but it has just about every other rare or odd animal imaginable. They are all stuffed, and most of them were collected in the nineteenth century by Walter Rothschild, a rich and eccentric Victorian. One of his better-known antics was riding in a wagon pulled by four zebras to Buckingham Palace. He dedicated his life and wealth to collecting and stuffing every species he could find. When he died in 1937, he gave the entire collection to the British Museum. Rothschild's collection includes a model of a dodo bird, the extremely long (up to eight meters) and extremely bony oarfish, and a group of fleas costumed in full Mexican dancing splendor. Although Doctor Dolittle might not have approved of stuffing these incredible specimens, he certainly would have enjoyed studying them.

Tring is on the A41, thirty-three miles north of London. It's an easy train ride from London, although the train station is about two miles from the museum. The museum itself is on Akeman Street, just off Tring High Street in the center of town. The museum is open from 10:00 to 17:00, Monday to Saturday; 2:00–5:00, Sunday. Children sixteen and under and seniors enter for free; adults pay £3.75. Telephone: (207) 942-6171. Web site: www.aylesburyvale.net.

LONDON ZOO, LONDON

One of the great urban zoos of the world, the London Zoo sits on the north side of Regent's Park along the Regent's Canal. For details, see the A. A. Milne chapter, page 81.

EDINBURGH ZOO, EDINBURGH

This zoo has a wonderful setting on a hillside on the outskirts of Edinburgh. For details, see the P. L. Travers chapter, page 140.

SHEEPDOG DEMONSTRATION, KINCRAIG, SCOTLAND

Shepherds can't exactly engage in small talk with their sheepdogs, but they do communicate with their animals with amazing clarity and precision about very complex tasks. This sheepdog demonstration provides an opportunity to visit a working sheep farm and watch shepherd and dog work together with great skill.

Neil Ross's farm at Kincraig near Aviemore in the Grampian Mountains of Scotland puts on a great show out in the fields. Up to ten dogs work in tandem as a single shepherd signals each dog with a distinct set of whistles and gestures. There are often puppies-in-training working as well. The dogs herd the sheep and a noisy bunch of ducks with impressive efficiency and enthusiasm. Anyone who loved the book or movie *Babe* by Dick King-Smith will enjoy this show as well, despite the absence of pig talent. Visitors can also have a go at sheepshearing and bottle-feeding lambs.

The demonstrations are held every day (except Saturday) at 12:00 and 4:00 P.M. Admission is £4/adults, £2/children. Telephone: (01540) 651310.

From the A9, take the B9152 to Kincraig. Follow the signs to the Highland Wildlife Park. Do not go into the new A9 at this point. One mile past the Highland Wildlife Park, look for signs saying WORKING SHEEPDOGS. Follow the dirt road, crossing the A9, through the open farm gate and on up to the farm. It's a confusing place to find but well worth the effort! You may want to call for local directions once you are in the area.

PET RESCUE

For an interesting look at the well-known British love affair with animals, turn on your television to Channel Four at 5:30 any weekday to watch *Pet Rescue*. This popular and long-running show follows real-life veterinarians and animal care workers as they do their work. One show may feature the hours'-long struggle to free a dog stuck in a drainage pipe, another might watch a horse whisperer at work. Every show includes the story of one animal in an animal shelter that needs a home. Interested viewers phone in, often by the hundreds, and a suitable home is chosen for the animal. Part of the fun is the follow-up they do weeks or months later to see how the animal and family are getting along. Telephone Channel Four in London at (207) 306-8333 for more information.

THE WINNIE-THE-POOH *and* CHRISTOPHER ROBIN BOOKS
by A. A. Milne

♣ Now one day Pooh and Piglet and Rabbit and Roo were all playing Poohsticks together. They had dropped their sticks in [the stream] when Rabbit said, "Go!" and then they had hurried across to the other side of the bridge, and now they were all leaning over the edge, waiting to see whose stick would come out first. But it was a long time coming because the river was very lazy that day, and hardly seemed to mind if it didn't ever get there at all.

—*The House at Pooh Corner,* 1928

$\mathcal{E}$NJOY A GAME OF POOHSTICKS, HUM A HUM AS YOU STROLL along the path with an eye out for heffalumps, visit Eeyore's Gloomy place, or just sit and think on a branch of the Lonely Pine as Christopher Robin and Pooh often did. Spending a few hours in Pooh's woods is a delightful and memorable experience for adults and kids.

Written in the 1920s and inspired by the author's young son, Christopher Robin Milne, the two books about the world of Pooh Bear, *Winnie-the-Pooh* and *The House at Pooh Corner,* are set in the forest and countryside around the Milne family's country cottage south of London. The area, known as Ashdown Forest, is well situated for a day trip by car from London or as a stop en route to the coast and is well marked but delightfully low-key and noncommercial. There are lovely hikes that are suitable for young children but also enjoyable for older kids/adults around the "100 Aker Wood," which features beautiful views out over the Downs and charming villages nearby. When we visited in the early spring, the gorse bushes (the prickly ones that Pooh falls into every now and again) were all blooming bright yellow and covering the hillsides. Most importantly, various features of the woods, such as the Poohsticks Bridge and the Lonely Pine, are very clearly linked with Milne's stories and with the wonderful illustrations that E. H. Shepard drew for the books after visiting the area. I loved the books when I was young, while my four-year-old has mostly known the Disney movies and spin-off books. But we both instantly recognized the various Pooh-related locations. We enjoyed figuring out where Roo liked to play, how Eeyore could have fallen into the stream by the bridge, and other favorite scenarios.

Both the Pooh stories and the two books of poetry by Milne, *When We Were Very Young* and *Now We Are Six,* also have some connections with London sights, especially the London Zoo.

Brief Biographies

The animals in the stories came for the most part from the nursery. My collaborator [Milne's wife] had already given them individual voices, their owner [Christopher Robin] by constant affection had given them the twist in their features which denoted character, and Shepard drew them, as one might say, from the living model. They were what they are for anyone to see; I described rather than invented them. Only Rabbit and Owl were my own unaided work.
—*A. A. Milne*

A. A. MILNE, 1882–1956

Alan Alexander Milne had a long and successful career writing light verse and sophisticated plays for adults, but he is remembered for the two story books and two books of poetry he wrote for children about his son, Christopher Robin. Born in 1882 in London, the third son of a schoolmaster, Milne was particularly close to his older brother, Ken. Separated in age by only sixteen months, the two brothers went for long walks, read books, and wrote stories, which they submitted (unsuccessfully) to magazines. They both won scholarships at a young age to Westminster School, where they discovered a talent for collaborating on writing humorous verse. They both continued their studies at Cambridge, Ken studying law and Alan studying math. They contributed joint work to the campus humor magazine, *Granta,* and Alan eventually became its editor. Ken drifted away from writing at this point, but Alan persisted; and after graduation in 1903, he moved to London to work as a freelance writer. He struggled a bit at the beginning but, by 1905, was contributing regularly to *Punch,* the leading magazine of sophisticated humor at that time. He became lifelong friends with playwright J. M. Barrie (the creator of Peter Pan) during these years. In 1906, he joined the permanent staff at *Punch* as assistant editor, and he remained there until the outbreak of World War I in 1914.

In 1913, Milne married Daphne de Selincourt, the goddaughter of the senior editor at *Punch.* Because she knew his work by heart and laughed at his jokes, he declared her to have "the most perfect sense of humour in the world." Milne volunteered for the army in 1915 and worked as an instructor in the Signal Corps, stationed on the Isle of Wight. He was sent to France in 1916 and was serving on the front lines when he contracted a fever and was sent back to England. He wrote of this time: "I should like to put asterisks here and then write, 'It was in 1919 that I found myself once again a civilian.' For it makes me almost physically sick to think of that nightmare of mental and moral degradation, the war."

Milne returned to civilian life to find that his position at *Punch* had been filled, so he set out to be a playwright. Nineteen-twenty turned out to be a banner year, with his first successful play, *Mr. Pim Passes By,* opening in London in January and with his son, Christopher Robin, being born in August. Milne continued to have success with his plays and branched out into writing novels. In 1923, he "wasted a morning" writing a children's poem called "Vespers," which began "Little boy kneels at the foot of the bed, droops on the little hands little gold head. . . ." He gave it as a present to Daphne and told her she could keep any money she might get for selling it. As Milne observed later, "It turned out to be the most expensive present I had ever given her." The poem was published in *Vanity Fair* and was an immediate hit. Milne was asked to write another poem for a new children's magazine, which became "The Dormouse and the Doctor." By 1924, he had published a book of poems for children, *When We Were Very Young,* illustrated by E. H. Shepard, who also worked for *Punch*. It was an immediate huge success.

Thanks to that success, the Milnes bought a weekend/summer home south of London in 1925 near the village of **Hartfield** and **Ashdown Forest,** while continuing to keep their home at **Mallord Street, Chelsea,** in London. *Winnie-the-Pooh* followed in 1926, *Now We Are Six* in 1927, and *The House at Pooh Corner* in 1928. All three were extremely successful, eventually being translated into twelve languages and selling over seven million copies.

Milne was the kind of author who needed new forms and new challenges. He didn't write for children again after 1928 except to adapt *The Wind in the Willows,* by Kenneth Grahame, into a children's play, *Toad of Toad Hall.* Milne shared a box with Grahame at the opening of the play, which was a success and is still performed at Christmastime in Britain.

Milne's brother, Ken, died in 1929. He had been quite ill with tuberculosis since 1924, and Alan had been helping out with educational and medical expenses for Ken's children. When he wrote his autobiography, *It's Too Late Now,* in 1939, he dedicated it to Ken.

A. A. Milne never again achieved the level of success that he had enjoyed in the 1920s. His last play was produced in 1938, and it was not a success. In his later years he came to resent the fact that his writing for adults was so overshadowed by the Christopher Robin books. In 1952, Milne suffered a stroke that left him partially paralyzed, and he died at the age of seventy-four, in 1956, at Cotchford Farm.

In 1961, Daphne sold the film rights for the Christopher Robin/Pooh books to Walt Disney.

CHRISTOPHER ROBIN MILNE, 1920–1996

As a child, Christopher Robin looked very much like the little boy in the famous illustrations, and he played with the real Winnie-the-Pooh, a bear his parents had bought at Harrod's and given to him for his first birthday. After the age of four, he spent much of his time at Cotchford Farm, near **Hartfield,** playing in the surrounding woods with his beloved Pooh, Eeyore, Kanga, Roo, and Tigger. His parents were somewhat removed from him during his "nursery years," and the center of his life was his much-loved nanny.

In his autobiography, *The Enchanted Places,* Christopher Robin says that his father wasn't very good at relating to children, and to make up for that he wrote stories about his son, his toys, and his games. Christopher Robin remembers his own eagerness to come up with ideas for games matching his father's eagerness for story ideas, and it's a bit unclear which came first for any given story.

However, it isn't easy to go through life with the whole world knowing you as a five-year-old. When Christopher Robin went to boarding school at age ten, he began to resent his fame and association with the stories. He encountered a lot of painful teasing, especially about the poem "Vespers." He eventually went on to Cambridge and studied math, as his father had. He left after eight months to join the army as World War II had begun. During the war he served in Iraq, Tunisia, and Italy, where he was wounded by a piece of shrapnel. He came to loathe war just as much as his father had before him.

After the war he returned to Cambridge and graduated in 1947, having switched his degree to English literature. He had difficulty settling into a job and went through a period of great bitterness toward his father. He writes: ". . . it seemed to me, almost, that my father had got to where he was by climbing upon my infant shoulders, that he had filched from me my good name and had left me with nothing but the empty fame of being his son."

In 1948, Christopher Robin married Lesley de Selincourt, his cousin. Lesley had spent a solitary childhood in the countryside much as Christopher Robin had done, and they found they "liked being solitary in each other's company." Because Lesley was the daughter of his mother's estranged brother, with whom the Milnes hadn't spoken for thirty years, she and Christopher Robin had never met as children. The Milnes were strongly opposed to the marriage. In 1951, Christopher Robin and Lesley moved across England to Dartmouth, Devon, and opened a bookstore there. In 1956, they had a daughter, Clare, and they spent the next twenty-odd years building up their business.

Christopher Robin saw very little of his parents after he left London. The last time he saw his mother was at his father's memorial service, even though she lived for another fifteen years. He was quite upset when Daphne sold the rights to his father's work. Eventually he wrote two volumes of autobiography, *The Enchanted Places* in 1974 and *The Path Through the Trees* in 1979. The writing of these books became a healing process for Christopher Robin and allowed him to come to peace with his relationship with his parents and his fame. In his later years he campaigned to preserve **Ashdown Forest** and worked with the Save the Children Fund. He died in 1996 at the age of seventy-six.

E. H. SHEPARD, 1879–1976

Ernest Howard Shepard was born in London in 1879, one of three children in an artistic family. He loved drawing as a child, and his talent was encouraged by both parents. His mother died when he was eight years old. In 1897, he won a scholarship to the Royal Academy schools. There he met Florence Chaplin, and in 1904 they were married. They had two children, Graham (born in 1907) and Mary (born in 1909). Mary grew up to become an artist herself, illustrating the Mary Poppins books in the 1930s.

E. H. Shepard's hopes of working for the magazine *Punch* were finally realized in 1907 when two of his drawings were accepted for publication. *Punch* had been the premier magazine for sophisticated cartoons in Britain for many years (much like the *New Yorker* magazine in the United States).

During World War I, Shepard served in the Royal Artillery at the Battle of the Somme. He returned home in 1919 with the rank of major. It was not until 1921 that Shepard was appointed to the regular staff of *Punch*. One of the other staff members suggested that he illustrate the book of poems A. A. Milne was working on, *When We Were Very Young*. Milne resisted the idea initially, and the editors were at first dismayed by Shepard's unframed illustrations, which were designed around the words on the page in unconventional ways. Shepard received a rather modest, flat fee for his work. However, the book was a huge success, and the partnership continued for the other three Christopher Robin books. Milne wisely acknowledged the importance of the illustrations to the books' popularity and insisted that Shepard be given a share of the royalties for the three subsequent books. This was highly unusual at that time.

Shepard visited the Milne family at Cotchford Farm to sketch Christopher Robin and the various spots in **Ashdown Forest** where he played with his toy friends. His son, Graham, accompanied him and played happily with Christopher Robin. However, Milne and Shepard were never close despite their successful collaboration. As Shepard put it, "I always had to start at the beginning with Milne, every time I met him."

Shepard's wife, Florence, died unexpectedly in 1927 during a small operation. After this Shepard threw himself into his work. He illustrated a new edition of *The Wind in the Willows* by Kenneth Grahame in 1931. He continued his work for *Punch* as a political cartoonist from

1935 to 1953 when, to his dismay, a new editor at the magazine dismissed him. At the age of seventy-five, he continued working, illustrating other children's books and writing his memoirs. He redid the Christopher Robin books with color illustrations, and he continued to provide colored drawings for new editions of the Pooh stories for many years. Like A. A. Milne, he became frustrated with the endless focus on what he called "that silly old bear." E. H. Shepard died in 1976 at the age of ninety-seven.

Places Connected with the Winnie-the-Pooh and Christopher Robin Books

ASHDOWN FOREST

Christopher Robin and his good friends Pooh Bear, Piglet, Eeyore, Kanga, Roo, and Tigger played in the area around the Milne home at Cotchford Farm (now a private residence) in what was then and is now Ashdown Forest. The forest was first fenced off in 1268 when John of Gaunt began its use as a royal hunting ground. The gates and hatches of the wall that surrounded the forest at that time are still present in many local names, and the name Hartfield also recalls hunting times. The area was preserved as an "Area of Outstanding Natural Beauty" by an Act of Parliament in 1885 and has been run since 1988 by the Ashdown Forest Trust as a preserved natural area.

The best place for information about the forest is the Ashdown Forest Information Centre near Wych Cross. The information center can supply you with a helpful pamphlet titled "Two Pooh Walks," which provides excellent information about the path to the Poohsticks Bridge and the path to the Enchanted Place, Lone Pine, and other Pooh-related spots at Gill's Lap. They also sell a general forest map, which will be useful if you are more ambitious and want to hike around the "100 Aker Wood" off the beaten path. Various "Pooh scenes" for young kids to color are also on sale. The information center has somewhat limited hours, especially on weekdays, so you may begin your visit with a stop at Pooh Corner, a shop in Hartfield (see page 83). They have a less informative, but also helpful, pamphlet about the Poohsticks Bridge walk.

To reach the Ashdown Forest area by car, follow the A22 south from London, through East Grinstead to Wych Cross. Turn left (go east) on the road toward Coleman's Hatch and Hartfield. About a mile down the road on the left is the Ashdown Forest Centre. The center is open weekdays, April through September, from 2:00–5:00 P.M. and weekends/holidays year round from 11:00–5:00 P.M. Telephone: (01342) 823-583.

By far the most convenient way to visit Ashdown Forest is by car. It is well worth renting a car in London for the trip. It is possible to visit the Ashdown Forest area by public transportation, but the links aren't smooth, and the distances once you arrive in the area are great enough that it would be quite difficult to do if you are traveling with children. If you do choose to go by public transport, travel by train from London (Charing Cross or Waterloo stations) to Tunbridge Wells. Take the No. 291 bus toward East Grinstead for approximately ten miles and ask to get off at High Street, Hartfield. The buses run from Monday to Saturday and leave approximately every two hours. For bus information, telephone (01342) 893-080.

Poohsticks Bridge: You can begin the walk to the Pooh-sticks Bridge at Pooh Corner in Hartfield, but the first part will be on a narrow, busy road and really doesn't work if you have young children with you. The alternative is to drive to  the Poohsticks Bridge car park about two miles up the B2026 from Hartfield. This will also shorten your walk to the bridge by a mile or so. The walk from the car park to the bridge is on a wide, well-marked path suitable for young children and baby strollers. It could be muddy at almost any time of year, so boots might be useful. The walk is through a quiet, gentle woods and past some lovely pastures. However, here, as in almost every English nature area, you are never far from a farm or a dirt road with vehicles going back and forth, so don't expect to have a private, out-in-the-wilderness kind of experience! Also, there is a lot of barbed wire along the path where it passes through private land and at the bridge itself. Despite these intrusions from the late-twentieth century, it's still a lovely walk, and the bridge and stream are a delightful scene straight out of the Pooh stories.

> They walked on, thinking of This and That, and by-and-by they came to an enchanted place on the very top of the Forest called Galleon's Lap, which is sixty-something trees in a circle; and Christopher Robin knew it was enchanted because nobody had ever been able to count whether it was sixty-three or sixty-four, not even when he tied a piece of string round each tree after he had counted it. Being enchanted, its floor was not like the floor of the Forest, gorse and bracken and heather, but close-set grass, quiet and smooth and green. It was the only place in the Forest where you could sit down carelessly, without getting up again almost at once and looking for somewhere else. Sitting there they could see the whole world spread out until it reached the sky, and whatever there was all the world over was with them in Galleon's Lap.
>
> —The House at Pooh Corner

Gill's Lap (Galleon's Lap): The area around Gill's Lap (called Galleon's Lap by Milne) provides access to several other places where Christopher Robin, Pooh, and friends played. An easy half-mile walk on a ridge top will take you to the Enchanted Place, the Lone Pine and Heffalump Trap, Roo's Sandpit, the North Pole, Eeyore's Sad and Gloomy Place, and the A. A. Milne Memorial. This walk also provides a view out over the "100 Aker Wood," which is called the 500 Acre Woods officially.

Some of these spots will jump straight out at you from the illustrations in the books and movies, others take a bit of imagination, but that's half the fun. There is a marker with a wonderful map drawn by E. H. Shepard of the path around this area next to the car park. The views out over the surrounding countryside are spectacular. It's a great area for a picnic, and true to Christopher Robin's observation, the

Enchanted Place is the only spot in the whole forest where you can sit down on the ground carelessly. (I sat down a bit too cavalierly at the Pooh Bridge and had nettle stings on my hand for the rest of the day.) The paths are unpaved but suitable for hardy baby strollers. All the Pooh-related spots listed above, except for the North Pole and Eeyore's Sad and Gloomy Place, are within a half mile of the parking lot.

To reach Gill's Lap, continue along the B2026 away from Hartfield. You will pass the Wren's Warren, Piglet, and Quarry car parks, and then you will see the Gill's Lap car park at the junction of the B2026 and Colemans Hatch Road.

"100 Aker Wood": If you feel like mounting your own "expotition" into the "100 Aker Wood" (called the 500 Acre Wood on the map), you can follow the marked path called the Weald Way, or you can strike out on your own. Be aware that you can only wander freely in the part of the wood that is within the boundaries of Ashdown Forest. A forest map from the Ashdown Forest Information Centre is a necessity for this. The Weald Way is most easily accessible from the Wood Reeves car park on the B2188. You might also follow the Vanguard Way across the B2026 from the Poohsticks Bridge car park. It skirts the 500 Acre Wood but intersects the Weald Way on the edge of it.

In the London Area

LONDON ZOO

A Canadian soldier left his pet bear cub, Winnie, with the London Zoo while he was fighting in France in World War I. The black bear cub was named for her hometown of Winnipeg, Manitoba. After the war the soldier gave Winnie to the London Zoo, and she lived there until her death in 1934. She was a great favorite with the young Christopher Robin Milne in the early 1920s, and his father even managed to arrange a visit for Christopher Robin with Winnie "behind the scenes," aided by one of the zookeepers. She was most certainly the inspiration for Christopher Robin's "Edward Bear" being dubbed "Winnie." ("The-Pooh" seems to have been a name first given by Christopher Robin to a favorite swan and then transferred to his beloved bear.) There is a statue of Winnie and the Canadian soldier near the Children's Zoo, which was given to the London Zoo by the people of Manitoba, a duplicate of one at the Assiniboine Park Zoo in Winnipeg. The bear exhibit at the zoo is newly renovated and quite good. However, it features sloth bears, which are adorable but not tremendously Pooh-like.

A read-through of "At the Zoo" from *When We Were Very Young* can set the tone for an enjoyable day out at the London Zoo. The zoo has updated and improved many of its enclosures and has a spacious, modern feel to it. It's a very popular family outing for Londoners and can get quite crowded despite the rather high admission price. In addition to a modest Children's Zoo, there are pony and llama rides and a couple of good play areas for kids. There is a playfully designed penguin area and lots of space for picnicking. The zoo also plays a role in the Mary Poppins stories (see the *Mary Poppins* chapter, page 137), and it is right across the street from Primrose Hill, with its *101 Dalmatians* connections (see *The 101 Dalmatians* chapter, page 206) and lovely views of the city. The Regent's Canal runs right through the zoo; and Regent's Park, which surrounds the zoo, is beautiful, spacious, and a great way to escape London traffic fumes and crowds.

The London Zoo is located at the north side of Regent's Park. It is open from 10:00 A.M. every day except Christmas Day. Admission is adults £9.00; children four and older £7.00. The nearest tube stop is Camden Town. It can also be reached by the C2 or the 274 bus. A waterbus runs between Camden Lock or Little Venice and the zoo on the Regent's Canal. The waterbus service is hourly from April through September, daily during October, and on weekends only from November through March. There is a parking area on Prince Albert Road (pay) for the zoo. Telephone: (207) 722-3333.

BUCKINGHAM PALACE

They're changing guard at Buckingham Palace—
Christopher Robin went down with Alice.

Alice is marrying one of the guard.
"A soldier's life is terrible hard,"
Says Alice.
—from "Buckingham Palace" in *When We Were Very Young*

It's unlikely that you'll need any extra reasons for visiting Buckingham Palace when you are in London, but it is a great opportunity to read the poem "Buckingham Palace," even if you do have to change the "king" references to "queen" these days.

Buckingham Palace is located at the end of the Mall between Green Park and St. James Park. The changing of the guard takes place at 11:30 A.M. daily from April 3 through August 3 and on alternate days the rest of the year. The event always draws a large crowd, so get there early if you want a good viewing spot. The closest tube stops for Buckingham Palace are Victoria, Hyde Park Corner, or Green Park. Telephone: (207) 930-4832.

Other Places Connected with A. A. Milne/ Christopher Robin Milne/E. H. Shepard's Lives

POOH CORNER, HARTFIELD

When Christopher Robin was a boy staying at Cotchford Farm up the road, he would ride his donkey in the company of his nanny down to the village of Hartfield. The donkey knew that the first stop was always at the sweets shop on the left as you enter the village, where Christopher Robin would buy a bag of peppermint bull's-eyes for sustenance before going on to do errands. The three-hundred-year-old shop is now known as Pooh Corner, and it sells an enormous variety of cards, books, stuffed animals, clothing, rugs, mobiles, and almost anything else you can think of related to Christopher Robin and his friends. The merchandise is heavily slanted toward the Disney version of Pooh, but they still sell bags of bull's-eye candies!

Pooh Corner is located on the High Street in Hartfield. The shop is open 9:00–5:00 P.M., Monday through Saturday all year; it is open 11:00–5:00 P.M. on Sundays/holidays from Easter through October and 1:30–5:00 P.M. Sundays/holidays the rest of the year. They have a free pamphlet that tells you how to get to the two Pooh paths described earlier in this chapter (to the Poohsticks Bridge and Gill's Lap). Telephone: (01892) 770-456.

MILNE HOUSE AT 13 MALLORD STREET, CHELSEA, LONDON

The house where the Milne family lived when in London is a private home now, marked with a blue plaque commemorating the Milnes' occupancy. The closest tube stop is South Kensington. You can take the No. 49 bus to Kings Road or make the twenty- to twenty-five-minute walk on foot. Get off the bus near King's College. Walk up Old Church Street from Kings Road for half a block to Mallord Street. Milne's house, at No. 13, is on the left about halfway down Mallord Street. It's an artsy area with lots of interesting shops, galleries, and restaurants.

SHEPARD HOUSE NEAR REGENT'S PARK, LONDON

The house where E. H. Shepard lived is located at 10 Kent Terrace just off Park Road on the western side of Regent's Park. It is an elegant town house in one of the impressive, cream-colored terraces that surround Regent's Park. It is particularly intriguing to make the connections between this setting and the illustrations Shepard's daughter, Mary, created for *Mary Poppins*.

The closest tube stop is Baker Street, and it can also be reached by the No. 274 bus, which runs to and from the London Zoo on Park Road.

Places to See Original Artwork/Manuscripts

BRITISH LIBRARY, LONDON

The new British Library has a wonderful, permanent display on the rich history of children's literature in the United Kingdom. Among the items featured is a copy of the first edition of *Winnie-the-Pooh* (1926) and a note written in 1934 by E. H. Shepard, in Pooh style, with illustrations, declining an invitation to a birthday party.

The British Library is located next to St. Pancras station at 96 Euston Road. It is open on Monday, Wednesday, Thursday, and Friday, 9:30–6:00 P.M.; Tuesday, 9:30–8:00 P.M.; Saturday, 9:30–5:00 P.M.; and Sundays/holidays, 11:00–5:00 P.M. There is no charge for admission. The closest tube station is Kings Cross/St. Pancras. Telephone: (207) 412-7332.

(*NOTE: The original Pooh, Piglet, Eeyore, Tigger, and Kanga toys that belonged to Christopher Robin Milne are part of the collection of the New York Public Library, far from their native land.*)

Other Places to Visit for Children Who Love Milne's Stories

THE HUNNY POT, AYR, SCOTLAND

If you find yourself in Ayr, Scotland, and you or your children are Pooh Bear fans, be sure to eat at The Hunny Pot. This small, homey restaurant is decorated with all sorts of Pooh paraphernalia and features a "Smack-

erels" section on the menu. This is a good place for a reasonably priced lunch or a cozy tea.

Ayr is on the southeast coast of Scotland near Robert Burns country and several well-known golf courses. The Hunny Pot is located in the center of town at 35-37 Beresford Terrace. Telephone: (01292) 263-239. Open Monday to Saturday, 9:00 A.M.–10:00 P.M.; Sunday, 10:30 A.M.–9:30 P.M.

THE BORROWERS *and*
BED-KNOB AND BROOMSTICK

by Mary Norton

"Borrowing", he said after a while, "Is that what you call it?"

"What else could you call it?" asked Arrietty.

"I'd call it stealing."

Arrietty laughed. She really laughed.

"But we **are** Borrowers," she explained, "like you're a—a Human Bean or whatever it's called. We're part of the house. You might as well say that the fire grate steals the coal from the coal-scuttle."

—*The Borrowers,* 1952

*T*INY POD, HOMILY, AND ARRIETTY MAKE A LIFE FOR THEM-
selves living under the floorboards of a spacious old house inhabited by
the dreaded "Human Beans." Ingenious and hardy, they "borrow"
everything they need from the world above. Their chest of drawers is
made of matchboxes, they cook in a pot made from a sewing thimble,
and they take their baths in a pâté tin. Although they live in dread of
being spotted, they make a comfortable life for themselves using their
wits and courage to get what they need. Their miniature world is
turned upside down when Arrietty befriends one of the Human Beans,
and they are forced to flee into the great world outside. The six books by
Mary Norton about these resilient little people and their fascinating
parallel world continue to intrigue each new generation of children.

The house that inspired the Borrowers' stories survives, now serving
as a school. If you don't find any Borrowers there, you might try a
miniature re-creation of British village life in the 1920s. A completely
different social class of Borrowers might have inhabited an amazing
dollhouse designed and built for a princess and on display in one of
England's grandest castles.

A Brief Biography of Mary Norton

I think the first idea—or first feeling—of *The Borrowers* came through
my being short-sighted: when others saw the far hills, the distant
woods, the soaring pheasant, I, as a child, would turn sideways to the
close bank, the tree roots, and the tangled grasses.
—Mary Norton, *Dictionary of Literary Biography*, Volume 160

Mary Norton (née Pearson) was born in London in 1903. Her childhood
was spent in **Leighton Buzzard, Bedfordshire,** living in the family's
imposing Georgian house. The family home and its surroundings later
became the setting for the Borrowers stories. Mary was extremely near-
sighted, a problem that wasn't detected until she went off to boarding
school. She described her young self as "an inveterate lingerer, a gazer

into banks and hedgerows, a rapt investigator of shallow pools, a lier-down by stream-like teeming ditches."

From the age of eight, Mary attended convent schools. Her family moved to Lambeth, a London suburb, when Mary grew older. She had aspirations to be an actress and spent a season as an understudy with the Old Vic theatre company. In 1927, she married Robert Norton, a wealthy shipping magnate. She lived with her husband in Portugal for several years, where they raised four children.

When World War II began, she moved back to London and worked for the War Office. After Robert joined the navy, Mary and the children moved to New York, where she worked for the British Purchasing Office. To supplement her income, she began writing. The family moved back to London in 1943 during the period when London was being heavily bombed. Mary's eyes were injured by an exploding bomb, but her sight was restored with surgery. Through it all she continued to write. Her first children's book, *The Magic Bed-Knob,* was published in 1943 to great critical success and was followed by *Bonfires and Broom-sticks* (1947). Eventually, these two books were combined into *Bed-knob and Broomstick* (1957), which was made plural, *Bedknobs and Broomsticks,* and into a musical starring Angela Lansbury by The Disney Studios in 1971.

However, Norton's biggest success came with *The Borrowers* in 1952. The book, illustrated by Diana Stanley, won the Carnegie Medal that year and was hailed as a classic. It was followed by *The Borrowers Afield* (1955), *The Borrowers Afloat* (1959), *The Borrowers Aloft* (1961), *The Borrowers Avenged* (1982), and *Poor Stainless,* which came out as part of a collection in 1966 and as its own book in 1994. The stories were made into a BBC television series in the 1980s. *The Borrowers Aloft* and *The Borrowers Avenged* were combined into a feature film starring John Goodman in 1997.

After the death of her first husband, Mary Norton married Lionel Bonsey in 1970. After living for many years in Essex, England, she moved with her new husband to county Cork, Ireland, in 1972. They eventually moved back to North Devon, England, where Mary died of a stroke in 1992.

Places Connected with The Borrowers

CEDARS HOUSE, LEIGHTON BUZZARD, BEDFORDSHIRE

Mary Norton described her childhood home, which she used as the setting for her Borrowers books, in a letter to a fellow Leightonian as being in ". . . what was then a sleepy and charming country town. A river ran through the bottom of our garden. There were two strange buildings in the garden: an orangerie, in which we kept a pet chameleon, and a 'temple' with palladium pillars, which was used as a billiard room—a wonderful place for midnight feasts."

The house, garden, and even the orangerie remain, but they have been transformed into the Leighton Middle School. In *The Borrowers Afield,* Mrs. May and Kate go to Leighton Buzzard to visit the house where the Borrowers had been spotted in Mrs. May's girlhood. The maid answers the door and tells them the house is now a school.

> . . . Kate, standing her ground, addressed the girl: "Can't we just see inside the hall?"
>
> "Help yourself," said the girl, looking mildly surprised. . . .
>
> Kate looked about her: [the front hallway] was wide and high and panelled and there were the stairs "going up and up, world upon world," as Arrietty had described them—all the same it was nothing like she had imagined it. The floor was covered with burnished, dark green linoleum; there was a sourish smell of soapy water and the clean smell of wax. . . . Mrs. May indicated a piece of wall, now studded with a row of coat pegs. "There; Pod's hole must have been just behind where the radiator is now. . . ."

And that is an amazingly accurate description of my visit to Cedars House in 2001 (with a very gracious school secretary replacing the maid)! However, the gardens are spacious and peaceful, with grand old trees and a lovely view of the local church steeple. One can almost imagine Arrietty gazing longingly out of one of the basement gratings toward the wide, sunny world outside. However, the setting for the house in the heart of the town is much less rural than the house the Borrowers occupied.

Visitors are welcome to explore the grounds of Leighton Middle School after registering at the school office. This gives you an opportunity to see the front hall, which still retains a charming, old tiled fireplace and a hint of what the house might have been like. You can contact the school in advance at Leighton Middle School, Church Square, Leighton Buzzard, Bedforshire LU7 7AE. Telephone: (01525) 374907. The local library sells a book titled *Four Walks with Viv Willis Around Leighton Buzzard* for those with a keener interest in the area. One of the walks includes Cedars House.

Leighton Buzzard is eight miles south of Milton Keynes. It can be reached by taking the A5 from junction 9 on the M1. Turn left onto the A505 and follow the signs to the town center.

Places Connected with Bed-knob and Broomstick

PORTOBELLO MARKET, PORTOBELLO ROAD, LONDON

The connection between the book *Bed-knob and Broomstick* and the Disney movie *Bedknobs and Broomsticks* is primarily in the basic plot premise: Three children befriend a woman who is taking a course in how to become a witch. Both stories include travel to a South Sea island, but that's where the similarities end. In the movie there's a wonderful scene set in the Portobello Market in London involving a sinister old bookseller and culminating in a rousing song-and-dance number, but you won't find a hint of it in the book.

Today's Portobello Market is just as lively and chaotic as it seems in the film. Everything from fine antique silk to an unending array of spoons is on display in street booths and in the shops behind them. The market stretches for over a mile down Portobello Road, beginning with a section of upscale antiques stores and stalls and moving on to crafts, artwork, and tourist kitsch. In the middle is a stretch of food and produce stalls, followed by an area that feels like a huge outdoor garage sale.

Saturday is the day to see the market in its glory. Take the tube to Notting Hill Gate station, walk up Pembroke Road, and turn left onto Portobello Road. Follow the crowds a few more blocks, and you are there. If you manage to go the entire length of the market, you can turn left after you pass under a highway and walk a block to the Ladbroke Grove tube stop. Several bus routes pass by there as well. The market is crowded and not easy to navigate with a stroller.

See the Paddington Bear chapter, page 166, for more information about the Portobello Market.

Places to See Original Artwork/Manuscripts

YOUNG BOOK TRUST, LONDON

The trust's collection includes some of Diana Stanley's original illustrations for *The Borrowers.* These are not on public display but may be viewed if requested in advance.

The Young Book Trust also has a library of every children's book published in the UK in the past two years. It is open to the public by appointment, but the books cannot be taken out. Contact Book House at 45 East Hill, London, SW18 2QZ. Telephone: 0181-516-2984.

THE BRITISH LIBRARY, LONDON

The Pearson Gallery of Living Words at the impressive new British Library (which used to be part of the British Museum) features a wonderful exhibit on British children's literature. Included in the display is a first edition of Mary Norton's *The Borrowers,* illustrated by Diana Stanley.

The British Library is located next to St. Pancras station at 96 Euston Road. It is open on Monday, Wednesday, Thursday, and Friday, 9:30–6:00 P.M.; Tuesday, 9:30–8:00 P.M.; Saturday, 9:30–5:00 P.M.; and Sundays/holidays, 11:00–5:00 P.M. There is no charge for admission to the exhibits. The closest tube station is Kings Cross/St. Pancras. Telephone: (0171) 412-7332.

Other Activities for Children
Who Love The Borrowers

QUEEN MARY'S DOLL HOUSE, WINDSOR CASTLE, WINDSOR, BERKSHIRE

Home to royalty for nine hundred years, Windsor Castle impresses with its size and grandeur. However, the most popular attraction within the castle exhibits grandeur on a very different scale, a scale that would put the Borrowers at ease. Queen Mary's Doll House was designed by Sir Edwin Lutyens, a famous architect, and presented to her in 1924. It is built on a 1:12 scale and is fully functional, with running hot and cold water, two working elevators, and a clock that chimes the hours. Every detail was specially designed, including miniature paintings on the walls and over two hundred tiny books in the library handwritten and autographed by the likes of Rudyard Kipling and Somerset Maugham. From the gold-leaf ceiling in the front foyer to the glass of wine by the queen's bedside, nothing is overlooked in this lavish dollhouse.

Overlooking the Thames, Windsor Castle is located just west of Heathrow Airport. Public areas are open from 10:00 to 5:00 P.M. from March through October, 10:00 to 4:00 P.M. the rest of the year. The changing of the guard takes place daily at 11:00 A.M., except Sundays. Admission is £9.80/adults, £5.60/children. Telephone: (01753) 831118.

BEKONSCOT MODEL VILLAGE, BEACONSFIELD, BUCKINGHAMSHIRE

Bekonscot, the world's oldest model village, is a replica of 1930s rural England in miniature. Covering an area of over forty thousand square feet, Bekonscot includes six tiny villages, which encompass every feature of British life of that era: a circus, a racecourse, a cricket pitch, a fishing village, an airfield, a coal mine, and a wonderful model steam railway running throughout.

Visitors to Bekonscot walk among all this activity on over two thousand feet of pathways. It's a delightful feeling to stand in the midst of this extensive and amazingly detailed landscape. Even the trees and landscaping have been scaled down to fit the tiny buildings.

There is a full-sized play area for young children, a picnic area, and a refreshments stand. Admission is £3.60/adults, £1.80/children, children under three free. The excess profits from Bekonscot are given to charity, with over a million pounds raised since its beginning in 1929.

Bekonscot is open from 10:00 to 5:00 P.M. every day from February 14 through November 1. Telephone: (01494) 675284. Web site: www .bekonscot.org.uk.

Beaconsfield is located just west of London at junction 2 on the M40. Follow the A355 and signs for the model village. It's a short train ride from London and an easy walk from the station to Bekonscot.

THE TALE OF PETER RABBIT
and OTHER STORIES
by Beatrix Potter

🍀 But Peter, who was very naughty, ran straight away to Mr.
MacGregor's garden, and squeezed under the gate! First he ate some
lettuces and some French beans; and then he ate some radishes; and
then, feeling rather sick, he went to look for some parsley. . . .
—*The Tale of Peter Rabbit,* 1902

Peter Rabbit, Benjamin Bunny, Mrs. Tiggywinkle, Jemima Puddle-Duck, Squirrel Nutkin, and Flopsy, Mopsy, and Cottontail—Beatrix Potter's characters and charming illustrations have been loved by generation after generation of children and adults around the world. Potter's rural world in the Lake District in northwest England and the house, garden, and villages that inspired much of her work have been preserved and are more accessible than that of any other well-known author of children's literature in the UK. This is both positive and negative for the visitor. On the positive side, there is a lot to see, much of it lovely and linked directly to Potter's much-loved stories and characters. The attractions are quite accessible and well documented, and there are good services (restaurants, B and Bs, etc.) to enjoy while you explore. The negative side is, of course, that you will find lots of other people visiting and enjoying the same sights! We visited in early October in the rain and still found ourselves waiting quite a while for a parking space. Although crowds are probable, they are there for a reason. Potter really did use the animals, house, village, and countryside around her in her precise and beautiful illustrations, and the house and countryside have been maintained much as they were in her day. Visiting the area in and around Near Sawrey truly gives you the experience of being in Potter's imaginary world.

A Brief Biography of Beatrix Potter

I am descended from generations of Lancashire yeomen and weavers; obstinate, hard-headed, matter-of-fact folk. . . . Your *Mayflower* ancestors sailed to America; mine at the same date were sticking it out at home, probably rather enjoying persecution.
—A letter from Beatrix Potter to the American magazine *The Horn Book*, May 1944

Beatrix Potter lived from 1866 to 1943, the daughter of well-to-do parents who had inherited fortunes from the Lancashire cotton industry. She spent the the first thirty-five years of her life in **Bolton Gardens, London,** living an isolated, dutiful existence with her parents. She had a gift for sketching from nature and loved to draw the animals at the **Natural History Museum** near her home. The family spent the summer holidays near **Birnam, Scotland,** when Potter was a child and in the **Lake District** in northern England during her teenage years.

In 1893, in her mid-twenties, she wrote a letter with pictures to her former governess's son, who was ill in bed. "I don't know what to write to you so I shall tell you a story about four little rabbits whose names were Flopsy, Mopsy, Cottontail and Peter," the letter began. And so the first and most famous of Potter's stories began to take shape. Friends urged her to publish the illustrated story. Seven years later, in her late thirties, after being unable to find a publisher for her "little book" based on the letters, she published 250 copies herself. Frederick Warne and Company then agreed to publish *The Tale of Peter Rabbit* if she would add color to her drawings. She did so, and the little book immediately became wildly popular. Potter herself then designed a Peter Rabbit doll, boardgame, and many other types of related merchandise, which were also (and still are) extremely popular. She wrote five more books in the next three years and became engaged to her publisher's son and her editor, Norman Warne. Just a few weeks after their engagement, he died suddenly of pernicious anemia. Potter had recently bought **Hill Top Farm** in the **Lake District**, and now she consoled herself by converting the seventeenth-century house into her home.

She wrote several books over the next seven years (1906 to 1913), including *The Tale of Tom Kitten, The Tale of Samuel Whiskers,* and *The Tale of Jemima Puddle-Duck,* all of which have Lake District connections. Her interest in farming, sheep breeding, and maintaining the traditional ways of the area deepened. At the age of forty-seven, Beatrix Potter married a local solicitor, William Heelis, and they lived at **Castle Cottage** in **Sawrey,** though Potter continued to use Hill Top as her studio and for entertaining guests. Potter wrote a few more books during those years, but the focus of her life became the local community and breeding prize-winning Herdwick sheep. She was a strong advocate of the work of the National Trust, an organization dedicated to the preservation of Britain's heritage. By the time of her death at age seventy-seven, Potter owned extensive landholdings in the Lake District, all of which she bequeathed to the National Trust. Beatrix Potter's legacy can be seen in her stories and artwork, her delightful home at Hill Top, and the beautiful countryside around her home, which has been preserved due to her generosity and foresight.

Places Connected with Beatrix Potter's Stories

THE LAKE DISTRICT

Considered by many to be the most beautiful area in England, this compact region contains dramatic mountains and lakes, expanses of open fell, and quaint farms and fields defined by drystone walls. Beatrix Potter's family spent their summer holidays here from the time she was sixteen years old, and it was here that she chose to settle as a successful author for the final thirty-seven years of her life. According to Potter's own letters, the sketches for *Peter Rabbit* were done in a garden in Keswick, a charming town in the northern part of the Lake District. Squirrel Nutkin sailed on the nearby lake, Derwentwater, and Mrs. Tiggywinkle lived in the Vale of Newlands down the road.

The Lake District is located in northwest England, twenty miles southwest of Carlisle. The main tourist center in the area is Windermere/Bowness. The area most directly associated with Beatrix Potter is around the villages of Near Sawrey and Hawkshead.

Places in the Lake District

SAWREY

Beatrix Potter first visited Sawrey (also called Near Sawrey) at age thirty while on holiday with her parents and accompanied by her pet rabbit, Peter. She fell in love with the area and wrote that "it is as nearly perfect a little place as I ever lived in, and such nice old-fashioned people in the village . . ." Nine years later, after the success of her first book, *The Tale of Peter Rabbit,* she returned to Sawrey to buy Hill Top (see below) in 1905. The village of Sawrey is pictured in *The Tale of Tom Kitten, The Tale of the Pie and the Patty Pan,* and *The Fairy Caravan.* Castle Cottage, where Potter moved with her husband, William Heelis, after their marriage, stands in the village, although it is not open to the public.

Sawrey can be reached by the B5285 from Hawkshead or by taking a short ferry ride across Lake Windermere from the Bowness pier. The ferry costs £2.00 for a car and occupants and leaves every twenty minutes. It takes less than ten minutes to cross the narrow lake. Continue on up the B5285 for two miles to Near Sawrey.

HILL TOP, SAWREY

As Potter wrote in a letter, "The books relating to Tom Kitten and Samuel Whiskers describe the interior of my old farm house where children are comically impressed by seeing the real chimneys and cupboards." A visit to Hill Top is a charming experience and lets you walk right into the illustrations in those books (for better or worse, without the rats and cats)! When Potter gave the farm to the National Trust, it was under the condition that it be left exactly as it was when she lived there from 1905 to the time of her marriage in 1913. Entrance to Hill Top is limited due to space restrictions in the house, so you may find yourself waiting awhile before you can go in. Luckily you can wait in the charming village nearby or in the excellent gift shop on site. You enter along a lovely garden path. In front of the house is "Mr. MacGregor's garden," complete with watering can. Visitors wander freely throughout the low-ceilinged, rather dark interior of the farmhouse. One can't help wondering how Potter managed to do such detailed drawings with so little light. The house is just as it was when Potter lived and wrote/drew there; and it is set up very effectively for children, with copies of Potter's books, especially *The Tale of Tom Kitten* and *The Tale of Samuel Whiskers,* available to read and compare with what you are seeing. My daughter and I read and looked at the pictures of Tom Kit-

ten sneaking up through the hearth into the chimney and Samuel Whiskers pilfering a rolling pin from the kitchen while we were in those very spots with those exact views ourselves. Interesting items from Potter's life include a dollhouse complete with tiny food and mice that she used as models for her illustrations.

Hill Top is open from April 1 through November 1 from Saturday to Wednesday, 11:00–5:00 P.M. Admission is £3.80 adults, £1.70 children. Telephone: (01539) 436269. There is a free car park in the village. If the weather is fine, leave your car in Windermere and take the lovely, two-mile walk along the road from the ferry to Sawrey. See directions under Sawrey (above).

HAWKSHEAD

Hawkshead, a delightful, but crowded, village two miles from Sawrey, is well worth a visit as the setting for *The Tale of Johnny Town-Mouse,* one of the last books Potter wrote before dedicating her time to farming and conservation. It's also home to the Beatrix Potter Gallery (see below). There are several tearooms and shops, including a National Trust shop. There is also a Lake District Tourist Information Centre in Hawkshead, which can help with booking accommodations. Telephone: (01539)-436525.

Hawkshead is two miles up the B5285 along Esthwaite Water from

Near Sawrey. The signpost to Hawkshead in Sawrey is depicted in *The Tale of Pigling Bland.* The lovely countryside between the two villages is the setting for *The Tale of Mr. Jeremy Fisher* and *The Tale of Mr. Tod.*

BEATRIX POTTER GALLERY

Located in the charming square in Hawkshead, the Beatrix Potter Gallery is housed in the building that Potter's husband used as an office until his death. The ticket office for the gallery is Tabitha Twitchit's shop in *The Tale of the Pie and the Patty Pan.* The exhibit inside is not to be missed: a wonderful display of Potter's original drawings and photos from her life. There is a "Discovery Quiz Sheet" available for children to have fun with as they go through the gallery. The gallery is run by the National Trust, open from April through October from Sunday to Thursday. There is an excellent gift shop about forty meters down the street, also run by the National Trust. Gallery admission is £2.80/1.40. Telephone: (01539) 436355.

Elsewhere in the UK

HOUSE OF THE TAILOR OF GLOUCESTER, 9 COLLEGE COURT, GLOUCESTER

One story by Beatrix Potter that is clearly connected to a location outside the Lake District is *The Tailor of Gloucester,* set in Gloucester in the South Midlands. Although Gloucester was bombed heavily during World War II and has therefore lost many of its older structures, you can still visit the quaint house Potter used as the setting for the story. It is located directly next to Gloucester Cathedral (see the Harry Potter chapter, page 196) on a narrow medieval street that leads through to the cathedral grounds. The street is part of a large pedestrian-only area in the center of the city. The first floor of the house is a shop selling all sorts of Potter merchandise, with a good amount of Pooh Bear and Thomas the Tank Engine paraphernalia as well. The gallery upstairs has both large-scale and miniature models of scenes from *The Tailor of*

Gloucester, including a replica of the mice finishing the coat. The house and the old gate to the cathedral are both pictured in Potter's book. Admission is £1/adults, children free. Telephone: (01452) 422-856.

Season's Restaurant across from the house is a good, inexpensive tearoom that's quite popular with local customers. There's also a pleasant café connected to the cathedral nearby. It's about fifteen minutes off of the M6 if you're coming by car or about a ten-minute walk through the town center from the Gloucester train station.

Other Places Connected with Beatrix Potter's Life Outside the Lake District

BOLTON GARDENS, LONDON

Potter's childhood home at 2 Bolton Gardens, her "unloved birthplace" as she referred to it, was destroyed by a bomb in World War II. Potter lived in that home with her parents until 1905, when the sales of *The Tale of Peter Rabbit* and her other early works allowed her some financial independence. In her late thirties, she was able to purchase Hill Top in the Lake District and gradually leave her parents' home. Although her childhood home no longer stands, there is an elementary school built on the site with a plaque commemorating Potter. The neighborhood is lovely, retaining the feel of well-to-do London at the turn of the century.

Walking along the rows of handsome homes, one can imagine Potter's isolated and strict childhood under the care of a string of governesses, and her dutiful life as an unmarried adult daughter.

Bolton Gardens is located in the Little Boltons area of London. The closest tube stop is Earl's Court.

THE NATURAL HISTORY MUSEUM, LONDON

Potter's artistic talent was encouraged by her parents, both of whom were accomplished artists. (Paintings by both her parents and one by her brother are hanging in the upstairs study at Hill Top.) The young Beatrix spent many hours as a young girl drawing the stuffed animals at The Natural History Museum not far from her home in London.

The museum continues to provide an excellent outing for children. It is across the street from the Victoria and Albert Museum (V&A), where some of Potter's original drawings are on display (see "Places to See Original Artwork/Manuscripts" section of this chapter, page 105). Admission is £5.50, free after 4:30 P.M. Telephone: (207) 938-9123. The closest tube stop is South Kensington.

BIRNAM, SCOTLAND

Beatrix Potter spent her summer holidays from childhood through adolescence in this area, and it was here that her love of the rural life took root. She wrote in later life that the inspiration for Peter Rabbit, Mrs. Tiggywinkle, Mr. Tod, and Mr. Jeremy Fisher came from this area. There is a Beatrix Potter Garden in the center of Birnam featuring an interesting display that includes an example of the coded diaries that Potter kept from the age of fifteen. The codes were finally deciphered in 1958, and the diaries were published in 1966. Also highlighted are the local folk who appear to have popped up in Potter's stories. There is an intriguing photograph of a local naturalist and friend of Potter's who does look strikingly like Mr. MacGregor, and the description of local washerwoman Kitty McDonald really does bring Mrs. Tiggywinkle to mind. The garden has replicas of the animals that inspired Potter in their natural surroundings, including a wee house with a true-to-life prickly hedgehog inside. The village library nearby (the Birnam Institute) has an exhibit about Potter's life, open sporadically from Easter through October. The Potter family stayed in many different places along the river Tay, including Eastwood, a grand house just south of Dunkeld, Birnam's lovely neighboring village just across the river. It was from Eastwood that Potter wrote the letter to her young friend that eventually became *The Tale of Peter Rabbit*.

Birnam is located twelve miles north of Perth, on the A9 just across the river Tay from Dunkeld. Both towns are quite picturesque and well worth a visit. On the Dunkeld side of the river, you will find excellent picnic facilities, a very good play area for children, and an historic cathedral. Dunkeld Tourist Information Centre, telephone: (01350) 727688.

Places in the Lake District

CASTLE COTTAGE, SAWREY

This is the home where Beatrix Potter and William Heelis lived after their marriage in 1913. Potter had purchased Castle Farm in 1909 because its fields joined those of Hill Top. The cottage is a private home now, but it can be seen across the fields from the entrance to the gift shop at Hill Top.

TROUTBECK PARK FARM, NEAR WINDERMERE

Potter purchased this farm in 1924 to breed her beloved Herdwick sheep. Now owned by the National Trust, the farm itself is not open to the public, but the beautiful area around it is accessible by public footpaths. Guided walks of the area are also available. Contact the Bridge House Information Centre, open April through October. Telephone: (01539) 432617.

Places to See Original Artwork/Manuscripts

BEATRIX POTTER GALLERY, HAWKSHEAD (SEE PAGE 101)
VICTORIA AND ALBERT MUSEUM (V&A), LONDON

The Beatrix Potter letters and papers, including some of her original artwork, are housed in the National Art Library, which is part of the V&A, although located at a different site from the main museum and not open to the general public. The main museum does have a small ongoing display of Potter's artwork, photos, and letters, taken from the archives, which changes periodically. It is located in a case near the restaurant in the museum. The museum gift shop is outstanding, with a great variety of items related to Potter's stories. Pooh Bear is well represented, too. There is also a special gift shop just for children's items.

Admission to the museum is £5, free for those under eighteen and for everyone after 4:30 P.M. It is directly across the street from The Natural History Museum (see page 103). The closest tube stop is South Kensington.

THE YOUNG BOOK TRUST, LONDON

An avid collector of Beatrix Potter artwork and paraphernalia named Linder bequeathed most of his two-thousand-piece collection to the Victoria and Albert Museum with the stipulation that three hundred objects be available for public viewing through the Young Book Trust (YBT). These may be seen by appointment. The small display includes beautiful original illustrations and drawings, valuable early "merchandise," and translations of Potter's books into many languages. The YBT also has a library of every children's book published in the UK in the past two years. It is open to the public by appointment, but the books cannot be taken out. Contact Book House at 45 East Hill, London, SW18 2QZ. Telephone: (208) 516-2977.

Other Activities for Children Who Love Potter's Stories

THE WORLD OF BEATRIX POTTER™ ATTRACTION, CRAG BROW, BOWNESS-ON-WINDERMERE

Our family was a bit wary of this "attraction," but it turned out to be quite informative and fun, although older children might find it a bit tame. Visitors are shown a short film about Potter's stories and then walk through an indoor area with re-created scenes from the books. The scenes are a bit like elaborate stage sets, and our three-year-old enjoyed finding the different characters. Each story is represented by only one or two scenes, so it helps to be familiar with the stories beforehand. There is also an exhibit and film about Potter's work as a farmer and conservationist. The gift shop is overflowing with Potterphernalia, and the tearoom is pleasant, serving children's meals. The attraction is located just off the A591 on Rayrigg Road in the center of town. Parking (for a fee) is located on the "lake" side a bit farther down Rayrigg Road. Admission is £2.99/adults, £1.99/children. Telephone: (015394) 88444. Open Easter through September 30, 10:00–5:30 P.M., off-season, 10:00–4:30 P.M.

FERRY RIDE ACROSS LAKE WINDERMERE

This short car-ferry ride is a treat for young children and makes the journey part of the fun of visiting Hill Top. It is also the easiest way to reach Sawrey and Hawkshead by car. (See the section on Sawrey, page 99, for details.)

WINDERMERE STEAMBOAT CENTRE, WINDERMERE

This is a wonderful museum for anyone who loves the boating life. It features a model boat pond and loads of historical boats. Beatrix Potter is represented by the little boat in which she used to sketch pond animals, most notably Mr. Jeremy Fisher. (See the *Swallows and Amazons* chapter, page 258, for more information about the center.)

TROTTERS & FRIENDS ANIMAL FARM, KESWICK

If you and/or your children are looking for a more direct, "hands-on" experience of some of the animals featured in Beatrix Potter's stories, this Lake District animal farm could be the answer. The farm is home to traditional farm animals and more-exotic species. There are daily "audience participation" events where the kids can hold a rabbit or milk a cow. British birds of prey and reptiles are also featured. There are free-roaming birds around the farm, and Jemima Puddle-Duck may waddle by and join your picnic lunch by the pond.

Trotters & Friends is located in the northern part of the Lake District between Keswick and Cockermouth just off the A66 near Bassen thwaite Lake. Summer hours: 10:00–5:30 P.M.; winter hours: 11:00–4:30 P.M. Admission: £3.30/adults, £2.20/children three–fourteen. Telephone: (01768) 776239.

> Rabbits are creatures of warm, volatile temperament but shallow and absurdly transparent.
>
> —Beatrix Potter, 1892 journal entry

RABBIT WORLD, AMESBURY, WILTSHIRE

If you aren't going to make it north to the Lake District, but someone in your party really loves Peter Rabbit, try a visit to Rabbit World instead. This is the world's largest collection of rabbit breeds, housing over fifty types of rabbits in pens in a covered area. Visitors have the opportunity to observe rabbit behavior up close, see babies in their nests, and pet a few bunnies.

Rabbit World is part of Cholderton Rare Breeds Farm Park, so there is the opportunity to see lots of sheep, goats, and—don't miss it—pig racing. The Ewe Tree Tea-rooms serve lunch and tea; there's a picnic area as well.

Rabbit World and the Cholderton Rare Breeds Farm Park are located near Stonehenge just east of the town of Amesbury, Wiltshire. Take the M3 south from the London area. Take the A303 west to the A338 south. Follow signs to the farm.

Admission is £4.25/adults, £2.75/children ages two–fourteen; a family ticket is £13. The park is open from 10:00 to 6:00 P.M., March 24 through November 4. Telephone: (01980) 629438. Web site: www .rabbitworld.co.uk.

THE LEGEND OF ROBIN HOOD

Robin Hood · meeteth · the · tall
Stranger · on · the · Bridge

In merry England in the time of old, when good King Henry the Second ruled the land, there lived within the green glades of Sherwood Forest, near Nottingham Town, a famous outlaw whose name was Robin Hood. No archer ever lived that could speed a gray goose shaft with such skill and cunning as his, nor were there ever such yeomen as the sevenscore merry men that roamed with him through the greenwood shades. Right merrily they dwelt within the depths of Sherwood Forest, suffering neither care nor want, but passing the time in merry games of archery or cudgel play, living upon the King's venison, washed down with draughts of ale of October brewing.

Not only Robin himself but all the band were outlaws and dwelt apart from other men, yet they were beloved by the country people round about, for no one ever came to jolly Robin for help in time of need and went away again with an empty fist.

—Howard Pyle, *The Merry Adventures of Robin Hood*, 1883

$\mathcal{R}$OBIN HOOD AND HIS MERRY MEN LIVING FREE IN SHERWOOD Forest, striking a blow for justice and right when they can, helping out those in need, and helping themselves to the king's deer, shooting arrows through willow twigs at one hundred yards, and seeking adventure when life gets too quiet . . . it's a tale that has come down to us from over six hundred years ago, but it continues to entertain and fascinate us into the twenty-first century.

The earliest written record of the legend, "Lytell Geste of Robyn Hode," dates from the 1400s but is written in reference to much older stories. The legend has been reworked in each century, coming together as we know it in the nineteenth century in Thomas Love Peacock's *Maid Marian* (1822) and Tennyson's play *The Foresters* (1881). Howard Pyle rewrote the stories for American children in 1883, a version that is still popular today, and illustrated his book with wonderful pseudomedieval drawings. The twentieth century saw a steady flow of movie versions, including five silent movies, the famous Errol Flynn and Olivia de Havilland film (1938), Walt Disney's rather odd cartoon version of the sixties with Robin as a fox and several characters voiced by Grand Ole Opry comedians, and Kevin Costner's *Robin Hood, Prince of Thieves* in 1991.

Did Robin Hood really exist, and if so, did he live the outlaw life the legends describe? This question continues to be debated. Even among those who are convinced of his historical reality, there isn't much agreement about where or even when he lived. Richard de Vries's *On the Trail of Robin Hood,* published by Crossbow Books in 1988, is an excellent introduction to these arguments.

Most of the main places mentioned in the various versions of Robin Hood exist to this day, albeit greatly altered. It's still possible to visit the oak tree under which the Merry Men may have feasted and to walk through the gates of Nottingham Castle. One is surrounded now by a fence, the other by a major, modern city, but they live on just as the legend does.

Places Connected with the Robin Hood Legend

NOTTINGHAM CASTLE AND CASTLE GREEN, NOTTINGHAM

This is the site of the evil Prince John's plotting against and eventual imprisonment of Robin Hood. However, the gatehouse (now the gift shop) is the only part of Nottingham Castle that Robin Hood might have known. The rest of the castle was destroyed in the 1600s and replaced with a mansion, which today houses the city's art museum. The historical Prince John (who then became King John) did visit the castle that stood on this site in Robin Hood's day while Richard the Lionheart was fighting in the Crusades. Admission to the castle museum is free on weekdays; £1.50/adults, 80 pence/children on weekends. The museum is open from 10:00 to 5:00 P.M. daily. Telephone: (01159) 483504.

The city's main tribute to Robin Hood stands in front of the castle on the Castle Green (which is mostly paved). A wonderful statue of Robin Hood shooting an arrow, erected in 1952, is surrounded by scenes from the legends in bronze.

Across the street stands one of the few medieval buildings still in existence in Nottingham, the Lace Market Centre. If you follow Castle Road to the right after exiting the Castle Gate, you will soon come to Ye Old Trip to Jerusalem pub. Worth a visit for the name alone, this pub was a stopping point for soldiers on their way to the Crusades. It dates from 1189 and may have been frequented by Robin and his men.

The Old Market Square, the center of urban Nottingham, is on the site where Robin Hood would have performed archery feats to win the

Silver Arrow in Prince John's contest. (This is according to Nottingham tourist information sources. Some stories place the contest clear across England in Cheshire.) To reach the Old Market Square, turn left as you leave the castle gate and follow Castle Road to Friar's Lane. Turn right and continue on for two long blocks to reach the Old Market Square. The Tourist Information Centre for Nottinghamshire is on the other side of the wide plaza.

SHERWOOD FOREST, NOTTINGHAMSHIRE

Twenty miles north of Nottingham is Sherwood Forest. Now only a shadow of its former glory, it once covered over one hundred thousand acres and served as the exclusive hunting ground for the king. Happily, however, everyone can enjoy it now without fear of being arrested by a warden for removing wood from royal land or shooting the king's deer. The Sherwood Forest Visitor Centre makes a good starting point for a visit to the forest, with exhibits about the ecology of the area and about medieval life in Sherwood.

The main vestige of Robin Hood's time in the forest is the Major Oak, a sprawling oak tree that may be almost one thousand years old. Legend points to this as the spot where Robin Hood and his men feasted and hatched plans for ways to separate the powerful and corrupt from their gold. This venerable tree needs some help to keep going, and the park has recently put in an unobtrusive support system for its limbs. By necessity, the tree is surrounded by a wooden fence as well. It's a short, wooded walk from the Visitor Centre to the Major Oak.

The 450-acre park features several well-marked trails and plenty of opportunity to be merry. The Robin Hood Way, a footpath that links many of the Robin Hood–related places in Nottinghamshire, also begins (or ends) in Sherwood Forest and covers almost one hundred miles before it reaches the gate of Nottingham Castle. There are plenty of small villages along the way for food and accommodation. The Nottinghamshire County Council offers a guide to the trail. Telephone: (01159) 823823.

The Forest Table restaurant is open for lunch and tea every day.

The Sherwood Forest Visitor Centre is located just north of Edwinstowe on the B6034. To get there by car from the center of Nottingham, follow the A60 out of the city. When it forks, take the A614. At the Ollerton traffic circle, pick up the B6034 towards Workshop. It's well signposted. Parking is free except on peak visiting days. For bus information, call (01159) 24000.

The center is open from 10:00 to 5:00 P.M. from April to October. It closes at 4:30 the rest of the year. Admission is free. Telephone: (01623) 824490.

EDWINSTOWE, NOTTINGHAMSHIRE

Located about a mile south of the Sherwood Forest Visitor Centre on the A6075 is lovely Edwinstowe. The legend says that Maid Marian waited to marry Robin until King Richard returned from the Crusades and declared that Robin was no longer an outlaw. She lived chastely in Sherwood Forest with Robin and his men perfecting her archery skills in the meanwhile. The Church of St. Mary in Edwinstowe is said to be where Robin and Maid Marian were finally married. The tower and parts of the nave date from Robin and Marian's time.

BLIDWORTH CHURCH

Tiny Blidworth has two claims to fame—as the hometown of Maid Marian and the final resting place of Will Scarlet. Will Scarlet is buried in the churchyard under an old yew tree. The stone marking his grave is a remnant of an older version of the church, which was rebuilt in 1739.

Maid Marian's home is reputed to have stood on the site of Ashfield Cottage, across from the Black Bull pub in Blidworth.

Blidworth is five miles southeast of Mansfield. Take the narrow road south from Rainworth on the A617. It's quite close to Newstead Abbey, Lord Byron's home.

ROBIN HOOD IN YORKSHIRE

Although the Robin Hood legend is most firmly entrenched in Nottinghamshire, there are those who make a strong case for Robin's connections with Yorkshire. The county of Kirklees, wedged in between Leeds and Manchester, claims Robin Hood's grave at Kirklees Priory. Unfortunately, the priory is in serious disrepair and not open to the public. Legend has it that Robin Hood was born in the town of Locksley, which may have been the village of Loxley, Kirklees. Nothing remains in Loxley to see except the Robin Hood pub. Researchers, scholars, and plain old fans of the famous outlaw will continue to debate whether Robin was an historical person or simply a powerful myth. Whether or not he was real and where and when he lived and died will continue to be debated as well. After seven hundred or more years, the only certainty is that the legend continues to delight our sense of adventure and satisfy our sense of justice.

Other Activities for Children Who Love Robin Hood

THE TALES OF ROBIN HOOD, 30–38 MAID MARIAN WAY, NOTTINGHAM

Since so many of the settings for the Robin Hood legend are no longer in their full glory, you may want to give this indoor re-creation of the legend a visit. Costumed guides walk you through replicas of the medieval streets and dungeons of Nottingham, an experience for the eyes and nose, and then put you onto a ride through the eerie depths of Sherwood Forest in Robin Hood's day. It's exciting enough for older children, but there may be a few scary moments for younger ones (a pair of vicious-looking wolves, a bit of gruesome fighting, some skeletons). After the ride visitors enter a gallery filled with kids' activities, including "Shoot the Sheriff" archery practice and "Pull the Sword from the Stone" (wrong legend but still fun!). While the kids have fun, adults can view some very informative exhibits about where the truth lies in the Robin Hood tales. There is also a good display about other Robin Hood–related sights in the area. A large indoor café features a big movie screen showing any one of the many movie versions of Robin Hood, from Errol Flynn to Kevin Costner. And, of course, everyone exits through a gift shop featuring an extensive collection of Robin Hood figurines, plastic longbow sets, knights' helmets, and Maid Marian dolls.

The Tales of Robin Hood attraction is located just down the hill from Nottingham Castle and the Castle Green. Follow Castle Road to Friar Lane and turn right. Walk one block to Maid Marian Way and turn left. The attraction will be on your left. There is pay parking located around the corner off of Friar Lane.

If you are coming from the M1, take the A52 east from junction 25. It takes awhile to get into the center of town, but The Tales of Robin Hood attraction is signposted once you get there.

The Tales of Robin Hood Attraction is open every day except Christmas and Boxing Day from 10:00 to 6:00 P.M. Admission is £5.95/adults, £3.95/children, £18.75/family ticket. Telephone: (01159) 483284. Web site: www.robinhood.uk.co.uk.

> *And yet I think these oaks at dawn and even*
> *Will whisper ever more of Robin Hood . . .*
> *. . . You, good Friar,*
> *You Much, you Scarlet, you dear Little John,*
> *Your names will cling like ivy to the wood.*
> *And here perhaps a hundred years away*
> *Some hunter in day-dreams or half asleep*
> *Will hear our arrows whizzing overhead*
> *And catch the winding of a phantom horn."*
> —Tennyson, *The Foresters,* 1881

ROBERT LOUIS STEVENSON'S WRITINGS FOR CHILDREN

❧ Looking out between the trees, we could see a great side of mountain, running down exceeding steep into the waters of the loch. It was a rough part, all hanging stone, and heather, and bit scrags of birchwood; and away at the far end towards Ballachulish, little wee red soldiers were dipping up and down over hill and browe . . . so we sat again, and ate and drank in a place whence we could see the sun going down into a field of great, wild and houseless mountains, such as I was now condemned to wander in with my companion.
                                                                              —*Kidnapped*, 1886

*F*ROM THE WILD AND REBELLIOUS HIGHLANDS OF SCOTLAND to the rough life of the English "gentlemen of fortune" (pirates) of the eighteenth century to the everyday joys of a child's life in Edinburgh in Victorian times, Robert Louis Stevenson's imaginative works bring alive the past with vividness, excitement, and charm.

Stevenson's roots were in Edinburgh, and anyone who is fond of *A Child's Garden of Verses* will find numerous connections between the poems and the poet's early years there. *Kidnapped* is set primarily in the Scottish Highlands and provides an adventurous and exciting view of Highland life in the 1750s, as well as a lively depiction of the historic tension between the Scottish Lowlands and Highlands. The story revolves around a kidnapping near Edinburgh and a real-life assassination that happened in the area between Glencoe and Fort William in the western Highlands. The hero of the book, David Balfour, makes a grueling passage on foot from a shipwreck near the Isle of Iona across the moors and mountains back to Stirling and Edinburgh. Stevenson's stories add a vivid dimension to a Scottish visit and make Scotland's turbulent and complex history come alive.

A Brief Biography of Robert Louis Stevenson

. . . no society of the wise and good, can repay me for my absence from my country. And though I think I would rather die elsewhere, yet in my heart of hearts I long to be buried among good Scots clods. I will say it fairly, it grows on me with every year: there are no stars so lovely as Edinburgh street-lamps. When I forget thee, Auld Reekie,* may my right hand forget its cunning!
—Robert Louis Stevenson, "The Scot Abroad" in *The Silverado Squatters,* 1883

*Auld Reekie is a nineteenth-century nickname for Edinburgh.

Stevenson was born in 1850 in Edinburgh into an upper-middle-class family. His father and paternal grandfather were distinguished engineers, well-known for building bridges and lighthouses throughout Scotland. His mother was the daughter of a church minister. They lived the respectable life of a prosperous family at 17 **Heriot Row** in the New Town section of the city. Stevenson spent much of his childhood in the company of his nurse, Alison Cunningham ("Cummy"), to whom he dedicated *A Child's Garden of Verses.* From his earliest years, he was plagued with weak lungs. He spent much of his childhood and adult life struggling with a tuberculosis-like ailment, which eventually brought about his early death.

As a teenager and university student, Stevenson became a well-known character in Edinburgh, nicknamed "Velvet Coat" for the unconventional jacket he wore regularly. He was extremely thin and wore his hair unusually long for the time. He had a fascination with the rougher parts of the Old Town of Edinburgh, which at that time was a seedy, crowded warren of brothels, pubs, and industrial poverty. As a student at the University of Edinburgh, he was increasingly rebellious, rarely attending class. He adopted a bohemian lifestyle, rejecting the stodgy respectability of Victorian Edinburgh and his parents and thumbing his nose at conventional morality. He had wanted to write from an early age and had his first publication, a pamphlet, published when he was sixteen. It described a religious uprising that had taken place in the Pentland Hills outside of Edinburgh near the Stevenson family's summer home at **Swanston.** At the age of twenty-one, determined to be a writer, Stevenson rebelled against the family's engineering tradition. His family, perhaps realizing that Stevenson's frail health wasn't suited to engineering, adjusted to the idea and provided financial support for the next fifteen years until Stevenson was able to support himself with his writing.

In his early twenties, Stevenson met the two loves of his life, two women with remarkably similar circumstances: both were called Fanny, both were married at age seventeen to husbands who proved to be louts, both were ten years older than Stevenson and still married when he fell in love with them, and both had one child who died at a young age.

The first was Mrs. Frances Sitwell, daughter of an old and wealthy

Irish family. Stevenson met her in London literary circles and spent three years writing her torrid love letters. Mrs. Sitwell, however, was in love with Sidney Colvin, head of the Slade School of Fine Art, and her relationship with Stevenson never amounted to much. (Twenty-five years later, when both were widowed, Mrs. Sitwell and Colvin finally were married.)

Stevenson met his second Fanny, Mrs. Frances (Fanny) Osbourne, at an artist's colony in France. She was a thirty-five-year-old married American who had just lost a four-year-old son to illness. Fanny was studying art in Europe while her estranged husband remained in California. Stevenson's affair with Fanny ended when she returned to America in 1878. After a miserable year, Stevenson followed her to Monterey, California, sailing over the Atlantic and making the overland journey across the United States in ill health. Fanny's divorce finally came through in 1880, and they were married in San Francisco. Penniless, they honeymooned in an old mining shack at Silverado in Napa Valley. At the time they expected Stevenson to die within a few months; however, their relationship must have done him some good because he lasted another fourteen years.

The Stevensons returned to Edinburgh to a warm reception and much-needed financial help from his parents. During this period Stevenson created the story of *Treasure Island,* perhaps inspired by a map drawn by his stepson, Lloyd. The next three years were spent in various places in Europe searching for a climate that would improve Stevenson's health. In 1884, the Stevensons rented a house on the south coast of England in Bournemouth named Skerryvore. During a three-year stay at Skerryvore, Stevenson was extremely productive, writing *A Child's Garden of Verses, Kidnapped,* and *The Strange Case of Dr. Jekyll and Mr. Hyde,* among other works. In 1887, Stevenson was acutely ill when he received word that his father had died. After a period of mourning and convalescence, the Stevensons again began wandering the world looking for a healthy climate.

As it turned out, Stevenson never returned to Britain again. He and Fanny spent time in the Adirondack Mountains of New York, on the coast of New Jersey, and in San Francisco. Finally, they set sail from San Francisco in the yacht *Casco* bound for the central Pacific. They were aboard the yacht for a year, with Stevenson writing regular travelogue letters to finance their journey. After a six-month stay in Honolulu, they boarded a trading schooner and set off for Samoa.

Stevenson's wandering life finally came to rest on the island of Upolu in western Samoa. Here, on four hundred acres of tropical mountainside, Stevenson spent the last five years of his life. They named their estate Vailima and built a large house run by a staff of Samoans. Stevenson quickly became a defender of the Samoan people's right to determine what happened to their islands. At the time, Germany, Britain, and the United States had decided to divide the islands among them. Stevenson wrote a book arguing against this onslaught of colonialism and was pleased to learn that it was burnt publicly in Berlin. In gratitude for his help, the Samoans built a road through the jungle to Vailima and called it "The Road of the Loving Heart."

Other than a few trips to Sydney, Australia, Stevenson spent these final years writing several stories of the South Seas and two novels set in Scotland while struggling with ill health at Vailima. He died suddenly in December 1894, at age forty-four, from a cerebral hemorrhage. He is buried in Samoa, on top of the mountain behind Vailima. His famous epitaph reads:

Under the wide and starry sky,
Dig the grave and let me lie.
Glad did I live and gladly die,
And I laid me down with a will.

This be the verse you grave for me:
Here he lies where he longed to be;
Home is the sailor, home from the sea,
And the hunter home from the hill.

Places Connected with Stevenson's Writings for Children in the Edinburgh Area

HAWES INN, SOUTH QUEENSFERRY, NEAR EDINBURGH, SCOTLAND

Sitting beside the Firth of Forth eight miles outside of Edinburgh, the three-hundred-year-old Hawes Inn has not changed much since Stevenson frequented it as a young man after a day out in his canoe. It is the setting for the kidnapping of David Balfour in *Kidnapped* and for his return in rags at the end of the story after his many adventures in the wilds of the Highlands. Modern times have seen the addition of a railway bridge and a dramatic road bridge crossing the Forth, but Hawes Inn, sitting between the two, holds its own. It remains a pleasant stop for a pint of beer at an outdoor table on the way back to Edinburgh after a day of touring.

> ♣ The Firth of Forth . . . narrows at this point to the width of a good-sized river. Right in the midst of the narrows lies an islet with some ruins; on the south shore they have built a pier for the service of the Ferry; and at the end of the pier, on the other side of the road, and backed against a pretty garden of holly-trees and hawthorns, I could see the building which they call the Hawes Inn.
>
> —*Kidnapped*

Hawes Inn is located on Newhalls Road in South Queensferry. From Edinburgh take the A90 motorway to the last exit before the bridge over the Firth of Forth. From elsewhere, take the M90 motorway. Buses No. 43 and 47 leave from the St. Andrew's Square bus station in Central

Edinburgh for the half-hour trip to the South Queensferry police station, which is a ten-minute walk from Hawes Inn. The inn is along the water between the motorway bridge and the railway bridge. Although this sounds unappealing, it is actually a very dramatic location, with the bridges adding to the impressive view rather than overwhelming it. In addition to the restaurant and pub, there are eight rooms available for overnight stays, including room 13, where Stevenson himself stayed. Address: Newhalls Road, South Queensferry, Lothian, Scotland EH30 9TA. Telephone: 0131-331 1990. (See the "Other Activities for Children" section at the end of this chapter for information about boat rides on the Firth from South Queensferry.)

EDINBURGH ZOO, EDINBURGH

The final scene in *Kidnapped* finds Alan Breck and David Balfour bidding each other an emotional, if low-key, farewell. The scene is set on Corstorphine Hill at a spot called "Rest-and-Be-Thankful." The name will make sense to anyone who has climbed from the entrance of the delightful Edinburgh Zoo up to the zebra enclosure at the top. Although the upper part of the zoo isn't at the precise summit of Corstorphine Hill, it is close enough to it to get a sense of the picturesque view that must have been in Stevenson's head as he wrote the scene. Luckily, there is a free shuttle bus between the zoo entrance and the zebra area on the hilltop.

The Edinburgh Zoo makes a delightful day out in its own right. It is located three miles west of the city center on eighty acres of hillside. Several buses run from Princes Street to the entrance. There is also a large parking lot that charges a nominal fee. Admission is £8/adults, £5/children over five. (For information about the Penguin Parade, see the Mary Poppins chapter, page 140.) Telephone: (0131) 334-9171.

In the Western Highlands, Scotland

APPIN/BALLACHULISH/GLENCOE

One of the pivotal events in *Kidnapped* is the assassination of Colin Roy Campbell, the Red Fox, a leader of the Campbell clan. Our unlucky hero, David Balfour, is present at the murder and subsequently is suspected of being the assassin. The assassination was an historical event that actually took place in the location and manner that Stevenson describes, making Balfour an eighteenth-century Forrest Gump! At any rate, the murder was controversial in its day and remains so, a sign that some ancient quarrels between Highland clans live on in modern times.

The site of "the Appin Murder," as it's known, can be visited near the town of Ballachulish, just north of Glencoe in the western Highlands. From the A82 in Ballachulish, take the A828 south toward Oban. Take the second left after the Ballachulish Hotel, approximately 1.9 miles from the A82. There is a small sign if you approach from the south. Turn left into a small parking area. A four-hundred-meter trail up the hillside is rather dull at first but then becomes quite lovely as it passes through a pine forest with nice views of Loch Linnhe. At the end of the trail is a cairn marking the spot of the Red Fox's assassination. Stevenson's tale of Balfour running for his life up the hillside takes on new meaning as you look up the exceedingly steep terrain. The trail is well maintained but not suitable for baby strollers. We visited in June, and there were some midges (insidious, tiny, biting insects) in the woods.

If you are interested in the other side of this controversy, you may want to stop just to the west of the bridge over the mouth of Loch Leven on the A82. Here there is a monument pointing to the spot where James of the Glens was executed for the Appin murder. The monument makes clear that many people feel that he was innocent and that Alan Breck was the actual assassin. But then James of the Glens didn't have a classic adventure tale written about him!

Clan Donald Visitor Centre, Isle of Skye

In *Kidnapped,* David Balfour is caught up in the conflict between the Campbell and Stewart clans that grew out of the unsuccessful clan uprising against the English in 1745. The intricacies of clan politics can be as confusing to the modern visitor as they were to Balfour. The Museum of the Isles at the Clan Donald Visitor Centre on Skye provides a dramatic and interesting presentation about the history of the clan system and its gradual dissolution. It's fascinating to hear the story from the old clan families' point of view, which gives the history a different spin than you'll find in places like the Museum of Scotland in Edinburgh or, certainly, in London! The center makes a great destination for other reasons as well: forty acres of beautiful woodland gardens, a lovely and reasonably priced restaurant/tearoom, and a family history research center for "the Scottish diaspora."

The Clan Donald Visitor Centre is located in Armadale on the Sleat Peninsula at the southern end of the Isle of Skye. It can be reached by ferry from Mallaig or by car on the A851 sixteen miles south of Broadford on Skye. The views across the Sound of Sleat are spectacular. Telephone: 01471 844-305 or 844-227. Address: Armadale Castle, Sleat, Isle of Skye IV45 8RS.

Rannoch Moor (West Highland Line by Train)

No one needs an additional reason to take the West Highland Line from Glasgow to Mallaig, one of the world's most famous and spectacular train rides. However, if you've read and loved *Kidnapped,* you can look forward to traveling across Rannoch Moor, just as David Balfour and Alan Breck did, but in considerably more comfort. The boggy expanse of Rannoch Moor is inaccessible by car and as close to an uninhabited area as you'll find on the mainland of Britain.

♧ The mist rose and died away, and showed us that country lying as waste as the sea; only the moorfowl and the peewees crying upon it, and far over to the east, a herd of deer, moving like dots. Much of it was red with heather; much of the rest broken up, with bogs and hags and peaty pools. . . .

—Kidnapped

For information, fares, and schedules for the West Highland Line, contact Rail Enquiries at 0345 484-950 or ScotRail telesales at (08457) 484950.

STIRLING, SCOTLAND

Today the dramatic sight of Stirling Castle can be seen day and night from miles away perched high on its solitary rock. That same sight greeted David Balfour and Alan Breck as a sign of hope that their long, difficult journey was almost at an end. In their day the bridge at Stirling was the only bridge across the lengthy Firth of Forth. That same bridge, which dates from 1500, is as picturesque today as it was when Balfour and Breck waited under cover of night to sneak across unnoticed. Now it functions as a pedestrian and bicycle crossing next to a much larger bridge for cars.

♧ The bridge is close under the castle hill, an old, high, narrow bridge with pinnacles along the parapet; and you may conceive with how much interest I looked upon it, not only as a place famous in history, but as the very doors of salvation to Alan and myself.

—Kidnapped

Although the bridge alone may not warrant a special trip to Stirling, the impressive castle and its surrounding medieval buildings most certainly do. You won't be able to miss the castle once you get near Stirling by car or train. The bridge is next to the A804 where it crosses the river. You can pick up the A804 from the M9 motorway.

A Child's Garden of Verses

The poems in *A Child's Garden of Verses,* though somewhat dated in both style and content, continue to be very appealing to children. They capture the anxieties and delights of childhood in a way that still rings true, from fear of the dark to the joy of going up in a swing. Stevenson's own Edinburgh childhood is reflected in the many references to the long winter nights and the endless summer sun that stays up long after the boy has gone to bed. The many poems about yearning to travel to faraway lands foretell Stevenson's adult wanderings.

In Edinburgh, Scotland

ROBERT LOUIS STEVENSON'S CHILDHOOD HOME, 17 HERIOT ROW

The Stevenson family moved to the New Town section of Edinburgh (new as opposed to the medieval Royal Mile area) when Robert was seven years old, and they remained there throughout his youth. They lived at 17 Heriot Row in a very comfortable, upper-middle-class home with access by key to the extensive private gardens across the road. Many of the memories that formed the basis for the poems in *A Child's Garden of Verses* are from this house. One of the most quaint is "The Lamplighter," with "Leerie" lighting the gas lamps each evening out in front. The house is privately occupied, but there is an interpretive plaque across the street.

Heriot Row can be reached easily on foot from Princes Street, the main shopping street in the New Town. Walk along Frederick Street, away from the Castle and Princes Street Gardens, until you reach Heriot Row. It will be just past the Queen Street Gardens. No. 17 is a few houses to the right.

Other Places Connected with Stevenson's Life in Edinburgh, Scotland

LADY STAIR'S HOUSE AND THE WRITERS' MUSEUM

This is a gem of a museum that focuses on Edinburgh's (and Scotland's) three most famous writers: Sir Walter Scott, Robert Burns, and Robert Louis Stevenson. Housed in a beautiful seventeenth-century merchant's house, the museum is located in the Lawnmarket section of the Royal Mile through Lady Stair's Close. (A "close" is an old term for a small alley constructed like a tunnel under the buildings that front the Royal Mile.) The courtyard around the museum has famous quotes from Scottish authors inscribed in the pavement. It contains the only collection of Stevenson memorabilia in Britain (the other main collections are in California and Samoa). It's a fascinating look at Stevenson's life, including a lock of his hair cut at age four. Don't miss the mahogany cabinet that stood in Stevenson's childhood bedroom. It was made by William Brodie, the real-life Jekyll/Hyde and Stevenson's inspiration for his tale. Deacon by day and burglar by night, Brodie was hung for his crimes in 1788 on gallows he himself had designed in his role as deacon. Brodie's Close is directly across the street from the museum where The Deacon's House café has murals depicting the whole, true, grisly story. Telephone: 0131 529-4901.

HIGH KIRK OF EDINBURGH, ST. GILES CATHEDRAL, ON THE ROYAL MILE NEAR GEORGE IV BRIDGE

Stevenson is buried in Samoa, halfway around the world from his birthplace. However, there is a memorial to him in St. Giles Kirk, a duplicate of the huge bronze plaque that stands at the foot of his burial hill in Samoa. The plaque depicts Stevenson reclining on a couch and bears the epitaph he wrote for himself. The Stevenson memorial is inside the church to the right and halfway up after you walk in the main door.

SWANSTON AND THE PENTLAND HILLS

Stevenson loved wandering the sweeping Pentland Hills six miles to the south of the center of Edinburgh. His family had a holiday cottage in Swanston, a tiny collection of farmhouses just at the foot of the Pentlands. His very first published work, a pamphlet called *Pentland Rising,* appeared when Stevenson was sixteen. It told of a religious conflict in the seventeenth century that occurred four miles from Swanston. At the end of his life, while living in Samoa, Stevenson wrote a nostalgic poem about his walks in the Pentland Hills. The family cottage still exists, but it is privately owned and not visible from the public road. However, there are excellent hiking trails with dramatic views of Edinburgh that begin where the road ends in Swanston and lead up into the Pentland Hills. There is a small parking area at the end of the road. Walk along the wooded stream for a few minutes, and you will see a picturesque grouping of thatched cottages. The trails begin just past the cottages and through the stile.

Swanston is located just off the A720 Edinburgh bypass. Exit at the Lothianburn junction and take the Biggar Road toward the city center. Turn left on Oxgangs Road and then left again on Swanston Road. Follow the road until it crosses the A720 and for another mile until it ends at the car park.

COLINTON

As a young boy, Stevenson often visited the home of his grandfather, Lewis Balfour, in the village of Colinton. The city has absorbed the village and grown beyond it now, but the area still retains its village feeling on the banks of the Water of Leith. His grandfather's house is the rectory for St. Cuthbert's Church, founded in 1095. The house is privately occupied but may be seen from the churchyard. A walk past the church leads to a lovely riverside walk and picnic area.

Colinton is quite near Swanston by car. Exit the A720 bypass at Dreghorn junction. Follow Dreghorn to Redford Road and turn left.

Redford ends at Colinton Road. Turn left again and follow Colinton for a quarter mile and make a sharp right on Spylaw Street. Spylaw becomes Dell as it crosses the Water of Leith. The church and rectory are just beyond the bridge. Parking is best on Spylaw Street.

Scottish National Portrait Gallery, Edinburgh

Stevenson's portrait by Count Pier Nerli hangs on the second floor of the National Portrait Gallery. Nearby is a portrait of his cousin, Andrew Lang, also a writer for children, who is best known for his series of folktales in *The Blue Fairy Book, The Red Fairy Book,* etc. The two men look startlingly alike. Admission is free. Open Monday through Saturday, 10:00–5:00 P.M.; Sunday, 2:00–5:00 P.M. Address: Corner of Queen Street and St. Andrew Street in New Town.

Other Activities for Children Who Love Stevenson's Stories in the Highlands

Boat Trips from Fort William on Loch Linnhe

Take a boat tour of Loch Linnhe to catch a view of seals, birds, and otters while sailing past the countryside where Alan Breck and David Balfour encountered their adventures. Seal Island Cruises offer boat tours that leave several times a day from the town pier in Fort William, with evening dinner cruises available during the summer. Tickets are £5/adults, £2.50/children. Telephone: (01397) 703919.

In or near Edinburgh

Boat Rides on the Firth of Forth

A variety of boat trips leave from the pier across from Hawes Inn in South Queensferry eight miles from Central Edinburgh.

Forth Jet offers high-speed thrill rides under the great bridges across the broad Forth and more-sedate trips down toward the sea. Bridge tours cost £5/adults, £3/children. A "Jet-boat Fun Ride" costs £6/adults, £4/children. Telephone: 0131-331- 4777. Reservations essential.

The Maid of the Forth offers wildlife cruises with the possibility of seeing seals, puffins, and dolphins. In conjunction with Historic Edinburgh, they also offer boat tours to Inchcolm Island with its medieval abbey, picnic area, and sandy beach. Fares are £9/adults, £4/children, and a family ticket for £22. Telephone: 0131-331-4857.

THE PENTLAND HILLS HIKE FROM SWANSTON

(See previous section on Swanston in this chapter for directions to hiking trails with lovely views of Edinburgh and the surrounding countryside.)

MUSEUM OF CHILDHOOD, ROYAL MILE

If you are interested in Stevenson's childhood experiences in the 1850s in Edinburgh or if you simply enjoy dollhouses, teddy bears, carousel horses, and toys in general, make a visit to the Museum of Childhood. The first museum in the world to specialize in the history of childhood, it's a fun place for kids to cut loose and for adults to marvel at ingenious toys from the past. The gift shop is a treat, too. It's located about halfway between the castle and Holyrood Palace on the Royal Mile. Admission is free. Open Monday through Saturday, 10:00–5:00 P.M. Address: 42 High Street, Royal Mile. Telephone: 0131-529-4142.

MARY POPPINS

by P. L. Travers

🍀 But at last they came to St. Paul's Cathedral, which was built a
long time ago by a man with a bird's name. Wren it was. . . .

"There she is!" cried Michael suddenly, and he danced on his toes
with excitement. . . .

"She's saying it! She's saying it!" cried Jane, holding tight to
herself for fear she would break in two with delight.

And she *was* saying it. . . . "Feed the Birds, Tuppence a Bag." . . .
Over and over again, the same thing, in a high chanting voice that
made the words seem like a song. And as she said it she held out
little bags of breadcrumbs to the passers-by. All around her flew the
birds, circling and leaping and swooping and rising.

—*Mary Poppins,* 1934

Mary poppins blows into no. 17 cherry tree lane on the east wind, slides up the bannister, unpacks a bed, chair, and clothing from an empty carpetbag, and proceeds to sort out the Banks family's lives while turning their world upside down. P. L. Travers created this stern, conceited, and absolutely magical nanny in 1934, and her staying power has been impressive. In addition to the eight books written by Travers over a fifty-year period, the classic Disney musical has proved an enduring favorite with new generations of children. And quite unusual for classic British children's stories, all the magic happens in the urban world of London.

Whether you come to Mary Poppins through P. L. Travers's books or through the Disney movie, you will find places in London where you can capture the feeling of delight that enlivens both. Fly a kite on Primrose Hill, enjoy Bert's counterparts at Covent Garden, or get up above the rooftops of modern London on a giant Ferris wheel. Children and adults hoping to find a bit of Mary Poppins's charm in London may have to search a bit, but it's still there for the finding.

A Brief Biography of P. L. Travers

I think the idea of Mary Poppins has been blowing in and out of me, like a curtain at a window, all my life. My sister assures me that I told her stories of Mary Poppins when we were very small children.
—P. L. Travers, *Saturday Evening Post*, November 7, 1964

Pamela Lyndon Travers (who preferred to be called "P.L.") was born Helen Lyndon Goff in Maryborough, Queensland, Australia, in either 1899 or 1906 (sources vary on this). Her Irish father, Travers Goff, was a sugar planter who settled in Australia after a stint growing tea in Ceylon. Her Australian mother, Margaret, hired a string of Irish nannies to care for their three daughters. One of these nannies had an umbrella with a parrot head that she kept wrapped in tissue paper and only used on her days off. Although P.L. couldn't recall inventing Mary Poppins in her youth, in later years she came across one of her childhood books with the inscription "M. Poppins" inside the cover. P.L.'s mother bought the book *Everything a Lady Should Know* from a door-to-door salesman and, like Mary Poppins, consulted it faithfully. A few other characters from P.L.'s childhood surfaced in the Mary Poppins stories, such as Andrew, Miss Lark's spoiled little dog, who belonged to P.L.'s great-aunt, and Mrs. Corry and her two huge daughters, who ran the general store in P.L.'s hometown.

P.L. later recalled the "blissful, forgiving moment" in her childhood nursery at bedtime when all was cozy and well. She would gaze at the mysterious view of her bedroom reflected in the mirror on the wall and wonder about the possibilities of two realities coexisting. Later in life that childhood memory inspired her description of Mary Poppins's final exit in her last book: through the reflection of the nursery door in a mirror on the wall.

Travers Goff died when P.L. was seven years old. The family moved to live with a great-aunt in New South Wales. As a teenager, P.L. began to publish stories in newspapers and magazines. After a short stint as an actress with a touring Shakespearean theater company, P.L. turned down a university scholarship and left Australia for Ireland in 1924.

In Ireland she became the devoted friend of George Russell, an Irish poet and journalist who was called AE. Through AE, P.L. became friends with Yeats and other influential Irish poets of the time. Her poems and theater reviews began to be published in Irish and English newspapers. She became interested in world mythology and fairy tales, an interest that influenced her writing for the rest of her life. She found her way to Fontainbleau, France, to study with the mystic thinker Georges Gurdjieff. On returning to London, she became an active, lifelong member of the Gurdjieff Society of London.

In the early 1930s, P.L. recuperated from a serious illness in an ancient thatched cottage in Sussex, England, known as the Pound House. The charming surroundings and the presence of two children eager for entertainment gave her an opportunity to use her storytelling talents, bringing forth stories about a wise, magical nanny named Mary Poppins.

Luckily for us she wrote those stories down, and the original book, *Mary Poppins,* was published in 1934 to immediate success. It was wonderfully illustrated by Mary Shepard, daughter of E. H. Shepard, who illustrated the Christopher Robin and Pooh stories of A. A. Milne (see the A. A. Milne chapter, page 76). A sequel, *Mary Poppins Comes Back,* came out in 1935. Two more books followed, *Mary Poppins Opens the Door* (1943) and *Mary Poppins in the Park* (1952). Travers wrote several other Mary Poppins–based books over the years, but the two that continue the story line begun by the original books were *Mary Poppins in Cherry Tree Lane* (1982) and *Mary Poppins and the House Next Door* (1989).

In 1944, Walt Disney Studios began negotiating with Travers for the right to make a film about Mary Poppins. Travers was no fan of the Disney approach to entertaining children, and it took her seventeen years to finally say yes. The Disney musical, *Mary Poppins,* came out in 1963. It was a huge success and won five Academy Awards. Although Travers was a consultant to the making of the film, she didn't care for the results, saying she was "disturbed at seeing it so externalized, so oversimplified, so generalized." Her ultimate hope was that the movie's popularity would bring more people to read the books.

Travers lived out her life in a small house in the Chelsea section of London. Although the homes of hundreds of famous authors are marked with blue plaques (historical markers) all over London, Travers's home remains unmarked as she kept the details of her personal life quite private. She was a founding editor of *Parabola,* a magazine focusing on myth and tradition. She wrote several books for adults, including *What the Bee Knows: Reflections on Myth, Symbol & Story* (1989), a collection of her essays for *Parabola.* She visited the United States frequently as a visiting writer and lecturer at Radcliffe, Smith, and Scripps Colleges. Travers also spent time living among the Navajo people to learn about their mythology. In 1977, she received the Order of the British Empire (OBE) from the British government.

Travers always insisted that she did not create Mary Poppins, but that Mary Poppins came looking for her. "All I know is that without a word of explanation, a character with a familiar name came in search of an author. And the one she picked on, for whatever incomprehensible reason, was glad, surprised and grateful." (*The Saturday Evening Post,* November 7, 1964.) P. L. Travers died in London in 1996.

Places Connected with the Mary Poppins Stories

REGENT'S PARK (NANNIES' PARK), LONDON

Jane and Michael Banks lived with their magical nanny, parents, and twin baby brother and sister (who were left out of the movie) at No. 17 Cherry Tree Lane. The lane is fictional, but the streets surrounding Regent's Park and Primrose Hill (see

page 138) certainly fit the description, especially in the springtime: ". . . where the houses run down one side and the Park runs down the other and the cherry-trees go dancing right down the middle." Lovely and spacious Regent's Park, with spectacular beds of flowers and walks lined with roses, even has an area designated as Nannies' Park inside the park's Inner Circle. Alas, we didn't see even one proper nanny carrying on the Mary Poppins tradition, but perhaps the wind wasn't blowing in the right direction.

You can enter the park near the Baker Street, Regent's Park, or Great Portland Street tube stations. If you are looking for some fresh air after the fumes of London's streets, you can walk the whole way through the park to the London Zoo.

LONDON ZOO, LONDON

The "Full Moon" chapter from the first Mary Poppins book highlights the contrast between the tone and style of the book *Mary Poppins* and the Disney movie. It's worth reading or rereading if you intend to visit the zoo while you are in London. Jane and Michael arrive at the London Zoo in the middle of the night to find everything reversed; people and children are in the cages being fed by the animals and a "fat old gentleman [is] walking up and down on all fours, and on his back, in two parallel seats, eight monkeys [are] going for a ride." From an adult perspective, there is an intensely mystical, surreal flavor to the whole episode. The Golden Cobra (Hamadryad), who is the acknowledged king of the zoo, tells the children, "It may be that to eat and be eaten are the same thing in the end. . . . We are all made of the same stuff, remember, we of the Jungle, you of the City. The same substance composes us—the tree overhead, the stone beneath us, the bird, the beast, the star—we are all one, all moving to the same end." It's certainly not the standard fare of children's stories from the 1930s!

The Zoo Green still exists much as it is described in "Full Moon," but the old Snake House has been replaced by a more modern facility. For fans of the movie *Mary Poppins* who can't make it to the Edinburgh Zoo (see below), the London Zoo features a striking penguin enclosure built in 1934. Sweeping, interlocking white ramps form an eye-catching backdrop for penguin antics.

The London Zoo is located at the north side of Regent's Park. It is open from 10:00 A.M. every day except Christmas Day. Admission is £9.00/adults, £7.00/children four and older. The nearest tube stop is Camden Town. It can also be reached by the C2 or the 274 bus.

A waterbus runs between Camden Lock or Little Venice and the zoo on the Regent's Canal. Camden Lock is a five-block walk up the Camden High Street from the tube stop. The waterbus service is hourly from April through September, daily during October, and on weekends only from November through March. There is a parking area on Prince Albert Road (pay) for the zoo. Telephone: (207) 722-3333. (See the *Winnie the Pooh* chapter, page 81 and the *Children of Green Knowe* chapter, page 224 for more information about the London Zoo.)

PRIMROSE HILL, LONDON

Primrose Hill is a park that adjoins Regent's Park directly across Prince Albert Road and Regent's Canal from the London Zoo. It is one of the rare hills in London and provides an excellent view of the city, including the dome of St. Paul's. This is the place you would go to find a steady breeze to fly a kite if you lived on Cherry Tree Lane. When you visit, bring your own kite, a picnic, and a scarf or hat. There is a children's playground with restrooms along Prince Albert Road at the bottom of the hill.

The closest tube stops are Camden Town or St. John's Wood, but neither one is very close. See the entry about the London Zoo (above) for bus and waterbus information. (Also see *The 101 Dalmatians* chapter, page 206 for more about Primrose Hill.)

BANK OF ENGLAND MUSEUM, BARTHOLOMEW LANE, LONDON

A visit to the area around Threadneedle Street certainly evokes the gray-suited, stodgy world of British banking as portrayed in the movie *Mary Poppins* (and less explicitly in the books). Sitting in the small, outdoor square in front of the Bank of England, you can feel the weight of the British Empire as it existed a hundred years ago represented in the solid, gray buildings that surround you. Hold on tight to your tuppence. The Bank of England Museum, which is just around the corner, is described in *The Wind in the Willows* chapter, page 42.

The museum is just a block from the Bank tube station. Take exit 2 and walk a block up Threadneedle Street, then left on Bartholomew Lane. Admission is free. Open Monday to Friday, 10:00–5:00; closed weekends and holidays. Telephone: (0207) 601-5545.

ST. PAUL'S CATHEDRAL, LONDON

The center for pigeon feeding in London seems to have shifted to Trafalgar Square (see "Other Activities for Children" section of this chapter), but a visit to St. Paul's, especially on a foggy day, will have you humming "Feed the Birds" nonetheless. The impressive cathedral was designed by Christopher Wren in the late 1600s after the Great Fire of London. Evensong, a short, peaceful service for the end of the day, is sung at 5:00 P.M. daily. No admission is charged at that time, and it's a lovely way to experience the cathedral's wonderful acoustics. Otherwise, admission is £4/adults, £2/children, or £7.50/£5.50 if you want to climb up into the amazing dome and Whispering Gallery. The lighting of the cathedral's exterior at night is also dramatic.

The closest tube stop is St. Paul's. Telephone: (0207) 236-4128.

Other Activities for Children Who Love Mary Poppins

EDINBURGH ZOO PENGUIN PARADE, EDINBURGH, SCOTLAND

In the animated portion of the movie *Mary Poppins,* the penguin waiters steal the show. They do the same at the Edinburgh Zoo. The zoo houses the largest exhibit of penguins in the world. Each day at 2:00 P.M., a keeper politely opens the enclosure door and checks to see if any of the penguins are interested in a stroll. The day we visited, most of the birds had better things to do, and only five penguins were inclined to parade. A couple hundred people gathered along the edge of a large, circular walkway and gaped and photographed as the birds meandered with great dignity and sangfroid through the crowd. When all was said and done, we weren't sure who was entertaining whom.

The Penguin Parade takes place daily at 2:00 P.M. from March through October. Get to the grassy areas by the enclosure early to claim a good viewing spot.

The Edinburgh Zoo is located three miles west of the city center on eighty acres of hillside. Several buses run from Princes Street to the entrance. There is also a large parking lot that charges a nominal fee. Admission is £8/adults, £5/children over five. (More information on the zoo can be found in the Robert Louis Stevenson chapter, page 123.) Telephone: (0131) 334-9171.

THE KITE STORE, 48 NEAL STREET, LONDON

If you really want the full Mary Poppins experience, pick up a kite and take it with you to Primrose Hill. The Kite Store is quite close to

Covent Garden. Follow James Street from the Covent Garden "plaza" to Long Acre. Jog a bit to the right and continue straight ahead on Neal Street, past all sorts of interesting shops and vegetarian restaurants, for two blocks. The store carries a wide range of kites, discs, and "any other interesting Thing that takes our fancy"! Telephone: (0207) 836-1666.

TRAFALGAR SQUARE, LONDON

If a visit to St. Paul's Cathedral (see above) doesn't satisfy your desire to feed the birds, try a visit to Trafalgar Square. Nelson's Column and four mighty bronze lions are the focus of the square, which is bordered by the National Gallery, the Church of St. Martin-in-the-Fields, Canada House, South Africa House, and Admiralty Arch. In 1999, there was a van selling bags of bird food to tourists and about 2 million pigeons flooding the square. By 2001, the van was gone, and the pigeon population was down to about 250,000. For better or worse, the experience is less overwhelming now, but it still provides an opportunity to mingle with London's bird population.

The closest tube stop is Charing Cross. Many bus routes pass through Trafalgar Square as well.

COVENT GARDEN, LONDON

If Mary Poppins's Bert were alive today, chances are he would be a street performer since there's not much call for chimney sweeps anymore. The best place in town for street performers of all types, including chalk artists, is Covent Garden.

This historic plaza used to be the fruit and vegetable market made famous by Eliza Doolittle in *My Fair Lady*. Since the mid-1980s, it's become a lively mix of restaurants and upscale shops. The street performers amaze and amuse the crowds gathered around them during the day and into the evening hours.

The closest tube stop is Covent Garden.

BRITISH AIRWAYS LONDON EYE, NEAR WESTMINSTER BRIDGE, LONDON

The best way to get a view out over the rooftops of London (aside from a parrot-handled umbrella) is one of London's newest landmarks, the London Eye. Built as part of the millennium celebration, it looks like a giant white Ferris wheel on the south bank of the Thames. Glass capsules holding up to twenty-five people rise to a height of 450 feet as they make the thirty-minute circuit around the wheel. You can rent binoculars in the Ticket Hall.

The London Eye web site (www.ba-londoneye.com) offers a webcam that gives a "real-time" picture from the Eye and changes positions every sixty seconds.

Tickets must be booked in advance, and you must arrive during the half hour before your "flight time." Make reservation more than three days in advance by calling (0870) 5000-600. (The number of zeros is correct!) You may also purchase tickets in advance or on the same day in the County Hall Building next door. Admission is £9.50/adults, £5/five–fifteen years old, £7.50/seniors; children under five ride free. The eye is in operation from 9:00 A.M. to 10:00 P.M., from April 1 through September 10, and from 10:00 A.M. to 6:00 P.M. from September 11 through March 31. It is closed Christmas Day. The closest tube stop is Westminster (a five-minute walk across the Thames) or Waterloo.

MORE-RECENT FAVORITES

II

WATERSHIP DOWN
by Richard Adams

♣ "Dandelion, get down!" [Hazel] said. "Why are you sitting up
there?"

"Because I can see," replied Dandelion, with a kind of excited joy.
"Come and look! You can see the whole world."

. . . They were on top of the down. Perched above the grass, they
could see far in every direction. . . . The height, the sky and the
distance went to their heads and they skipped in the sunset. "O Frith
on the hills!" cried Dandelion. "He must have made it for us!"

—*Watership Down*, 1972

$\mathcal{A}$ STORY OF EPIC PROPORTIONS WITH BATTLES, SPIES, BLOOD-shed, heroes, and psychopaths—and it's all about rabbits. Not only that, the main characters are endearing and memorable rabbits: Hazel, the born leader; Fiver, brilliant and psychic; Bigwig, brave and tough; Blackberry, an inventive genius. The story of their journey to found a new warren takes place over twelve miles of lovely Hampshire countryside. It's an area that hasn't changed much in the thirty years since the story was written. The rabbits' numerous progeny could reenact their ancestors' courageous adventure again today if they were so inclined.

For human admirers, the Watership Down area is well worth visiting for a few days of exploration or as a great picnic spot on the way to Stonehenge or other points west of London. Richard Adams set the story in his boyhood haunts, where it fits the landscape quite precisely, right down to the copse of beech trees that mark the Honeycomb Warren. By car, on foot, or by bicycle, following the path of Hazel and his heroic band provides a great day out in the picturesque countryside surrounding Watership Down.

A Brief Biography of Richard Adams

A lot of people have said this is a political fable or even a religious fable or social comment. I promise you it is not a fable or an allegory or a parable of any kind. It is a story about rabbits, that is all.
—Richard Adams in the *Pittsburgh Press*, 1974

Richard Adams was born in 1920, the fourth child of a doctor and his wife. He grew up in a large house surrounded by three acres of spacious gardens outside of **Newbury**, Berkshire, at Wash Common. From his bedroom window he could see out across the woods and fields to **Watership Down** a few miles away. Richard's brother and sister were significantly older than he was; his second brother, two years older than Richard, died in the great influenza epidemic of 1919. Richard was left to play in solitude a great deal, roaming the fields and woods nearby. One of his favorite children's stories was Hugh Lofting's *Dr. Dolittle*.

Like the good doctor, Adams loved animals and the study of local plants. In his teenage years Adams became an ardent fly fisherman on the nearby river Kennet, a hobby that he was to keep for life.

At age eight Adams entered Horris Hill Preparatory School, a boarding school close to Newbury. This was followed by Bradfield College, a boarding school for older boys. He entered Worcester College, Oxford, in 1938, but his studies were interrupted by the war in 1940. Adams served in the army and then in a parachuting platoon for the remainder of the war, returning to finish his degree in history at Oxford in 1946.

After graduating in 1948, Adams married Elizabeth Acland, a neighbor from Wash Common. He entered the British civil service, where he worked for the next twenty-four years. His work within the Department of the Environment during those years included slum clearance, coastal erosion prevention, and air pollution control.

A great admirer of Shakespeare, Adams named his two daughters Juliet and Rosamond. In order to instill a love of the Bard in them, he often drove them to Stratford to see live Shakespeare performed. The drive was lengthy, so Adams invented stories for the girls to pass the time. One of them, which he told when the girls were ages seven and nine, was about a group of rabbits caught in a Greek tragedy–inspired situation. The story was so engrossing that the girls urged Adams to write it down. Eventually he did so in the evening hours after work.

After being turned down by several publishers, Adams was on the brink of publishing the tale himself so he could give it to his daughters when a small publisher agreed to put it out. The result, *Watership Down,* came out in 1972. The initial print run was two thousand copies. The book was a surprise hit, winning the Carnegie Medal. It eventually sold well over ten million copies in over twenty languages, making Adams a wealthy man at age fifty-two. Although much of its success came when it was marketed as a book for young people, Adams has always insisted that it is an adult book, appropriate for readers aged eight to eighty-eight. The story of *Watership Down* was made into an animated movie in 1978 by Martin Rosen. A TV series of the story was produced in 2000 for British and Canadian audiences.

Adams left the civil service in 1974 to focus on writing. *Shardik* came out in 1974, followed by *The Plague Dogs* in 1978. The latter, about dogs used for scientific experimentation who escape to freedom, reflects Adams's work for animal rights, which included serving as vice president of the Royal Society for the Prevention of Cruelty to Animals. Adams continued to write novels, children's books, and nature books through the 1970s and 80s. His autobiography, *The Day Gone By,* which covers his life from his childhood near Newbury until he returned home from serving in the army, came out in 1990.

Adams and his wife, Elizabeth, now live in an eighteenth-century house in Whitchurch, Hampshire, just a hop, skip, and a jump from Watership Down.

Places Connected with Watership Down

NOTE: Hazel, Fiver, Bigwig, and company probably didn't realize that their epic journey leaped right over the border between Berkshire and Hampshire. This can be confusing when looking up places on maps and inquiring at Tourist Information Centres (which tend to focus only on the county in which they are located). The boundary between the two "shires" is the river Enborne just south of Newbury. Watership Down itself is in Hampshire, but it is considered a continuation of the Berkshire Downs.

No matter which county you are in, this is lovely, rolling English countryside. Any of the walks described below will give you a feel for the settings described in the book. The one exception is the Sandleford Park area, which is really right on the edge of a large town. If you only have time for one walk, be sure to catch the view from the top of Watership Down itself.

Sandleford Park, Newbury, Berkshire

Newbury is three miles south of the M4 at junction 13. On the south side of Newbury, quite near the Tesco Retail Park (complete with Pizza Hut), a bit of countryside has yet to be dug up by developers despite Fiver's prophecies. Here you can stroll across the area of the Sandleford Warren, Hazel and Fiver's home at the beginning of *Watership Down.* These are also Richard Adams's childhood haunts; his home was on the nearby Andover Road. Pick up the footpath marked TO WARREN ROAD just across from St. Gabriel's School on Newton Road. It leads across an open, cultivated area to Warren Road next to the Park House School on Andover Road, about a twenty-minute walk.

Newtown Churchyard/Ecchinswell/ Nuthanger Farm Area, Hampshire

The rabbits crossed the river Enborne just beyond the roundabout where the Newtown Road meets the A339. Blackberry's innovation, a floating board, gets the weaker rabbits across the stream; then they make their way through Newtown Churchyard and across Newtown Common, heading toward Ecchinswell. To walk the area today without fear of crossing someone's private property, pick up a copy of *Rambling for Pleasure: Kennet Valley & Watership Down,* put out in 1999 by the East Berkshire Ramblers Association. It's available at the Tourist Information Centre in Newbury (The Wharf, Newbury, telephone: (01635) 30267) and costs £3. Ramble 13 begins just past the church and will lead you across Newtown Common with a lot less stress than Hazel and the gang experienced. If you do the whole loop, you will also see the Horris Hill School, which Richard Adams attended as a boy.

As you meander on toward Ecchinswell, you will most likely pass through parts of the Sydmonton Court Estate, currently owned by songwriter Andrew Lloyd Weber. You may also see elegant-looking horses grazing or being trained. This area has been famous for its race horses for decades and is crisscrossed by "gallops" where the horses are run.

Ramble 17 in *Rambling for Pleasure: Kennet Valley & Watership Down* begins at the village hall car park in Ecchinswell. The loop trail passes Nuthanger Farm, the setting of two exciting moments in the story: the raid to liberate the domesticated doe rabbits and the heroic attempt to lure the farm dog into chasing the enemy rabbits away at the end of the book. Although the public right-of-way passes nearby, the farm is private property and not open to the public. If you want to see the area by car, follow the road from Kingsclere (on the A339) to Ecchinswell. Although you won't see the farm buildings, you can follow the country lanes and take in some great views of Watership Down itself and the lovely countryside surrounding it.

Watership Down, near Kingsclere, Hampshire

Kingsclere is located on the A339 about eight miles south of Newbury and ten miles north of Basingstoke. Follow the B3051 from the roundabout toward Overton. About a mile south of Kingsclere, the road goes steeply up the down, which is easily the biggest hill around. When Fiver urged Hazel to lead the rabbits to the hills, this three-hundred-foot ridge loomed (from a rabbit's point of view) on the horizon. At the top there is a pull-out area for cars marked WAYFARER'S WALK. Follow the path west about two hundred yards to find the Honeycomb area by the copse of beech trees. The views out toward Oxfordshire are impressive, and it's easy to see how a rabbit would feel as if it were on the roof of the world here. There is a picnic area on the other side of the B3051 a bit farther along the Wayfarer's Walk.

Continue south on the B3051. You will soon pass through "Caesar's Belt" (which is called Robley's Belt on the current map), where the rabbits encounter a fox. The B3051 crosses over the "Iron Road" and the river Test on its way into Overton. The B3400, a left turn in the center of town, leads toward Laverstoke (about a mile away). The river Test between Overton and Laverstoke is a beautiful, well-tended trout stream with paths along each side for the fisherfolk to use.

This is the part of the river the Watership Down rabbits encounter while coordinating their raid on the Efrafra warren. The small plank bridge they hop across to discover that rabbit mind–blowing contraption, a boat, and the two bridges they float under as they escape General Woundwort's forces, are all there exactly as in the story.

> The bridge stretched from bank to bank between two low abutments. It was not arched. Its underside, made of iron girders, was perfectly straight—parallel with the surface and about eight inches above it. Just in time Hazel saw what Kehaar meant. If the punt did pass under the bridge without sticking, it would so do by no more than a claw's breath. Any creature above the level of the sides would be struck and perhaps knocked into the river. He scuttered through the warm bilgewater to the other end and pushed his way up among the wet, crowded rabbits.
> "Get down in the bottom! Get down in the bottom!" he said.
> —*Watership Down,* chapter 39

Other Activities for Children Who Love Watership Down

RABBIT WORLD, AMESBURY, WILTSHIRE

As beautiful and evocative as the countryside is around Watership Down, younger travelers may want to see some real bunnies. The place to do that is Rabbit World, home to the world's largest collection of rabbit breeds. Over fifty types of rabbits are housed in pens in a covered area. It's not exactly Hazel and friends fending for themselves in the wild, but it does provide the opportunity to observe rabbit behavior up close, see babies in their nests, and pet a few bunnies.

Rabbit World is part of Cholderton Rare Breeds Farm Park, so there is the opportunity to see lots of sheep, goats, and—don't miss it—pig racing. The Ewe Tree Tea-room serves lunch and tea; there's a picnic area as well.

Rabbit World and the Cholderton Rare Breeds Farm Park are located near Stonehenge just east of the town of Amesbury, Wiltshire. It's about twenty miles from the Watership Down area. Follow signs from the A303 for the A338 south.

Admission is £4.25/adults, £2.75/children two–fourteen; a family ticket is £13. The park is open from 10:00 to 6:00 P.M., March 24 through November 4. Telephone: (01980) 629438. Web site: www .rabbitworld.co.uk.

Thomas the Tank Engine *and* Other Stories

by the Reverend W. Awdry

❧ [Thomas] was a fussy little engine, always pulling coaches about. . . . He was a cheeky little engine, too. He thought no engine worked as hard as he did. So he used to play tricks on them. He liked best of all to come quietly beside a big engine dozing on a siding and make him jump.

"Peep, peep, peep, pip, peep! Wake up, lazybones!" he would whistle, "why don't you work hard like me?"

Then he would laugh rudely and run away to find some more coaches.

—*Thomas the Tank Engine*, 1946

When the Reverend Wilbert Awdry began writing down simple stories about trains for his son, the steam train was still very much a part of everyday life in Britain. The stories, which were technically accurate in every way (except for the talking engines), were immediately popular, but steam locomotion began to fade. The first steam railway preservation efforts began about five years after the first Thomas books were published in 1945, as diesel power began to take over. Thomas and his friends became a voice for preservation, and they have continued to inspire the imaginations of new generations of young railway enthusiasts. Today, with more than one hundred preserved railways run by volunteers all over Britain, Thomas and all his fellow steam trains have no more worries about being left on the sidings and forgotten.

The opportunities for experiencing a ride on a steam train from a vintage station are numerous in all parts of Britain. Thomas makes the rounds each year, and "Thomas Days" are extremely popular events at many of the preserved railways and railway museums. The cloud of steam billowing across the sky, the expressive hisses and chugs as the engine puffs along, add a dimension to a train ride that shouldn't be missed by anyone of any age who loves train travel.

A Brief Biography of the Reverend Wilbert Awdry

It needed little imagination to hear, in the sounds they made, the engines talking to each other. From that time there developed in my mind the idea that steam engines all have personality.
—The Reverend W. Awdry, describing the sounds made by freight engines outside his bedroom window when he was a boy

Wilbert Vere Awdry was born in Ampfield, Hampshire, in 1911. His father, a clergyman with a keen interest in railroads, was called "the Railwayman Parson" by his many parishioners who worked for the railways. The family had a model train set in their yard with a working steam engine two-and-a-half inches long. The family moved to Box, Wiltshire, where they lived by the main train line from London to Bristol. The sounds of the trains passing by provided the first bit of inspiration to young Wilbert for what would later become the world of Thomas the Tank Engine and his friends.

Awdry attended St. Peter's College, Oxford, where he received his B.A. and M.A. degrees. He followed in his father's footsteps by becoming an ordained priest of the Church of England in 1937. During a short teaching stint overseas in Jerusalem, he met Margaret Wale, also a teacher; they were married in 1938. Upon returning to England, Awdry took a position as curate at St. Nicholas's Church, King's Norton, Birmingham, in 1940. In that same year their son, Christopher, was born.

When Christopher had an attack of the measles in 1942, his father drew him a picture of six train engines with faces, each with a different expression, to entertain him. That picture became the basis for the story "Edward's Day Out." Young Christopher liked the details of his father's stories to be the same with every telling, so Wilbert Awdry began to write the stories down. Mrs. Awdry insisted that her husband send three of the stories to a publisher, and they came out in 1945 as *The Three Railway Engines.* It featured three steam engines, Edward, Gordon, and Henry.

When his son recovered from the measles, the Reverend Awdry built him a small blue model of a tank engine. Christopher named it Thomas and soon, another set of stories had emerged. They became *Thomas the Tank Engine* (1946). The Reverend Awdry dedicated the book to Christopher because "you helped me make them."

Britain's railways were nationalized in 1948, and in the next book in the series, *James the Red Engine* (1948), Awdry notes that "we are nationalized now, but the same engines still work the region." Awdry became vicar of a parish in Emneth, Norfolk, in 1953. He continued to publish stories throughout the 1950s and on until 1972. The books reflect the growing dominance of diesel power over steam engines on British trains during this period, with Awdry often casting the diesel engine as the (very mild) villain. With the last steam engine being phased out of use in Britain in 1968, Awdry's books became more and more a plea for preserving and honoring this colorful and much-loved period of Britain's past.

Train enthusiasts praise Awdry's stories for their realistic details and adherence to the real functions of each type of engine. Each character was based on a real prototype engine. Many of the stories have been about the fictional Skarloey Railway, which is based on the historic **Talyllyn Railway** in Wales. The Reverend Awdry and his son visited Talyllyn often on vacations. As the stories became more involved, Awdry sketched out an imaginary world, the Island of Sodor, for his trains to inhabit. Sodor is supposed to be located in the Irish Sea, between the Isle of Man and the Lancashire coast.

The Reverend Awdry retired from the parish ministry in 1965 and from writing in 1972. He and his wife moved to Stroud, Gloucestershire, where Awdry enjoyed building model railways, which he displayed around the country to promote steam railway preservation. He was awarded an OBE in 1996. The Reverend Awdry died peacefully at home in March 1997, at the age of eighty-five.

Christopher Awdry has continued the family tradition by writing stories about Thomas and his friends since 1983. His young son, Richard, provided a "test audience" for the new stories, just as Christopher had once done for Wilbert. Christopher, his wife, and son continue to visit Talyllyn Railway each summer as volunteers who help run and maintain the narrow-gauge, steam-driven line.

The stories about Thomas and his railway world continue to be popular with young children around the globe. The Thomas stories have been made into a popular TV series for children narrated by Ringo Starr. A feature film called *Thomas and the Magic Railroad,* starring the voices of Alec Baldwin and Peter Fonda, came out in 2000.

In the stories about Thomas and his friends, the highest praise that the Sir Topham Hatt gives is: "You are a Really Useful Engine." In much the same tone, Christopher Awdry describes his father as being grateful for a life in which he could be useful to the cause of railway preservation.

Places Connected with Thomas the Tank Engine

National Railway Museum (NRM), York

For a few weekends each year, the National Railway Museum welcomes Thomas and his friends into its railyard. Sir Topham Hatt comes along to make sure everything is done properly and to read some stories to the  kids. For 50 pence you can even have a ride on Thomas! The museum has a twenty-four-hour Thomas event hot line at (01904) 686282 to find out the dates of Thomas's upcoming visits.

If you aren't lucky enough to be in York when Thomas is in town, don't despair. The National Railway Museum is a treasure trove of trains. From Stephenson's historic "Rocket" to the "palace on wheels" of the royal family to the ride on the miniature train out back, this museum will fascinate train lovers of any age. There are several gleaming steam locomotives (polished weekly) and a working turntable, which is demonstrated at 3:30 P.M. daily. This is just like the turntable James the Red Engine was sitting on when the wind spun him around, an event that wasn't uncommon in the days of steam.

The museum is extremely kid-friendly, with a picnic area and an Interactive Learning Centre. You can ride a "road train" from York Minster (York's magnificent cathedral) to the National Railway Museum and back. It costs £1/adults, 50 pence/children. The tram runs every thirty minutes from April through October, less frequently in the off-season.

The National Railway Museum is open from 10:00 to 6:00 P.M. daily. Admission is £6.90/adults; children sixteen and under are free. The gift shop carries plenty of Thomas items.

The museum is located on Leeman Road about a half mile across the river from the museum gardens. Pedestrians can follow the posted signs from anywhere in the center of York. If you are arriving by train, it is an easy walk from the York train station. Although it is best to avoid driving into the center of York if possible, there is long-term parking (fee) at the museum. Follow the signs from the Ring Road. Telephone: (01904) 621621.

TALYLLYN RAILWAY, TYWYN, WALES

Talyllyn calls itself "The World's First Preserved Railway," saved from destruction in 1950 by the Talyllyn Railway Preservation Society. The all-volunteer society continues to maintain and operate the line to this day. The seven-mile line was opened in 1865 to transport slate. The original equipment still chugs its way through the Fathew valley at about nine miles per hour. The Reverend Awdry loved visiting the railway with his son, and his family continues to help out each year with the work of maintaining the line. Talyllyn's official Children's Favourite Engine is Peter Sam, whom Reverend Awdry included in some of his stories. When, as in 2001, Peter Sam has boiler trouble and needs to be mended, his friend Duncan takes his place. Peter Sam and Duncan are known to their close friends at the Talyllyn line by their real names, Edward Thomas and Douglas, but they keep that quiet to protect their privacy.

The Talyllyn Railway has special days for Peter Sam and/or Duncan each summer, occasionally with Christopher Awdry and his family in attendance. The engines also work on designated weekends and holidays. The railway's web site, www.talyllyn.co.uk, is extremely informative and can furnish the exact dates.

Tywyn is located in the middle of the west coast of Wales about twenty miles north of Aberystwyth. From Aberystwyth, follow the A487 north to Machynlleth, then take the A493 west to Tywyn. The Talyllyn line begins at Tywyn Wharf. There is a car park and easy access to the main railway line for those coming by train. The Narrow Gauge Railway Museum and Talyllyn gift shop are also located at Tywyn Wharf. The train line follows the B4405 out of Tywyn, and the train can be boarded at four stops en route. The station the farthest inland with road access is at Abergynolwyn, which has restrooms, a shop, picnic facilities, and a car park.

Almost the entire Talyllyn line lies within the boundaries of spectacular Snowdonia National Park. Several beautiful walking trails connect with the railway stops along the line. They make excellent day hikes if you take an early train out in the morning and reboard the train later in the day.

A Day Rover ticket allows for unlimited travel on the line all day, costing £9/adults, £2 children five–fifteen; under five travel free. Trains run every fifty minutes during the high season, beginning at 9:45 A.M. More-limited schedules are available during other seasons. Telephone: (01654) 710472.

Other Places Connected with the Reverend Awdry's Life

THE MUSEUM IN THE PARK, STROUD, GLOUCESTERSHIRE

The Reverend Awdry and Mrs. Awdry retired to the Stroud area, living nearby at Rodborough. There is a small, Thomas-themed playroom in the local museum. See the *Cider with Rosie* chapter, page 238 for more information.

Other Activities for Children Who Love the Thomas the Tank Engine Stories

PRESERVED RAILWAYS, EVERY PART OF BRITAIN

For railway enthusiasts young and old there is a wealth of restored railways with steam locomotives in every part of Britain. The Reverend Awdry himself put together a book on the subject that is well worth consulting: *A Guide to the Steam Railways of Great Britain,* edited by Reverend Awdry and Chris Cook, London: Pelham, 1979; revised edition, 1984. The latest edition of *Heritage Railway* magazine lists 107 active preserved railways in Britain and Ireland in its "Up and Running" column. Seventeen railway museums are listed as well (see http://ukh/rail.uel.ac.uk for up-to-date information). No matter what part of the country you are planning to visit, you'll be able to ride on an historic steam train if you are so inclined. Many of these preserved railways feature "Thomas Days" when you will be lucky enough to ride on Thomas and talk with Sir Topham Hatt, the Fat Controller.

Three steam railways of special interest:

1. One of the restored railways, the Keighley & Worth Valley Railway in West Yorkshire, has the added attraction of a connection with another children's classic, *The Railway Children* by Edith Nesbit. It also stops in Haworth, Yorkshire, home of the Brontë family of *Jane Eyre* and *Wuthering Heights* fame. The KWVR has regularly scheduled "Thomas Days" and an impressive wall of Thomas items for sale in the gift shop. (See the chapter about Edith Nesbit's book, *The Railway Children,* page 245, for details.)

2. *Stepney the "Bluebell" Engine* by the Reverend Awdry (1963) features the real-life Bluebell Railway in East Sussex. The Bluebell Railway is accurately portrayed as a place for old steam engines to retire, a refuge from being "cut up" by the engineers at the Other Railway who no longer use steam. The Bluebell Railway is still thriving, with regularly scheduled "Thomas" weekends. In 2001, they featured Stepney and Fenchurch shunting some "Troublesome Trucks" as well as a Bedtime Train for kids that included a Thomas bedtime story. (See the web site at www.bluebellrailway.co.uk for exact dates.)

   The Bluebell Railway runs between Kingscote and Sheffield Park in Sussex. Trains operate from April 7 through the end of September each year. Take a regular train to East Grinstead and then transfer to the No. 473 bus to Kingscote station. By car, the easiest access is at the Sheffield Park station on the A275, two miles north of the junction with the A272. The way is signposted from the A23. Telephone: (01825) 722370.

The Bluebell Railway is located close to Ashdown Forest, the home of Winnie the Pooh and friends (see the A. A. Milne chapter, page 78 for more information). For a certain age group, it's hard to beat Thomas and Pooh all in one day! It would make a wonderful day trip from London if traveling by car.

The Bluebell trains and stations were also used in a production of *The Railway Children* by Edith Nesbit produced by Carlton TV. The show aired in the United States on public television in 2000.

3. If you are planning to visit the setting that inspired Frances Hodgson Burnett's *The Secret Garden* in Kent, you may also want to enjoy a ride on the Kent & East Sussex Railway, a steam railway that originates in nearby Tenterden. They offer a "Thomas Day" every February and lots of Thomasphernalia as well. Take the A28 northeast from Rolvenden about six miles to Tenterden. Follow the signs from the High Street in Tenterden. Trains run every weekend from April through October, every day in July and August. The line passes through seven miles of beautiful, rolling countryside. Parking is free. Telephone: (01580) 765155.

BEKONSCOT MODEL VILLAGE, BEACONSFIELD, BUCKINGHAMSHIRE

For seventy years, Bekonscot, the world's oldest model village, has given visitors a chance to step back in time into 1930s rural England in miniature. Covering an area of over forty thousand square feet, Bekonscot includes six tiny villages that encompass nearly every feature of British life of that era: a circus, a racecourse, a cricket pitch, a fishing village, an airfield, a coal mine, and a wonderful model steam railway running throughout. The model trains travel to seven stations, all controlled by illuminated track diagrams and levers that are operated from a signal house visible to the public. The gift shop by the entrance is even housed in an old railway carriage.

Visitors to Bekonscot walk among all this activity on over two thousand feet of pathways. It's a delightful feeling to stand in the midst of this extensive and amazingly detailed landscape. Even the trees and landscaping have been scaled down to fit the tiny buildings.

There is a full-sized play area for young children, a picnic area, and a refreshments stand. Admission is £3.60/adults, £1.80/children, under three free. The excess profits from Bekonscot are given to charity, with over a million pounds raised since its beginning in 1929. Bekonscot is open from 10:00 to 5:00 P.M. every day from February 14 through November 1. Telephone: (01494) 675284.

Beaconsfield is located just west of London at junction 2 on the M40. Follow the A355 and signs for the model village. It's a short train ride from London and an easy walk from the station to Bekonscot.

LONDON'S TRANSPORT MUSEUM, LONDON

Although this museum doesn't have any specific exhibits about Thomas or steam trains, it does feature lively, interactive exhibits about the London underground, double-decker buses, and all the other types of transport that have kept London running for the last two centuries. Kids will enjoy the bus-driving simulators and the model tube trains that run on a track suspended from the ceiling. The gift shop offers loads of Thomas merchandise and a café overlooking the busy plaza outside.

The London Transport Museum is located at Covent Garden, in the corner of the plaza area between Russell Street and Southampton Street. The museum is open daily from 10:00 to 6:00 P.M., Fridays 11:00–6:00 P.M. Admission is £5.95/adults; children under sixteen are free. The closest tube stops are Covent Garden or Charing Cross. Telephone: (0207) 565-7299. Web site: www.ltmuseum.co.uk.

THE PADDINGTON BEAR STORIES

by Michael Bond

❧ "I'm glad I emigrated," said Paddington, as he reached out a paw and pulled the plate [of buns] nearer. "Do you think anyone would mind if I stood on the table to eat?"

Before Mr. Brown could answer he had climbed up and placed his right paw firmly on the bun. It was a very large bun, the biggest and stickiest Mr. Brown had been able to find, and in a matter of moments most of the inside found its way on to Paddington's whiskers. People started to nudge each other and began staring in their direction. Mr. Brown wished he had chosen a plain, ordinary bun, but he wasn't very experienced in the ways of bears. He stirred his tea and looked out the window, pretending he had tea with a bear on Paddington Station every day of his life.

—*A Bear Called Paddington*, 1958

$\mathcal{A}$ BEDRAGGLED LITTLE BEAR IN A STRANGE HAT SITS ON HIS suitcase in Paddington station wearing a tag that says, "Please look after this bear. Thank you." Mr. and Mrs. Brown, kindhearted people that they are, take the scruffy stowaway home with them. He needs a name, and Paddington seems to have the right amount of dignity to it. This polite, determined little bear proceeds to turn their lives upside down, almost always with good results. In the forty years since Paddington arrived on the scene, he has become a fixture of childhood, second only to Pooh in international bear popularity and immediately recognizable in his Peruvian hat and duffle coat.

Paddington fans might take a few minutes to look around London's Paddington Station in case there might be a stowaway in need of a home, shop for bargains at the Portobello Market—perhaps a jar of marmalade might come in handy—or get a taste of the British seaside just as Paddington did on his first trip to the beach. If you are interested in bringing Paddington home with you, there are a few specialty shops that can provide just the bear for you.

A Brief Biography of Michael Bond

[Paddington] lives in a very contemporary world, yet he goes back to the safe pre-war world. When Paddington goes back home, it's the world that I remember from my childhood. In England, if you try to make a telephone call now, you find that the telephone box has been vandalized. Paddington lives in a world where that hasn't happened yet.

—Michael Bond in *Contemporary Authors*, New Revision Series, Vol. 24, Gale Publications, 1987

Born in Newbury, Berkshire, in 1926, Michael Bond grew up in nearby Reading. He spent his childhood with three guinea pigs, Pip, Squeak, and Winifred, and a dog. Bond was only an average student, with one teacher complaining that Bond suffered from an overdeveloped sense of humor. He attended Presentation College, a preparatory school, from age eight to fourteen. At age eighteen, in 1943, he joined the Royal Air

Force and continued serving in the British army after the war ended.

While stationed in Egypt, Bond sent a short story to a British magazine, and it was accepted for publication. Thus encouraged, he set his sights on being a writer. Upon leaving the army in 1947, Bond began a long association with the BBC, initially as a cameraman. He married Brenda Johnson in 1950, and they had two children, Karen and Anthony.

While looking for a Christmas present for his wife in 1957, Bond noticed a little bear all alone on the shelf of a London department store. The bear came home to their one-room apartment. He was named Paddington because they lived quite close to **Paddington Station.** The little bear stared down at Bond as he sat at his typewriter one evening. Hoping only to get his writing juices flowing, Bond typed, "Mr. and Mrs. Brown first met Paddington on a railway platform." Bond got swept up in the fun of writing about the self-possessed little bear from Darkest Peru. *A Bear Called Paddington* was published in 1958. Immediately successful, it became the first of thirteen Paddington books that came out over the next two decades. Peggy Fortnum's ink drawings captured the humor and the dignity of the little bear in the duffel coat and Wellington boots. Over the years the Paddington books have sold over thirty million copies and have been translated into twenty languages. The stories have also been made into an animated TV series.

Michael Bond gave up his job at the BBC to become a full-time writer in 1965. A second series of Paddington stories for younger children began in the early 1970s, illustrated by various artists. Bond's daughter, Karen, collaborated with her father on a series of Paddington activity books in the late 1970s and 1980s.

Michael Bond's prolific career has continued with the popular series about Olga Da Polga, a guinea pig inspired, perhaps, by his childhood companions. In the late 1980s, Bond made the transition into adult fiction with a successful series of books about a French food inspector, Monsieur Pamplemousse, and his faithful dog, Pommes Frites. Pamplemousse tackles lighthearted mysteries set in various regions of France. Bond himself continues to live in London with a flat in Paris. He was awarded the OBE in 1997.

Places Connected with the Paddington Bear Stories

PADDINGTON STATION, LONDON

The station's only nod toward its famous namesake is the Paddington Stand at Paddington Station, located between platforms 8 and 9. Open from 7:30 A.M. to 7:30 P.M. daily, it sells Paddington duffel coats, rain slickers, books, tapes, dishes, and even bibs for your marmalade-loving cub. And if you are looking for your own Paddington bear, this is the truly authentic place to find him. Telephone: (0207) 706-0268.

If you arrive in Britain by plane from Darkest Peru or other points west, you will probably land at Heathrow Airport. If you take the Heathrow express train into town from the airport, you also may find yourself sitting on your suitcase in Paddington Station. It's one of those grand old train stations with a huge, arched roof that lets you know you're not in Kansas anymore. If you are already in London, the station can be reached by four different tube lines, including the Circle and District lines.

PORTOBELLO MARKET, LONDON

The Brown family lives at No. 32 Windsor Gardens, a street not far from the Portobello Road. Paddington visits the Portobello Market every Saturday to buy his buns and to do some shopping for Mrs. Brown. He makes friends with Mr. Gruber, an antique dealer, and joins him regularly for buns and cocoa.

> Now Paddington spent a lot of his time looking in shop windows, and of all the windows in the Portobello Road, Mr. Gruber's was the best. For one thing it was nice and low so that he could look in without having to stand on tiptoe, and for another, it was full of interesting things. Old pieces of furniture, medals, pots and pans, pictures; there were so many things it was difficult to get inside the shop, and old Mr. Gruber spent a lot of his time sitting in a deck-chair on the pavement.
>
> —*A Bear Called Paddington,* chapter 5

Paddington becomes such a "regular" on Portobello Road that the merchants all chip in to buy him a new shopping cart for his first birthday with the Browns.

Today's Portobello Market is a hodge-podge of people selling everything under the sun. The market stretches for over a mile down Portobello Road, beginning with a section of overflowing antiques stores much like Mr. Gruber's and moving on to crafts, artwork, and tourist kitsch. In the middle is a stretch of food and produce stalls, followed by an area that feels like a huge outdoor garage sale.

Saturday is the day to see the market in its glory. Take the tube to Notting Hill, walk up Pembroke Road, and turn left onto Portobello Road. Follow the crowds a few more blocks, and you are there. If you manage to go the entire length of the market, you can turn left after you pass under a highway and walk a block to the Ladbroke Grove tube stop. Several bus routes back into the center of the city pass by here as well. Please note that the market is crowded, and it will be easier to take little ones on your back than in a stroller.

THE SEASIDE AT BRIGHTON, EAST SUSSEX

When the Browns take Paddington for his first trip to the seaside, they go to "Brightsea," a dead ringer for the real seaside resort of Brighton. For your own taste of this traditional British outing, take the hour-long train ride from London or drive south on the A23 from junction 8–7 on the M25, which circles London. Set up a blanket on the beach near the Palace Pier and see who can build the biggest sand castle. Paddington gave it a try but took a brief bear nap as the tide came in and ended up floating in his bucket all the way around to the tip of the pier.

The pier is a lively, if slightly seedy, place these days, divided between arcade games and junk food stands.

If you need some inspiration before you design your sand castle, visit the Royal Pavilion, Brighton's other landmark. This fantastical-looking former royal residence is about as different from Buckingham Palace as two buildings can be. The interior is just as exotic and fun to explore for kids and adults. The Royal Pavilion tearoom is a good place to retreat from the elements if the weather takes a turn. Telephone: (01273) 292592. There are also plenty of restaurants and shops to explore in the pedestrian area called The Lanes, which lies west of East Street, as most everything should.

Places to See Original Artwork/Manuscripts

DE GRUMMOND COLLECTION, UNIVERSITY OF SOUTHERN MISSISSIPPI, HATTIESBURG, MISSISSIPPI

The de Grummond Collection at the McCain Library, University of Southern Mississippi, includes the works of American and British children's writers. The Michael Bond Papers include a set of galleys for *A Bear Called Paddington* and some of the sketches drawn by Peggy Fortnum for *Paddington at Work*. The collection is open to researchers by appointment only. Please call 601-266-4349. Web site: www.lib.usm.edu/~degrum.

Other Activities for Children Who Love the Paddington Bear Stories

THE ENGLISH TEDDY BEAR COMPANY, 42 PICCADILLY, LONDON

If you or your children like bears you can squeeze, The English Teddy Bear Company is the place to go. The shop features a range of stuffed Paddingtons, from a tiny bear in a bag to a Paddington so large you'll need to buy him a separate plane ticket to get him home. Take the tube to Piccadilly Circus and walk a short distance up Piccadilly (the street). Open Monday to Saturday, 10:00–8:00 P.M.; Sunday, 11:00–5:30 P.M. Telephone: (207) 491-2091.

PADDINGTON AND FRIENDS SHOP, BATH, SOMERSET

If you didn't make it to the Paddington Stand at Paddington Station in London, you can find all the Paddington paraphernalia you could hope for at this shop. Although Paddington would certainly enjoy exploring this lovely town, he wouldn't approve of its name. Paddington and Friends can be found at 1 Abbey Street quite near The Pump Room. Telephone: (01225) 463598.

Charlie and the Chocolate Factory *and* Other Stories

by Roald Dahl

♣ "And then again", Grandpa Joe went on speaking very slowly now so that Charlie wouldn't miss a word, "Mr. Willy Wonka can make marshmallows that taste of violets, and rich caramels that change colour every ten seconds as you suck them, and little feathery sweets that melt away deliciously the moment you put them between your lips. . . . And, by a most secret method, he can make lovely blue birds' eggs with black spots on them, and when you put one of these in your mouth, it gradually gets smaller and smaller until suddenly there is nothing left except a tiny little pink sugary baby bird sitting on the tip of your tongue."

—*Charlie and the Chocolate Factory*, 1964

$\mathcal{A}$ GROUP OF CHILDREN WIN A CHANCE TO TOUR THE MOST amazing candy factory in the world. As they do, they disappear one by one, victims of their own greed and willfulness. A boy crawls into a humongous peach and has an adventure with the giant insects that live inside it. An orphan is snatched by a gentle giant and held prisoner in his cave surrounded by more brutal giants who eat a steady diet of children. No one can accuse Roald Dahl of being overly sweet. With the fiendish glee of childhood, he mixes humor, imagination, and retribution into every one of his children's stories. The result is a body of work that has delighted generations of children and shows no signs of going out of vogue. Chances are at least one of Dahl's books is on a list of your or your children's favorites: *Charlie and the Chocolate Factory, James and the Giant Peach, The BFG, Matilda, The Witches, The Magic Finger, Fantastic Mr. Fox, The Twits,* and on and on.

Dahl fans can enliven a trip to Britain by tracing the steps (rather leaps) of the Big Friendly Giant on his way to give the Queen a nightmare, by walking into an actual Giant Peach to learn about insects, or by visiting the factory that inspired the creation of Willie Wonka.

A Brief Biography of Roald Dahl

[The children who write to me] invariably pick out the most gruesome events as the favorite parts of the books. . . . They don't relate it to life. They enjoy the fantasy. And my nastiness is never gratuitous. It's retribution. Beastly people must be punished.
   —Roald Dahl in the *New York Times Book Review,* 1977

Roald Dahl was born in 1916 in Llandaff, Cardiff, Wales, to Norwegian parents. His father was a wealthy shipbroker, an adventurous, self-made man. Roald was christened in the **Norwegian Church** on Cardiff Bay. His description of his childhood in his autobiography, *Boy: Tales of Childhood* (1984), reads like one of his children's books, full of mischief (putting dead mice in the candy jars at the local store to scare the shopkeeper) and magic (the family trips each summer to an isolated island in

Norway). Like his stories, his childhood also had a definite dark side. His young sister died when Dahl was only three, and his father died just weeks later of pneumonia and grief.

Dahl was sent to Repton, a famous private school (which the British call a "public" school) near Derby at age twelve. The brutal canings and mental agonies the boys were put through stayed with Dahl for the rest of his life. In later years he was outspoken in his disdain for that type of education. He did enjoy, however, the boxes of Cadbury chocolates the boys were given frequently. These contained twelve Cadbury bars, eleven of them new products. **The Cadbury company** asked the boys to give written comments on each bar, and Dahl recalled writing, "Too subtle for the common palate" for one bar. This early introduction to "new product development" by the candy industry came out on paper as Willie Wonka's wonderful confections years later.

At age eighteen Dahl turned down the option of attending Oxford or Cambridge for the excitement of seeing the world: He went to work for Shell Oil in Tanzania. With the beginning of World War II, Dahl joined the Royal Air Force in Kenya. He became one of a small band of fighter pilots who flew dangerous missions in the eastern Mediterranean, described vividly in *Going Solo* (1986), Dahl's second autobiographical book. A near-fatal crash in Egypt in 1941 left him with injuries that plagued him for the rest of his life.

Dahl was then appointed assistant air attaché in Washington, D.C. C. S. Forester, the author, interviewed Dahl about his war experiences and urged him to write them up. Dahl's "notes" were printed without change in the *Saturday Evening Post,* and Forester wrote to Dahl, "Did you know that you are a writer?" Dahl claimed to have lost the whole fee he was paid for that story in a poker game with then-senator Harry Truman.

And so began Dahl's writing career. He spent the next twenty years successfully writing darkly comic short stories for adults. The one exception was his first children's story, *Gremlins,* in which Dahl coined the term. Gremlins, he explained, were little creatures who lived in fighter planes and caused them to crash. Eleanor Roosevelt liked the story so much she invited Dahl to dinner at the White House.

In 1953, Dahl married movie actress Patricia Neal. Their married life hit what Dahl called "the Disasters" in the early 1960s after their son was left brain damaged by a traffic accident in New York City and their seven-year-old daughter died from the measles. She was the same age that Dahl's sister had been when she died. Patricia Neal suffered a massive stroke and required constant care. Dahl responded to each of these difficulties by actively participating in finding a cure. He invented a valve to help other children with the same condition as his son. The regimen he used to help his wife recover, the Patricia Neal Therapy Extension Program, is used today by stroke centers worldwide.

In the midst of these crises, Dahl wrote his first wildly popular children's books: *James and the Giant Peach, Charlie and the Chocolate Factory,* and *The Magic Finger.* These books and the fourteen that followed made Dahl the world's most successful living children's writer. The first printing of *Charlie and the Chocolate Factory* in China set a world record at two million books. Successful movie versions of *Willie Wonka and the Chocolate Factory, The Witches,* and *James and the Giant Peach* increased Dahl's popularity. Dahl cowrote the screenplay for the movie *Chitty Chitty Bang Bang* and for the James Bond movie *You Only Live Twice.*

In his later years, Dahl and Patricia Neal were divorced, and Dahl married Neal's friend Felicity Ann Crosland. They lived near **Great Missenden, Buckinghamshire,** where Dahl continued to write in a dusty, spider-filled brick hut in the orchard. Shortly before his death from leukemia in 1990, Dahl donated the rights to one of his books, *The Vicar of Nibbleswicke,* to The Dyslexia Institute in Britain. His books continued to top the bestselling children's book lists. In 1997, Dahl's *Matilda* was voted the "nation's favorite children's book" by British children.

A Brief Biography of Quentin Blake

Quentin Blake's illustrations capture the humor and energy of Roald Dahl's stories in *Charlie and the Chocolate Factory, The BFG, Matilda, Fantastic Mr. Fox,* and *James and the Giant Peach* among others. As Dahl himself said, "There's no one to touch him. He has a magic gift of drawing a character on the page exactly as you imagined it."

Blake was born in Sidcup, Kent, in 1932. After studying English literature at Cambridge, Blake found work as a cartoonist for *Punch* and other magazines while taking art classes at the Chelsea Art School in London. He illustrated his first children's book in 1960, *A Drink of Water*, by his friend John Yeoman. In addition to several books by Dahl, he has illustrated over one hundred children's books, including books by Russell Hoban, Joan Aiken, and Dr. Seuss. He has written and illustrated several children's books as well, including *Clown* and *Zagazoo*.

He served as head of the Illustration Department at the Royal College of Art from 1978 to 1986, when he stepped down to concentrate on illustration work. In 1988, Blake was awarded the OBE for his contributions to children's literature, and in 1999, he was named Britain's first Children's Laureate.

Quentin Blake continues to work and live in London.

Places Connected with Charlie and the Chocolate Factory

CADBURY WORLD, BIRMINGHAM

A massive, innovative candy company that sends its chocolate treats all over the world, Willie Wonka's fictional factory can only be the Cadbury company on the outskirts of Birmingham. To satisfy the demand for tours of their facility, the good people at Cadbury have created Cadbury World. A mecca for Willie Wonka fans and chocolate lovers of all kinds, Cadbury World has something for everyone who has even the vaguest interest in chocolate. For young kids there's Cadbury Land, with a fun live show and playground area and the Cadabra ride, a cute but incomprehensible ride through a world of singing cocoa beans. For older kids there's a walk-through history of chocolate with a live magician doing tricks and two intereactive stage productions. (Interactive means the audience members get roasted and shaken in their seats as if they were a tray of cocoa beans.) A self-paced tour of part of the production and packaging area, which may or may not be in operation on any given day, features lots of tastes and samples from the workers. One visitor reported hearing mysterious singing from the part of the factory not open to the public. Draw your own conclusions.

For adults, the Cadbury Collection presents the history of this socially progressive, family-run company, who built "The Factory in a Garden" and provided housing, health care, and child care for their workers when sweatshop conditions prevailed elsewhere. There's also a fascinating look at the funny, creative TV advertisements that Cadbury has run over the last several decades.

And if you aren't in a complete chocolate stupor after all this, you'll want to see the set of the popular British soap opera *Coronation Street* re-created in detailed miniature and made out of (what else?) chocolate!

The average visit to Cadbury World lasts three hours. It can easily fill the better part of a day, depending on the depths of your feelings about chocolate. When it's all over, join the crowds in the giant gift shop for chocolate bargains to take home to those unable to make the pilgrimage themselves.

Admission to the whole spectacle is £8.50/adults, £6.25/children. Families of four can enter for £25 and families of five for £30. There is also a cafeteria that, surprisingly, serves decent Indian food. Cadbury World is located southwest of Birmingham in the suburb of Bournville. Follow the signs from the M5, junction 4 or the M42, junction 2. When you reach the factory area, follow the purple railings to Cadbury World. Parking is free. It's a signposted walk from the Bournville train station.

The twenty-four-hour information line: (0121) 451-4180. To reserve tickets, which is highly recommended, call: (0121) 451-4159.

Places Connected with Other Roald Dahl Stories

BUCKINGHAM PALACE/HYDE PARK CORNER, LONDON

The BFG by Roald Dahl (1982) tells the story of the Big Friendly Giant, his little friend Sophie, and their cunning plan to save the children of the world from the other nasty giants who like to eat children by the dozens. It sounds gruesome, but it turns out to be one of Dahl's sweeter stories. Part of their plan involves the giant making an impressive leap clear across Hyde Park Corner en route to an unannounced visit with the queen of England in her second-floor bedroom at Buckingham Palace. When you visit the palace, the height of those windows gives you a new respect for the BFG's stature.

Buckingham Palace is located at the end of the Mall between Green Park and St. James Park. The changing of the guard takes place at 11:30 A.M. daily from April 3 through August 3 and on alternate days the rest of the year. The event always draws a large crowd, so get there early if you want a good viewing spot. It's a bit difficult with very young children because of the waiting and the huge crowds.

You can get a real feel for the BFG's trek in August or September when the palace interior and gardens are open to the public. Hours are 9:30–4:30 P.M. Tickets can be purchased at a booth in Green Park. The closest tube stops for Buckingham Palace are Victoria, Hyde Park Corner, or Green Park. Telephone: (0171) 930-4832.

Hyde Park Corner is located at the southeast corner of Hyde Park, adjacent to the gardens of Buckingham Palace. The grand Constitution Arch with its statue of Peace in her chariot stands in the middle of the traffic. Note the special stop-and-go lights for horse traffic. Although there is a pedestrian underpass, it would be much easier to cross sitting in a giant's ear.

BUCKINGHAMSHIRE COUNTY MUSEUM, AYLESBURY, BUCKINGHAMSHIRE

This small county museum opened the delightful Roald Dahl Children's Gallery in 1996, thanks to a gift from Dahl's widow and a pile of money from the National Lottery. The gallery features interactive displays based on Dahl's books, with an emphasis on creativity and imagination. Young visitors can crawl through Fantastic Mr. Fox's tunnel and discover buried treasure, pop inside a TV show like Mike Teavee in the Chocolate Factory, explore the Twits's upside-down room, ride Willie Wonka's glass elevator (only up and down, unfortunately), and have fun interacting with insects inside James's Giant Peach. A giant walk-through book leads into Matilda's library, and there's a wonderful, kid-oriented display about Dahl's life as well.

The museum is located on Church Street in the center of Aylesbury. Follow the signs on foot from the Market Square. There is a small café, a gift shop, and a garden area with benches. The museum is open from 10:00 to 5:00 P.M., Monday to Saturday; 2:00–5:00 P.M., Sundays. NOTE: The Roald Dahl Gallery is only open from 3:00 to 5:00 P.M. on school days. Admission is £3.50/adults, £2.50/children three–sixteen. Admission prices are £1 less on school days during the school year. The Children's Gallery is very popular, and entrance tickets are good only for an hour during busy periods. Telephone: (01296) 331441.

Aylesbury is eighteen miles east on the A41 from junction 9 of the M40 or twenty-five minutes northwest on the A41 from junction 20 of the M25. It's about a forty-minute drive from Oxford taking the A34 north and then the A41 east. Aylesbury is an hour from London (Marleybone station) by train, and the museum is an easy walk from the train station.

And above all, watch with glittering eyes the whole world around you because the greatest secrets are always hidden in the most unlikely places. Those who don't believe in magic will never find it.
  —*Roald Dahl, quoted on the wall of the Roald Dahl Children's Gallery*

Other Places Connected with Roald Dahl's Life

NORWEGIAN CHURCH ARTS CENTRE, CARDIFF, WALES

Cardiff Bay is being redeveloped and restored on every side, with new restaurants, shopping areas, museums, and even a new Welsh Parliament Building springing up. In the midst of it all, on the edge of the water stands a small, unassuming wooden church, reminding the bay of its hardy seafaring past. This used to be a place of worship for Norwegian sailors. For Roald Dahl's Norwegian parents, the chapel was a connection to their homeland, and they had their son baptized here as in infant.

Sixty years later Dahl played a large role in setting up a trust fund to help restore the church for its current use as an arts center. There's a warm and friendly café inside should the Welsh winds be blowing. The center hosts art exhibits, concerts, and plays throughout the year. It's open every day from 10:00 to 4:00 P.M. It's located at the very end of Harbour Drive in Waterfront Park on Cardiff Bay. Telephone: (01222) 454899. Admission is free.

Dahl's widow, Mrs. Felicity Dahl, generously opens the garden of the home she and Dahl shared to the public for several Wednesday afternoons each summer. The money raised from these events goes to charity. Admission is £2/adults; 50 pence/children. Tea and cake are also available. Visitors are able to get a good look at the garden hut in the apple orchard where Dahl wrote every day. Fans of *Danny the Champion of the World* (1975) will see that Dahl got his inspiration for Danny's home from the gypsy caravan that sits in the garden.

Great Missenden is just off the A413, about halfway between junction 1 of the M40 and Aylesbury. The High Street was the setting for the very beginning of *The BFG*, where Sophie sees the Giant blowing dreams through a long trumpet into the children's bedrooms in the night. Follow the High Street south from the town center to Whitefield Lane. Follow Whitefield Lane under the railway overpass and continue on the extremely narrow lane. Gipsy House is on the right. It is a private home and only open to the public on specific afternoons.

For dates and information, contact The National Gardens Scheme. Telephone: (01483) 211535. Web site: www.ngs.org.uk.

RING OF BRIGHT WATER/THE OTTER'S TALE

by Gavin Maxwell

🍀 Mij seemed to regard me closely as I composed myself on my back with a cushion under my head; then, with an air of knowing exactly what to do, he clambered up beside me and worked his body down into the sleeping bag until he lay flat on his back inside it with his head on the cushion beside mine and his forepaws in the air. In this position he heaved an enormous sigh and was instantly asleep.

—*The Otter's Tale,* 1962

$\mathcal{R}_{ING}$ OF BRIGHT WATER, THE STORY OF TWO OTTERS brought from far-off lands to live and frolic in the seas off the west coast of the Scottish Highlands, charmed the world when it was published in 1960. These clever, playful animals are part of the natural world of coastal Scotland, but Gavin Maxwell's pet otters were transplanted thousands of miles from Iraq and Africa. As Maxwell describes it, they fit into the landscape so perfectly that it came to seem incomplete without their lively presence. Maxwell essentially redesigned his house and his life around these wild animals, an eccentric accomplishment that is all the more amazing because he was living in a house with no electricity or running water located over a mile from any road at the time. A children's version of the story, *The Otter's Tale*, followed in 1962 and a movie version in 1969.

Ring of Bright Water is about the fascinating details of life with otters, but it is also about existing with nature in an isolated Scottish cottage and all the wonder and struggle that entails. Camusfearna, the house Maxwell and the otters lived in, burned down in 1968. It is still possible to make that hike through the forest and down the steep burnside to the site of the house and the beautiful, isolated Bay of the Alders, where the otters loved to swim. As Maxwell described it in a sequel: "To the most turbulent of lives come unforeseen periods of calm and tranquility . . . such a season of fair weather, an idyll belonging more properly to childhood or to old age, I described in *Ring of Bright Water*." A visit to the area will heighten your appreciation for Maxwell's determination to live at Camusfearna and for the idyll that was his reward.

A Brief Biography of Gavin Maxwell

Camusfearna, I have called it, the Bay of the Alders, from the trees that grow along the burn side; but the name is of little consequence, for such bays and houses, empty and long disused, are scattered throughout the wild sea lochs of the Western Highlands and the Hebrides, and in the description of one the reader may perhaps find the likeness of others of which he has himself been fond, for these places are symbols. Symbols, for me and for many, of freedom . . .

from the prison of adult life and an escape into the forgotten world of childhood, of the individual or the race.

      —Gavin Maxwell in the Foreword to *Ring of Bright Water*, October 1959

Gavin Maxwell was born in southwest Scotland in 1914. His father was a lieutenant colonel in the army who was killed in World War I. Maxwell's mother was the fifth daughter of the duke of Northumberland. She raised her four children at Elrig, the family home in the countryside near Mochrum, Scotland. The children were educated by governesses and led an isolated life. Maxwell's intense love of nature began on the Scottish moors around Elrig.

After graduating from Hertford College, Oxford University, Maxwell became a freelance journalist, participating in an ornithological expedition to Scandinavia. He served in the Scots Guards during World War II. The horror and destruction he witnessed in the war heightened his longing to live away from "civilized" life. On his return home, he retreated to the Hebridean island of Soay off the coast of western Scotland and started up a shark fishery. The business eventually failed, but he published his first book, *Harpoon Venture,* about the experience in 1952.

After a stint as a professional portrait painter, Maxwell went on to write several books, among them a description of peasant life in Sicily, a history of one of the leading families of Morocco, and an account of his time spent in the marshes of southern Iraq. It was in those marshes that Maxwell acquired a pet that would change the direction of his life and his writing, a marsh otter named Mijbil.

   ... and there squatting on the floor were two Marsh Arabs; beside them lay a sack that squirmed from time to time ... With the opening of that sack began a phase of my life that in the essential sense has not yet ended, and may, for all I know, not end before I do. It is, in effect, a thraldom to otters, an otter fixation, that I have since found to be shared by most other people who have ever owned one.

      —*Ring of Bright Water*

Maxwell brought Mijbil home to London with him in the cabin of a commercial airliner on a trip that lasted well over twenty-four hours.

With typical otter ingenuity, Mijbil was out of his box and wreaking havoc among the other passengers within thirty minutes of takeoff. They both survived the journey (although no one mentions what happened to the other passengers) and ultimately settled at Maxwell's West Highland retreat of **Camusfearna.** Maxwell's description of his year with Mijbil and another otter named Edal at Camusfearna became *Ring of Bright Water,* published in 1960. It was a huge success, selling over a million copies, and continues to be a classic of British nature writing. Maxwell wrote a children's version of the book, titled *The Otters' Tale,* in 1962. A popular family movie of *Ring of Bright Water* came out in 1969, produced by the same people who had made the hit movie about lion cubs in Africa, *Born Free.*

Maxwell continued to live at Camusfearna, writing two sequels to *Ring of Bright Water* titled *The Rocks Remain* and *Raven Seek Thy Brother.* The sequels tell the stories of an otter named Teko, who joined Edal at Camusfearna, and of the death of Edal in a fire that leveled the house in 1968. Edal is buried at Camusfearna under these words. "Edal, the otter of Ring of Bright Water, 1958–1968. Whatever joy she gave to you, give back to nature."

Maxwell went on to purchase the island of **Eilean Ban,** located a bit north of Camusfearna in the waters between Kyle of Lochalsh and the Isle of Skye. His efforts to found a zoo of native highland wildlife there were cut short by his sudden death from lung cancer, in 1969, at the age of fifty-five. The island was sold to settle his affairs after his death. However, in 1998, Maxwell's dream was partially realized when Eilean Ban was placed under the management of a community trust as a nature reserve and museum. Maxwell's ashes are buried on the site of Camusfearna.

Places Connected with Ring of Bright Water in Scotland

CAMUSFEARNA

Ring of Bright Water and *The Otter's Tale* are almost as much about Camusfearna and the beauty of living on the coast in the Scottish Highlands as they are about the otters. After the success of the books, Gavin Maxwell found himself interrupted on a  daily basis by fans interested in seeing his animals and his home. He soon became frustrated with the situation and tried to keep Camusfearna unmarked and off the map. It remains unmarked to this day, but thirty years after Maxwell's death, it is no longer an intrusion to hike down to the Bay of Alders as long as it is done with respect for the natural areas involved. It is a beautiful hike, even on a very rainy day, as we discovered. However, it is a steep, slippery descent down the side of a ravine and involves crossing a rather high creek on a double-rope bridge, so it is not suitable for younger children. As mentioned before, the house itself burned down in 1968, and Edal, the otter, was killed in the fire. Both Edal's and Maxwell's ashes are buried on the site.

🌿 When I missed Mij from his accustomed haunts I would go first to the waterfall, for there he would spend long hours alone. . . . Once, I remember, I went to look for him there and at first could not find him; then my attention was caught by something red in the black water at the edge of the foam, and I saw that Mij was floating on his back, apparently fast asleep, with a bunch of scarlet rowan berries clasped to his chest with one arm.

—*Ring of Bright Water*, chapter 9

GAVIN MAXWELL 🌿 185

Camusfearna is located on the western edge of Scotland across the Sound of Sleat from the Isle of Skye. The closest village is Glenelg. To reach Glenelg from Inverness, take the A82 along the north shore of Loch Ness, ever watchful for a glimpse of Nessie. At Invermoriston, turn onto the A887, which travels through Glenmoriston. The A887 joins the A87 and continues on around Loch Cluanie and through Glen Shiel. At Shiel Bridge, turn onto the narrow road to Glenelg. As you wind up and over the hills, the views are stunning. Glenelg is about nine miles from Shiel Bridge, although the drive takes about thirty-five minutes.

To find the trail to Camusfearna, follow the road south out of Glenelg. About five miles out of town, you will see a gate across a lumber road on the right. If you pass a large pond next to a white house on the Sound of Sleat side, you've gone too far. You will need to park along the roadside. Follow the lumber road on foot for half a mile until a smaller trail splits off to the right. Take the smaller trail. You will soon come to a cairn (stack of stones). Take the small path that leads down the steep hillside next to the cairn. The trail was very muddy in June, so boots are a good idea. The trail proved a bit much for an intrepid four-year-old but suited a seven-year-old friend perfectly. Follow the trail another half mile or so to the bottom of the slope. Here you will see the creek that is fed by the waterfall where Mijbil and Edal loved to play. There is a single rope to help you cross the creek—not for the faint-hearted. There is a lovely white cottage that has been built near the site of Camusfearna and a rock memorial for Maxwell. The spot is as beautiful as Maxwell's descriptions of it.

GLENELG

Glenelg is the closest village to Maxwell's Camusfearna. Sadly it seems to fit the description of the spot where Maxwell's first otter, Mijbil, was killed. The book describes a sharp bend in the road with a small church between the water and the road as the unfortunate spot. Aside from this sad association, it is a very pleasant village and makes an excellent jumping-off point for exploring Maxwell's area as well as the Isle of Skye. The Strupag Café is a pleasant spot for an inexpensive lunch along the water, and Glenelg Candles has an interesting gift shop and delicious homemade food that may be eaten in front of a warm fire on a rainy day.

The car ferry to Kylerhea on Skye runs every fifteen minutes from Glenelg. The ferry operates Monday to Saturday, 9:00 A.M.–8:30 P.M.; Sunday, 10:00 A.M.–6:00 P.M., mid-May through August; Monday to Saturday, 9:00 A.M.–6:00 P.M., the rest of the year. It does not operate from mid-October through mid-March. It will take you directly over to the Kylerhea Otter Haven (see below for description).

EILEAN BAN, OFFSHORE FROM KYLEAKIN, ISLE OF SKYE, SCOTLAND

In 1995, the Skye Bridge was built between Kyle of Lochalsh and the Isle of Skye. The bridge passes right over Eilean Ban (White Island), the tiny lighthouse island where Gavin Maxwell spent the final years of his life. Since 1998, the island has been managed by the Eilean Ban Trust, a group comprised of representatives from local communities and The Born Free Foundation.

The trust has opened the Bright Water Visitor Centre on the pier in Kyleakin. There are interactive exhibits about lighthouses, Maxwell, and local plants and animals. Younger children will enjoy the puzzles and sandpit area. Boat trips run from the centre to Eilean Ban from April through October. Visitors to the island can see a memorial stone for Teko the otter, hike the island's nature trails, and spend time in the "wildlife hide" observing the local animals. The roof of the hide is thatched with heather to help it blend in with the landscape. The trust has painstakingly re-created Gavin Maxwell's cottage, including the forty-foot-long sitting room Maxwell constructed. Here he displayed artifacts from his world travels.

Admission to the Bright Water Visitor Centre is free, but donations go to help maintain the centre and island. Boats run on various schedules, and it's best to call ahead if your schedule is tight. The crossing takes fifteen minutes, and visitors have an hour and a half to enjoy the island. There are a wide range of local crafts for sale at the centre as well. Telephone: (01599) 530040. Web site: www.eileanban.com.

Other Activities for Children Who Love Otters

KYLERHEA OTTER HAVEN, ISLE OF SKYE

If reading the book or watching the video of *Ring of Bright Water* has piqued your interest in seeing otters in the wild, the Kylerhea (pronounced kile-ray) Otter Haven is the place to visit. The Forestry Commission of Great Britain has set up an otter "hide" overlooking a quiet section of the Sound of Sleat that is open to the public. It's a pleasant quarter-mile walk from the parking lot to the hide. There are excellent interpretive displays about how otters live and how to catch sight of one. Bring your binoculars and allow a bit of time to sit quietly and observe. If you don't get to see an otter, chances are you will see some of the other local wildlife, including seals, falcons, eagles, and/or herons. We actually had better luck with seeing otters near the ferry dock, but the visit to the hide made a lovely walk.

Kylerhea is located on the Isle of Skye at the narrowest point in the Sound of Sleat, where the car ferry from Glenelg docks. It can also be reached by taking the A850 off of the A87, Skye's main highway. The turnoff for the Kylerhea Otter Haven is well marked, about a quarter mile from the ferry dock. For more information, contact the Forestry Commission at (01320)-366-322. The Otter Haven is open from 9:00 A.M. until one hour before dusk each day.

The Harry Potter Stories

J. K. Rowling

THE HARRY POTTER STORIES TOOK THE WORLD BY STORM IN the late 1990s, topping both the children and adult bestseller lists internationally and winning scores of literary prizes. Suddenly wizard costumes became a standard feature at every Halloween celebration; and the game of quidditch, with its golden snitch and Nimbus Two Thousand brooms, became part of popular culture. The ongoing stories about Harry Potter's adventures at Hogwarts School of Witchcraft and Wizardry have seized our imaginations with their humor, mystery, and amazing array of magical creatures.

The wizards and witches in the Harry Potter books go to great lengths to keep their world secret from the nonmagic Muggles. They do a good job of it, so the best we can hope for are glimpses of the wizard life that J. K. Rowling has created so vividly. When we catch a glimpse in the echo of footsteps while wandering through a cathedral cloister or in a moment of feeling lost in a puzzling hedge maze, the drama and magic of Harry's ongoing story can come to life for a fan of any age.

A Brief Biography of J. K. Rowling

Hermione was very easy to create because she is based almost entirely on myself at the age of 11. She is really a caricature of me. I wasn't as clever as she is, nor do I think I was quite such a know-it-all, though former classmates might disagree. Like Hermione, I was obsessed with achieving academically, but this masked a huge insecurity.
                    —J. K. Rowling *in Salon* magazine, March 31, 1999

Joanne Kathleen Rowling was born in Chipping Sodbury, South Gloucestershire, about ten miles northeast of Bristol, in 1965. Her father was an aircraft mechanic, her mother a lab technician. A younger sister, Di, came along two years later. The family moved three times to various towns outside of Bristol before Joanne reached the age of nine. They finally settled into a cottage in the little village of Tutshill, near Chepstow, across the river Severn from Bristol. Joanne was a true bookworm, always reading or writing a story. She loved *The Wind in the Wil-*

lows, the books of E. Nesbit, *The Chronicles of Narnia,* and the James Bond books. Her ultimate favorites as she grew up a bit were Jane Austen and Jessica Mitford. She later said that all she ever wanted to be was a writer, but she was too shy to tell anyone.

After graduating from Wyedean Comprehensive School with high honors, Rowling went on to study French and literature at Exeter University in Devon. Her parents encouraged her in this direction, hoping she might become a bilingual secretary. After an exhilarating year studying in Paris, Rowling graduated with honors from Exeter. She moved to London and began a series of secretarial jobs, including a stint at Amnesty International. The positions went against the grain of Rowling's creative and self-admittedly terribly disorganized character. She continued to write short stories and novels, but she didn't feel any of them were good enough to show anyone, much less attempt to publish.

After a trip to Manchester, where she was planning to move, Rowling was traveling back to London when her train experienced a very long delay. Staring out the window at some cows in a field, Rowling suddenly had the idea of a story about a boy who didn't know what he was. By the time the train finally made it to London, the basic outline of the first Harry Potter book was formed in Rowling's mind.

This coincided with a difficult period in Rowling's life. Her mother had been diagnosed with multiple sclerosis. The condition worsened quickly, and her mother died unexpectedly at the age of forty-five. Soon after, Rowling lost her new job in Manchester and her apartment was robbed. The burglars took everything Rowling's mother had left to her. She later said that the only event in her life that really influenced the direction of the Harry Potter stories was the death of her mother.

Through it all Rowling kept working on her new story idea, developing detailed outlines for each year that Harry would spend at Hogwarts, filling notebook after notebook with ideas and details. At age twenty-six, she took a look at her life and decided to go abroad once again. She took a position teaching English as a Second Language in Oporto, Portugal. A chance meeting with a Portuguese television journalist led to a whirlwind romance and marriage. Daughter Jessica came along soon afterward, but the marriage didn't last.

Rowling returned to Britain with five-month-old Jessica and settled in Edinburgh, Scotland, to be close to her sister. The financial pressures were ever present. Rowling told the *School Library Journal,* "I thought it would be selfish for my daughter if I could earn a better living doing something else. If writing wasn't helping to buy new shoes, then it just felt very self-indulgent. What I was praying for was to just make enough for me to continue to write."

Rowling finally shared a bit of her Harry Potter work with her sister, who responded in just the right way—she laughed. Rowling decided to take a real risk and give over a year to finishing the book without trying to work at the same time. She went on public assistance, which meant that paying the rent and buying enough food were often a challenge. She couldn't afford a typewriter, so the entire story was handwritten. As soon as the baby would fall asleep in her stroller, Rowling would dash over to **Nicolson's Café,** settle in with the one cup of coffee she could afford, and write for an hour or two until Jessica woke up.

The book was completed in the spring of 1994. Financially, things improved tremendously with a grant from The Scottish Arts Council. Rowling managed to get a used typewriter and typed out two copies of the book, photocopying being too expensive. She sent the copies off to two literary agents and then found herself a job as a French teacher. One of the agents, Christopher Little, took on the book and, after being turned down by several publishers, eventually sold it in 1997 to Bloomsbury Publishing. *Harry Potter and the Philosopher's Stone* (the British title) was a word-of-mouth success in Britain. It went on to win a long list of literary prizes. The American publisher, Scholastic, paid $105,000 for publication rights in the United States, the highest advance ever paid to a first-time British author. It came out as *Harry Potter and the Sorcerer's Stone* in the States and soon topped the bestseller list.

The second book, *Harry Potter and the Chamber of Secrets* (1998), was an even bigger success on both sides of the Atlantic, and the books began to cross over into the adult market. As fans around the world anxiously awaited book three, *Harry Potter and the Prisoner of Azkaban* (1999), and book four, *Harry Potter and the Goblet of Fire* (2000), it became clear that the Harry Potter books were an unprecedented publishing phenomenon. The first printing in the United States for book four was a record-breaking 3.8 million copies. A Warner Brothers film of the first book came out in 2001 to great fanfare. More than 100 million Harry Potter books have been sold worldwide.

Rowling has moved from obscurity to fame and has become the third wealthiest woman in Britain. She made a special visit to her daughter's school in Edinburgh to explain to the kids that daughter Jessica doesn't know anything about future Harry Potter plots so could they please stop asking her about them. When asked about her future plans in *Salon* magazine, Rowling responded, "Well, I'll be writing, and that's about all I know. I've been doing it all my life, and it is necessary to me—I don't feel quite normal if I haven't written for a while. I doubt I will ever again write anything as popular as the 'Harry' books, but I can live with that thought quite easily. By the time I stop writing about Harry, I will have lived with him for thirteen years, and I know it's going to feel like a bereavement. So I'll probably take some time off to grieve, and then on with the next book." In 2001, Rowling began a new chapter in her life by marrying Neil Murray, an anesthetist, in a quiet ceremony at her home in Scotland.

Places Connected with the Harry Potter Stories

KINGS CROSS STATION, LONDON

The Wizard community certainly picked the least impressive possible location for students to board the Hogwarts Express. Platform 9¾ is invisible to us Muggles, but platforms 9 and 10 couldn't be more mundane! They are located in a nondescript, modern annex to Kings Cross station, used primarily by commuter trains. When Harry can't find platform 9¾ on his first trip to school, Ron's mother advises him to "walk straight at the barrier between platforms nine and ten. . . . Best do it at a run if you're nervous." Railway personnel discourage the curious visitor from giving this a try. The older and more atmospheric part of the station, built in 1851, was used for the movie version.

Kings Cross station and St. Pancras station are located right next to each other on the Euston Road just a block from the British Library. Follow the signs back and to the left of the main entrance to Kings Cross for platforms 9 and 10. The closest tube stop is Kings Cross/St. Pancras.

AUSTRALIA HOUSE, THE STRAND, LONDON

Australia House, the home of the Australian Embassy in London, was transformed into stodgy Gringotts Bank, the place where all the best wizard families keep their fortunes, for the film of *Harry Potter and the Sorcerer's Stone.* The building itself is located on The Strand right next to the BBC's Bush House, home to the BBC's World Service, near The Strand's intersection with Aldwych. A public tour is given every Thursday at 1:15, advanced booking required. Tours can be booked over the Internet at www.australia.org.uk. Australia House is a short, although congested and fumy walk from the Covent Garden area.

BODLEIAN LIBRARY, OXFORD

In 2002, the Bodleian Library will celebrate its four hundredth anniversary as one of the great scholarly libraries in the world. But its claim to fame in 2001 was its appearance in the movie version of *Harry Potter and the Sorcerer's Stone.* Both the Divinity School and Duke Humfrey's Library were used for some interior scenes at Hogwarts, including, appropriately enough, the Hogwarts library.

The clerics and scholars who sponsored the building of the Divinity School between 1427 and 1488 would probably be aghast at its use in depicting a school for wizards, but the intricate carving on the ceilings and walls of the main hall show that the artisans of the time had imaginations as lively as J. K. Rowling's. The owl on the right side near the windows seems particularly appropriate.

The only way to get a good look at the Divinity School is to take a guided tour that begins in the main hall just beyond the gift shop. The tour includes the Convocation House and the impressive Duke Humfrey's Library. The Bodleian Library quadrangle is located off of Broad Street between the Sheldonian Theatre and the Radcliffe Camera. Telephone: (01865) 277188. Web site: www.bodley.ox.ac.uk.

The Hogwarts Express, Severn Valley Railway, between Bridgnorth, Shropshire, and Kidderminster, Worcestershire

In the summer of 2000, J. K. Rowling rode the Hogwarts Express all around Britain on a book-signing tour. Thousands of children and adults flocked to small local train stations to meet the author and talk about Harry Potter's world. The Hogwarts Express locomotive used for that tour now resides at the Severn Valley Railway in Shropshire. The public can ride on a train pulled by the bright red engine along the sixteen-mile route between Bridgnorth and Kidderminster. The line follows the river Severn through lovely, unspoiled countryside. Passengers can get on and off the train at several country stations and walk along the river.

The Severn Valley Railway can be boarded at either Bridgnorth or Kidderminster. Day Rover tickets cost £10/adults, £5/children five–fifteen years old. Be aware that the Hogwarts Express doesn't pull trains every day. It's best to call ahead to be sure when it is running. However, the railway runs trains every day between Easter and the end of September and on weekends and holidays the rest of the year. Telephone: (01299) 403-816. Web site: www.svr.co.uk.

To experience the general atmosphere of Hogwarts School of Witchcraft and Wizardry, take a stroll around the cloisters of Gloucester Cathedral, where several of the movie's scenes were filmed. Construction of this magnificent Gothic cathedral began in 1089, and its massive pillars have stood for over nine hundred years. It houses an effigy of William the Conqueror's son and the grave of Edward II among many other treasures. The cloisters, formerly the monks' living quarters, contain dramatic fan vaulting from the fourteenth century. The peaceful inner courtyard provides a good picnic spot with an impressive view of the cathedral's tower. A "lavatorium" attached to the cloisters contains a trough where the monks bathed and niches where they hung their towels.

A passageway from the cloisters leads to a pleasant restaurant and modern lavatoria. The cathedral is open daily from 8:00 A.M. to 6:00 P.M. Gloucester Cathedral tower rises up from the town center. It's about a fifteen-minute drive from the M6 if you're coming by car. Park in one of the public car parks and walk through the pedestrian-only area to the cathedral. It's about a ten-minute walk through the town center from the Gloucester train station. Telephone: (01452) 528095. Web site: www.gloucestercathedral.uk.com.

See the Beatrix Potter chapter, page 101, for information about the nearby *Tailor of Gloucester* house.

ALNWICK CASTLE, ALNWICK, NORTHUMBERLAND

Alnwick Castle (pronounced "annick") stands impressive and foreboding overlooking the river Aln. It has been the home of the Percy family since the twelfth century and retains its massive medieval exterior. Although Hogwarts School of Witchcraft and Wizardry seems from its description in the books to be located amid the mountains and lochs of Scotland, Alnwick Castle, just fifty miles south of the Scottish border, "played" the outside of the school in the first Harry Potter movie. The extensive grounds around the castle provided the ideal fields for the gripping quidditch matches. The inside of the castle is worth a look, too, with a real dungeon to tour and a valuable collection of Italian paintings and antiques.

Alnwick Castle and the charming village of Alnwick are located forty miles north of Newcastle-upon-Tyne just off the A1 motorway. Follow the B6341 into town, then follow the signs. The castle is open from April 1 through the end of October, daily from 11:00 to 5:00 P.M. Admission is £6.75/adults, £3.50/children five–sixteen years old. A family ticket costs £15.50. Telephone: (01665) 510777. Web site: www.alnwickcastle.com.

Other Places Connected with J. K. Rowling's Life

NICOLSON'S CAFÉ, 6A NICOLSON STREET, EDINBURGH, SCOTLAND

Just across from the Edinburgh Festival Theatre in the ancient part of Edinburgh sits a bright, pleasant café located over some shops. Just a few years ago you might have spotted a redhead with a sleeping baby sitting in a back corner of the café sipping a cup of coffee as she wrote in her notebook. It would've been hard to believe at the time that this woman was creating a book that would eventually become one of the most popular children's books of all time, but that's just what J. K. Rowling was doing.

Nicolson's Café is open from 9:00 A.M. until midnight and serves everything from breakfast to a late dinner. Prices are reasonable, and there's no one to hurry you along if you feel like spending some time drinking a cuppa and contemplating your next bestseller. Telephone: (0131) 557-4567.

Other Activities for Children Who Love the Harry Potter Stories

HEDGE MAZES

In *Harry Potter and the Goblet of Fire,* Harry is one of two boys representing Hogwarts in the Triwizard Cup Competition, a sort of Olympic Games between the great wizarding schools. There is a dangerous edge to the tasks involved in the competition, the final one being a nighttime race through a hedge maze filled with spells and creepy creatures. The mazes described below are much less menacing, but they provide an excellent challenge for older children and plenty of opportunities to run around and make lots of noise.

Leeds Castle, Maidstone, Kent: Leeds Castle, which calls itself "the Loveliest Castle in the World," has something for every member of the family: an historic castle surrounded by beautiful grounds, an aviary, shops and restaurants, even a dog-collar museum (see *The 101 Dalmatians* chapter, page 209). It also offers a challenging hedge maze that, like the maze in *Harry Potter and the Goblet of Fire,* provides a reward for those who find their way through to the middle. I won't spoil the surprise, but luckily it isn't a visit with Lord Voldemort.

If one of your loved ones attempts the maze and doesn't return, there is a map of the maze in the lobby of the nearby tearoom to assist a search party. There is also potential for some good spectator sport from the hillside behind the maze, where onlookers can watch the befuddled "maze-goers" try to find their way.

Leeds Castle lies just off the main highway (the M20) between London and Dover, about a forty-minute trip from London. There is ample free parking. Admission is £10/adults, £6.50/children age four–fifteen; £29/family ticket. Telephone: 0870-600-8880. Web site: www .leeds castle.co.uk.

Hampton Court Palace, Surrey: For five hundred years, since Henry VIII's time, Hampton Court Palace has been considered a showplace of English gardening. Its famous maze was planted in 1702 in the Northern Gardens. The paths in the maze cover half a mile, so give yourself time to wander through.

There's an endless amount to see both inside the palace and out, including a tennis court that has been in use since the 1620s. The palace makes a great day trip from London, either by train or boat. Trains leave frequently from Waterloo station and take thirty minutes. Boats leave from Westminster Pier, near Big Ben, and cost £14/adult, £7/child for a round trip. The boat trip is an excellent way to get a feel for the Thames and arrive, as royalty often did, at Hampton Court Landing. To travel by the tube, take the District Line to Richmond and then catch the R68 bus from the tube station directly to the palace.

Admission to Hampton Court Palace is £10.80/adult, £7.20/child, children under five free. A family ticket costs £32.20. The palace is open from 9:30 to 6:00 P.M. from March 25 through October 27. The rest of the year it closes at 4:30 P.M. The opening time is pushed back to 10:15 on Mondays. Telephone: (0208) 781-9500. Web site: www .hrp.org.uk.

BRITISH BOARDING (OR "PUBLIC") SCHOOLS

For all its dazzle and magic, Hogwarts is in many ways a basic British boarding school. For a taste of what real boarding school life is like, try a tour of one of these prestigious Muggle schools:

Rugby School, Rugby, Warwickshire: Rugby School, of course, has its own claim to fame as the place where the sport of rugby originated back in 1823, when a student had the audacity to pick up the ball and run with it. Lewis Carroll and Arthur Ransome (see appropriate chapters, page 32 and page 261 for more information) both attended Rugby and lived in the same rooms, although fifty years apart.

Public tours of Rugby School take place daily at 2:30 P.M., leaving from the Rugby School Museum. The museum is located at 10 Little Church Street in the town of Rugby, immediately next to the school campus. Fee parking is available across the lane. The museum is open from 10:30 to 12:30 P.M. and from 1:30 to 4:30 P.M., Monday to Saturday; 1:30–4:30 P.M. only on Sundays. Telephone: (01788) 556109. Web site: www.rugbyschool.net.

Eton College, Eton, Berkshire: Eton has been educating the children of Britain's ruling class since 1440, including eighteen prime ministers and the sons of the current prince of Wales, Prince William and Prince Harry. It is located just west of London across the Thames from Windsor Castle. Several of the original buildings and classrooms are still in use.

The public can get of taste of Eton's atmosphere by taking a tour of the campus. Tours are offered at 2:15 and 3:15 daily and last about an hour. Tickets cost £4. Groups of eight or more are required to book in advance. Telephone: (01753) 671177.

If you come by car, you must park in Windsor and walk across the Thames pedestrian bridge into Eton, then continue up the High Street. Eton is a mile from the M4, junction 5. Follow the signs through Slough to Eton.

Trains leave London's Waterloo station every thirty minutes on weekdays and Saturdays, every hour on Sundays. The trip takes fifty minutes. The walk from the train station across the Thames to Eton takes about twenty minutes.

TWO PLACES FOR SEEING OWLS OF EVERY SORT, FROM HEDWIG TO PIGWIDGEON

The Owl Centre, Muncaster Castle, Cumbria: Run by the World Owl Trust, the Owl Centre is on the wooded grounds of Muncaster Castle in the Lake District. Over one hundred owls from fifty different species are on display, including the huge eagle owl and the tiny pygmy owl. A "Meet the Birds" presentation is held each day at 2:30 on the castle lawn. During breeding season, you can watch owls' nests up close through a closed-circuit TV system. The wild herons are fed each day at 4:30.

There is an adventure playground and a café on the grounds. Admission is £5/adult and £3/child, £15 for a family ticket. Children under five are free. For £1.50 extra you can also tour the castle. Telephone: (01229) 717393. Web site: www.owls.org.

National Birds of Prey Centre, Newent, Gloucestershire: One of the oldest and largest collections of birds of prey in the world, the centre features three hundred birds from over eighty species of owls, hawks, eagles, and falcons. Flying demonstrations are given three times each day.

The National Birds of Prey Centre is twenty-five minutes west of Gloucester, just outside Newent. Take the A40 toward Ross-on-Wye, turn right onto the B4215, and follow the signs. The centre is open from 10:30 A.M. to 5:30 P.M. daily from February 1 through November 30. There is a picnic area, café, and children's playground. Admission is £5.75/adults, £3.50/children four–fifteen. A family ticket is £16.50. Telephone: (0870) 990-1992. Web site: www.nbpc.co.uk.

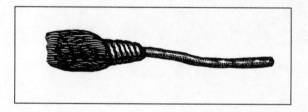

THE 101 DALMATIANS
by Dodie Smith

🍀 From the first, it was quite clear the dogs knew just where they wanted to go. Very firmly, they led the way right across the park, across the road, and to the open space which is called Primrose Hill. . . . [The dogs] stood side by side and they barked. They barked to the north, they barked to the south, they barked to the east and west.

"Anyone would think they were signaling," said Mr. Dearly. But he did not really mean it. And they *were* signaling. . . . Within a few minutes, the news of the stolen puppies was travelling across England, and every dog who heard at once turned detective.

The 101 Dalmatians, 1956

CRUELLA DE VIL—IF SHE DOESN'T SCARE YOU, NO EVIL THING will! Dodie Smith's *The 101 Dalmatians* and the 1961 animated Disney movie based on the book introduced one of the great villains in children's literature: the zebra-coifed Cruella De Vil. She's an outrageous fiend who wants to make a coat out of puppy skins. Two brave dalmatians, Pongo and Missis (called Perdita in the movie), heroically rescue their puppies and eighty-four others with the help of the entire dog community, thwarting Cruella's plan. The story has remained popular for decades, with a live-action movie version that came out in 1996 and a sequel, *102 Dalmatians,* in 2000.

The story is set in London, where Pongo and Missis live with their two "pets," owners Roger and Anita. Seeking out the settings for *The 101 Dalmatians* provides the perfect excuse to spend time in some of London's loveliest parks. As a tourist you can pass your entire stay in museums, theaters, and restaurants and go home wondering if you've actually seen anything of the real life of London. Get out into a park and enjoy mingling with the British and their dogs! From the more formal St. James Park, set amid some of Britain's grandest buildings, to the open fields of Primrose Hill, a visit to Pongo's haunts will be a breath of fresh air.

A Brief Biography of Dodie Smith

> I consider myself a lightweight author, but God knows I approach my work with as much seriousness as if it were Holy Writ.
> —Dodie Smith, *Something About the Author*

Dorothy Gladys (Dodie) Smith was born in Whitefield, Lancashire, in 1896. Her father died when she was only eighteen months old. Dodie and her mother moved in with Dodie's grandparents, three uncles, and two aunts, who lived in an old house in a suburb of Manchester. It was a very artistic household where, according to Dodie, "everyone sang and played some musical instrument . . . and one uncle, an admirable amateur actor, was often to be heard rehearsing, preferably with me on hand to give him his cues." Bitten at this tender age by the theater bug, Smith had written a forty-page play by the time she was nine.

After attending school in Manchester and St. Paul's Girls' School in London, Smith was admitted to the Royal Academy of Dramatic Arts at the age of eighteen. She pursued an acting career after finishing her studies and traveled with a theater company entertaining the soldiers during World War I. In 1923, she gave up on acting and for eight years worked as a buyer for a furniture store. During these years she wrote plays and had her first professional production in 1931 with *Autumn Crocus.* She went on to write several more light domestic comedies under the pseudonym C. L. Anthony. *Call It a Day,* which opened in London in 1935 and New York in 1936, was the most successful.

She purchased a cottage near Finchingfield, Essex, called "The Barretts," and settled in to write a more complex play. She dropped her pseudonym and began writing as Dodie Smith. The play was called *Dear Octopus* for a toast given by one of the characters: "To the family— that dear octopus from whose tentacles we never quite escape, nor, in our inmost hearts, ever quite wish to." Smith traveled to New York in 1938 to help cast the production of *Dear Octopus* and ended up staying in the United States for the next fourteen years. She married her business manager, Alec Beesley, in 1939. The couple moved to California, where Smith worked for Paramount Pictures as a screenwriter. Two of her scripts became films, *The Uninvited* (1944) and *Darling, How Could You!* (1951). The latter is an adaptation of a James Barrie work (see *Peter Pan* chapter, page 3). They also spent a year in Doylestown, Pennsylvania, where Smith wrote her first and most successful novel for adults, *I Capture the Castle.* During her time in the United States, Smith and her husband drove across the country six times accompanied by their beloved pet dalmatians.

Smith returned to England and wrote five more novels. In 1956, inspired by her pets, she wrote her first children's book, *The 101 Dalmatians.* The book was a success and became even more popular when Walt Disney Studios made it into an animated film in 1961. The book's less-successful sequel, *The Starlight Barking,* came out in 1967. Smith wrote her third and last children's book, *The Midnight Kittens,* in 1978. Smith's final output includes her four-volume autobiography, *Look Back with Love* (1974), *Look Back with Mixed Feelings* (1978), *Look Back with Astonishment* (1979), and *Look Back with Gratitude* (1985). She died in 1990.

Places Connected with
The 101 Dalmatians

PRIMROSE HILL, LONDON

Primrose Hill is a small, windswept park attached to Regent's Park directly across Prince Albert Road and the Regent's Canal from the London Zoo. It is a modest hill, but it provides an excellent view of the city in several directions. This is also the spot Pongo and Missis chose for the Twilight Barking, so that they could contact the Great Dane at Hampstead and all the other dogs in London. It's a great place for kite flying (see the *Mary Poppins* chapter, page 138). There is a children's playground with restrooms along Prince Albert Road at the bottom of the hill.

The closest tube stops are Camden Town or St. John's Wood, but neither one is very close. It can also be reached by the C2 or the 274 bus. A waterbus runs between Camden Lock or Little Venice and the London Zoo on the Regent's Canal. Camden Lock is a five-block walk up the Camden High Street from the tube stop. The waterbus service is hourly from April through September, daily during October, and on weekends only from November through March.

REGENT'S PARK AREA, LONDON

The Dearlys lived in "a small house on the Outer Circle of Regent's Park—just the right house for a man with a wife and dogs." When Pongo and Missis (Perdita in the movie) set out to find their puppies, they ran across the wintry Regent's Park, passing the zoo, and traveling on into Camden Town. It seems that Roger and Anita must have lived somewhere along the western edge of the park, perhaps in one of the impressive terraces designed by John Nash in the early 1800s. It's a lovely walk to retrace Pongo and Perdita's route, starting at the Clarence Gate off of Cornwall Terrace, heading up past the zoo, and stopping at Primrose Hill along the way for a good bark. It would be too long a walk for young children, however. (E. H. Shepard, who illustrated the Christopher Robin/Winnie the Pooh books, really did live in this area, at 10 Kent Terrace. His daughter Mary illustrated the *Mary Poppins* books. See the A. A. Milne and P. L. Travers chapters for more information.)

You can enter the park near the Baker Street, Regent's Park, or Great Portland Street tube stations. Baker Street is closest to the west side terraces (and an added bonus if you are a Sherlock Holmes enthusiast).

ST. JAMES PARK, LONDON

One of the grand strolls in London is from Buckingham Palace through St. James Park toward either Westminster Abbey or Trafalgar Square and Whitehall Street. St. James Park is full of blossoming trees and exotic waterfowl. A small bridge crosses the lake in the center of the park, providing a wonderful photo spot with Buckingham Palace in the background. The people who made the live-action version of *The 101 Dalmatians* liked the scenery, too, and made the south side of the bridge the setting for Roger and Pongo to meet Anita and Perdita. Take one look at the water-fowled water, and you'll realize the actors really earned their salaries when they fell into the drink. It's a great picnic spot, but you'll need to bring your own supplies as there is no food for sale in the park.

The closest tube stop is St. James Park. If you want to begin at Buckingham Palace, the closest tube stop is Victoria, Hyde Park Corner, or Green Park. See the *Charlie and the Chocolate Factory* chapter, page 177 for more information about Buckingham Palace.

Other Activities for Children Who Love
The 101 Dalmatians

THE CRUFTS DOG SHOW, BIRMINGHAM

If you are a dog lover and you happen to be in Britain in March, make plans to be in Birmingham at the granddaddy of all dog shows, Crufts. It's an opportunity to see more than 101 dalmatians, with 230 of the breed participating in 2001. This venerable dog show has been an annual event since an entrepreneur named Crufts began organizing it for profit in 1891. It was taken over by The Kennel Club in 1948, and proceeds are now given to charity. Over 21,000 dogs take part in the four-day show each year. It is held in The National Exhibition Center (NEC) on the southeast side of Birmingham. The NEC is adjacent to both the train station and the airport. By car, it can be reached from the M6 or the M42. There is ample parking (pay). In 2001, a four-day pass to Crufts cost £30. Single-day passes were £8–£9.50/adults; £5–£6.50/children. Telephone for The Kennel Club in London: 0870-606-6750.

Crufts usually is scheduled for early March. If your itinerary doesn't include Birmingham, The Kennel Club also offers the smaller Discover Dogs show in London for two days in early November of each year. Check the extremely informative web site for exact dates: www.crufts.org.uk.

LEEDS CASTLE, MAIDSTONE, KENT

Some visit Leeds Castle out of historical interest; others want to enjoy the elaborate gardens or take on the challenge of the maze. But for the dog-oriented, the attraction has to be what the brochure calls "one of the world's few museums dedicated entirely to the collection of antique dog collars." The museum features an amazing array of collars: spiky ones that must have been worn by real brutes, delicate golden ones for the more courtly dog, and huge, iron ones that must have been put on for life. It's housed in the castle's gatehouse by the gift shop and included in admission to the castle grounds.

For more information about Leeds Castle, see the *Harry Potter* chapter, page 198.

Leeds Castle lies just off the main highway (the M20) between London and Dover. There is ample, free parking. Admission is £10/adults, £6.50/children age four–fifteen, £29/family ticket. Telephone: 0870-600-8880. Web site: www.leeds-castle.com.

BRITISH FAVORITES FOR AMERICANS TO ENJOY

III

GREYFRIARS BOBBY

by Eleanor Atkinson

♣ When the time-gun boomed from Edinburgh Castle, Bobby gave a startled yelp. He was only a little country dog—the very youngest and smallest and shaggiest of Skye terriers—bred on a heathery slope of the Pentland hills. . . . That morning he had come to the weekly market with Auld Jock, a farm labourer, and the Grassmarket of the Scottish capital lay in the narrow valley at the southern base of Castle Crag. . . . In any part of the city the report of the one-o'clock gun was sufficiently alarming, but in the Grassmarket it was an earth-rending explosion directly overhead. . . . Bobby had heard it many times, and he never failed to yelp a sharp protest at the outrage to his ears. . . .

—*Greyfriars Bobby*, 1912

$\mathcal{I}$N THE HEART OF EDINBURGH'S OLD TOWN, PERCHED ON A pedestal, is a statue of a small Scottish terrier named Bobby. Bobby was a real dog who lived in the mid-1800s in what was then the squalid tenement district of Edinburgh. His master was either a constable or a penniless farm laborer (versions of the story vary) who died in 1858. Bobby was so devoted to his master that he stayed by his grave in Greyfriars Kirk churchyard for fourteen years until his own death in 1872. During those fourteen years, he became a much-loved local celebrity of sorts. He was given a special collar and special permission to stay in the graveyard, and upon his death, a statue was erected in his honor next to the graveyard.

Bobby's story has been retold in many print and film versions for all age groups. Eleanor Atkinson's book achieved the greatest popularity of all of them, even though Atkinson was an American and had never even visited Edinburgh! Atkinson's book is written at a teenage or adult level, but there are also excellent versions of the story for younger readers.

Edinburgh is as charming and distinctive a city as you'll find anywhere, with Scottish history at every turn. As you stroll from the heights of Edinburgh Castle down to the stunning new Museum of Scotland, a quick stop to see Bobby's statue and Auld Jock's grave brings the sweep of history down to the more comprehensible size of a little dog's love for his master.

A Brief Biography of Eleanor Atkinson

I think it was fortunate that I did not know that young people were going to care for my stories. I might have made the mistake of writing down to them. An author never knows his luck!
—Eleanor Atkinson in *Twentieth Century Authors,* 1942

Eleanor Stackhouse was born in 1863 in Rensselaer, Indiana. After passing a happy childhood in northwestern Indiana, she attended and graduated from Indianapolis Normal Training School, a teaching college.

She struggled to become a writer while working as a teacher in Indianapolis and Chicago. After four years, she was able to break into journalism as a special writer for the *Chicago Tribune* under the pen name of Nora Marks.

In 1891, she married a news editor named Francis Blake Atkinson. They decided to combine their talents and began publishing a weekly newspaper for high school students called *The Little Chronicle.* Unable to find suitable stories for their paper, Eleanor began writing them herself and was as surprised as anyone when they were published as books. The Atkinsons eventually sold their paper and went to work for the Compton Encyclopedia company. Eleanor worked as a contract writer and editor while she stayed home to care for their two daughters.

Eleanor's first books were about Abraham Lincoln and Chicago, and there is no explanation for why she decided to write about Scotland, a place she never visited, for her fourth book. *Greyfriars Bobby* came out in 1912 and was an immediate success. It has remained in print ever since. A movie version of the book was made in 1961. The only other book of note by the author was *Johnny Appleseed,* published in 1915.

The author's two daughters both grew up to become writers. The Atkinsons retired to Nyack, New York, and Eleanor Atkinson died in 1942 at the age of seventy-nine.

Places Connected with the Story of Greyfriars Bobby in Edinburgh, Scotland

GREYFRIARS BOBBY'S STATUE, CORNER OF CANDLEMAKER ROW AND GEORGE IV BRIDGE

This winsome little statue was sculpted using the real Bobby as a model shortly before his death and erected in 1872. The inscription on the base describes it as a "tribute to the affectionate fidelity" of the little dog.

George IV Bridge is the first major right turn as you head down the Royal Mile from the Castle toward the Palace of Holyroodhouse. Follow

George IV Bridge for about a quarter mile. Bobby's statue and the other places described below will be on the right, where Candlemaker Row joins the main street at a sharp angle. If you reach the new Museum of Scotland, you have gone a bit too far.

Greyfriars Bobby's Bar, 34 Candlemaker Row

Just across Candlemaker Row from Bobby's statue is Greyfriars Bobby's Bar. In the nineteenth century, this was the "dining-room" where Auld Jock and Bobby were treated with great kindness in Atkinson's story. Today it is a comfortable pub that caters mainly to tourists.

Greyfriars Kirkyard

The entrance to the churchyard is just beyond Greyfriars Bobby's Bar. There are signs pointing the way to Auld Jock's (also known as John Gray's) grave. Bobby stayed beside this grave faithfully for fourteen years, determined not to leave his master. As the innkeeper says in Atkinson's version of the story, "Ay, terriers are sonsie, leal dogs," which translates to "splendid, loyal dogs" for the non-Scottish among us.

Bobby's Bothy

Bobby's Bothy is a small gift shop just by the entrance to the church-yard. If you are looking for Bobby-related items, including easier versions of the story to read to younger children, this is the place to visit.

Huntly House Museum, 142 Canongate, Royal Mile

This local history museum occupies an aristocrat's mansion built in 1570. On display is the special collar that Greyfriars Bobby wore in the final years of his life and his wee feeding bowl. The museum is open Monday to Saturday, 10:00–5:00 P.M. Admission is free. It's located on the end of the Royal Mile nearest to Holyroodhouse called the Canongate, across from the Canongate Tollbooth. Telephone: (0131) 529-4143.

If dog collars happen to be of general interest to you, don't miss the Dog-Collar Museum at Leeds Castle. See *The 101 Dalmatians* chapter, page 209, for details.

Other Activities for Children Who Love Greyfriars Bobby or Scottish Terriers

CRUFTS DOG SHOW, BIRMINGHAM

If you are a dog lover and you happen to be in Britain in March, make plans to be in Birmingham at the granddaddy of all dog shows, Crufts. It's an opportunity to see more than twenty-six different types of terriers, with seventy-six individual Scottish terriers participating in 2001. The show has been an annual event since an enterprising man named Crufts began organizing it for profit in 1891. It was taken over by The Kennel Club in 1948, and proceeds are now given to charity. Over-twenty-one thousand dogs take part in the four-day show each year. It is held in The National Exhibition Centre (NEC) on the southeast side of Birmingham. The NEC is adjacent to both the train station and the airport. By car, it can be reached from the M6 or the M42. There is ample parking (pay). In 2001, a four-day pass to Crufts cost £30. Single-day passes were £8–£9.50/adults, £5–£6.50/children. Telephone for The Kennel Club in London: 0870-606-6750.

Crufts usually is scheduled for early March. If your itinerary doesn't include Birmingham, The Kennel Club also offers the smaller Discover Dogs show in London for two days in early November of each year. Check the extremely informative web site for exact dates. Web site: www.crufts.org.uk.

Sheep Dog Demonstration, Kincraig, Scotland

They may not be terriers, but the dogs at Neil Ross's farm in the Grampian Mountains of Scotland display the intelligence and intensity that Bobby must have had. A single shepherd communicates with up to ten dogs working in tandem by using a distinct set of whistles and gestures for each dog. There are often puppies-in-training working as well. The dogs herd the sheep and a noisy bunch of ducks with impressive efficiency and enthusiasm. Visitors can also have a go at sheepshearing and bottle-feeding lambs.

The demonstrations are held every day except Saturday at 12:00 and 4:00 P.M. Admission is £4/adults, £2/children. Telephone: (01540) 651310.

From the A9, take the B9152 to Kincraig. Follow the signs to the Highland Wildlife Park. Do not go onto the new A9 at this point. One mile past the Highland Wildlife Park, look for signs saying WORKING SHEEPDOGS. Follow the dirt road, crossing the A9, through the open farm gate, and on up to the farm. It's a confusing place to find but well worth the effort, especially if your children are also enchanted by the story of *Babe*, the sheep-herding pig! You may want to call for local directions once you are in the area.

THE CHILDREN OF GREEN KNOWE STORIES
by Lucy Boston

♣ The room seemed to be the ground floor of a castle, much like the ruined castles that he had explored on school picnics, only this was not a ruin. It looked as if it never possibly could be. Its thick stone walls were strong, warm and lively. It was furnished with comfortable polished old-fashioned things as though living in castles was quite ordinary. Toseland stood just inside the door and felt it must be a dream.

—*The Children of Green Knowe*, 1954

$\mathcal{L}$UCY BOSTON WROTE A SERIES OF SIX BOOKS ABOUT AN AMAZ-ing house called Green Knowe. Built almost nine hundred years ago, the house is not just the setting for the books, it is almost another character in them. Its four-foot-thick walls, ancient fireplaces, old moat, and magical topiary gardens are a living presence in the stories. The patchwork quilts, toys, furnishings, and paintings it contains provide a connection between the generations of children that live in the house. From the boy who lives in Norman times and sees the house being built to the one who visits his great-grandmother in the post–World War II years, the children who live at Green Knowe experience the continuity of the house's history by crossing over into each other's lives, if only fleetingly.

Perhaps the most wonderful thing of all about Green Knowe is that it really exists. Lucy Boston bought an old Norman manor house near Cambridge called Hemingford Grey in 1939. She lovingly restored it and, at the age of sixty, began to write books for children set at Hemingford Grey (Green Knowe) that were true to the actual history and layout of the house and garden. The books are considered classics in Britain but are not well-known in the United States. They are wonderful stories and well worth reading on their own account, but they will be especially intriguing to older children and adults who are planning a visit to the Cambridge area. Hemingford Grey, the oldest continuously inhabited house in England, has witnessed a lot in its nine-hundred-year life. A tour of the house and garden guided by its current occupant, Lucy Boston's daughter-in-law, Diana, brings English history alive in a much more personal way than visits to famous castles and great estates ever can. It's one of those rare places that appeals to all ages: history and beauty for the adults, lots of intriguing items from the stories for older children to puzzle out and recognize, and a spacious garden and river path with ducks for the younger kids to explore.

A Brief Biography of Lucy Boston

I believe that one place closely explored will yield more than continents passed through. Now I have found the place I need . . . this is where I stay, getting deeper in it every moment and always surprised. This is the house that all the books describe. If I were a historian, a lifetime could be spent researching into it. But I just sit and talk to it. I live in it alone and find it good company.

—*Lucy Boston*

Lucy Boston was born in 1892 in Southport, Lancashire. Her family was wealthy but extremely strict, or as she put it, "rigidly, rabidly puritanical." Lucy spent the rest of her life rebelling against her upbringing and credited that rebellion with her love of parties and dancing. She began studying classics at Oxford in 1914, but her studies were interrupted to train as a nurse for the war effort. She served in a French military hospital near Le Havre and married her cousin, Harold Boston, an army officer, in 1917. They lived in Europe and had one son, Peter. The marriage was dissolved in 1935, and Lucy returned to England and purchased **Hemingford Grey** in 1939. She put her heart and soul into restoring the house and its surrounding gardens. She and her son discovered a pile of rocks in a corner of the garden and thought they might be of use in restoring the old Norman fireplace. When they tried them out, they fit precisely into the gaps in the wall, forming a beautiful arch. They realized that they had found the remains of the old fireplace that had been sitting in a heap untouched for five hundred years!

Paranoia ran high during those early years of World War II, and Lucy was regarded with suspicion by her new neighbors. The fact that she wore clothing she had acquired when she lived in Austria didn't help matters, and when she left her lights on twice during blackout periods, the neighbors became convinced she was a spy. As time went on and people became better acquainted, these feelings evaporated. Lucy invited the men and women serving at the local army base over for a weekly "music evening" to listen to the huge gramophone in her sitting room. One of the highlights of a tour of Hemingford Grey today is listening to the old gramophone playing with its bamboo needle. It produces a surprisingly good sound, not much different from that of a modern CD player.

In the early 1950s, when Lucy Boston was just over sixty years old, she began writing *The Children of Green Knowe,* a book about the children who had lived in the house in the 1600s and a boy visiting his great grandmother in modern times. It featured illustrations by Lucy's son, Peter Boston, and was published in 1954 by Penguin Books. It was followed by *The Chimneys of Green Knowe* (1958), *The River at Green Knowe* (1959), *A Stranger at Green Knowe* (1961), which won the Carnegie Medal, and *An Enemy at Green Knowe* (1964). The series finished in 1976 with *The Stones of Green Knowe,* the story of the boy who first lived in the house in Norman times. The series has had enduring popularity in Britain and continues to be reprinted up to the present day.

Lucy Boston wrote other stories for children, including *The Sea Egg* (1967) and *The Castle of Yew,* and two novels for adults, *Yew Hall* (1954) and *Persephone* (1969), which was published in the United States as *Strongholds.* She also published a collection of poems she had written over a fifty-year period, *Time Is Undone* (1977). She continued writing on into her eighties with a book about the restoration of Hemingford Grey, *Memory in a House,* and her autobiography, *Perverse and Foolish: A Memoir of Childhood and Youth* (1979).

In addition to her writing, Lucy produced beautiful and creative patchwork quilts for family and friends right up to the end of her life. Some of these are on display at Hemingford Grey. They bring to mind ancient Mrs. Oldknow, a central character in several of the books, stitching away at her patchwork while she tells stories of earlier times to her great grandson.

Lucy Boston died at the age of ninety-seven, in 1990, at Hemingford Grey.

Places Connected with Lucy Boston's Stories and Life

THE MANOR HOUSE, HEMINGFORD GREY, CAMBRIDGESHIRE

The Manor House at Hemingford Grey is not an exact match for the fictional Green Knowe, but it comes so close that it is a magical place to visit. The river slips quietly by the topiary gardens; the drooping branches of the old beech tree form a hidden room for children of any era to play in; the huge old rocking horse in the attic bedroom makes the floorboards creak; and the wide chimney leading from the front room hearth to the bedrooms looks like a perfect passageway for a young boy to climb. Judging from the reaction of two eight-year-old American boys who had read some of Boston's Green Knowe stories before visiting, it's terrific fun to discover how much of Green Knowe really exists.

A tour of the house, usually given by a family member, begins with a brief description of the ways the configuration of the building has changed over nine centuries. Imagine living in a time, as the first occupants did, when the front door of a house needed to be one floor above the ground and reached by a ladder that could be pulled in for defensive purposes. The remains of the old moat and the extraordinary thickness of the walls are also remnants of less secure times.

Lucy Boston's personality and impact on the house are everywhere. Visitors are treated to a look at several of her beautiful patchwork quilts. There are pictures of the empty fields that she transformed into the lovely garden that surrounds the house. And everywhere are the details she wove into her stories, from the cherub faces on the beams in the front hall to the carved Japanese mouse whose wooden back feels as soft as real fur.

A walk around the garden will eventually lead you to the only topiary animal from *The Children of Green Knowe* that really exists, the fawn with the tail that wags when you touch its nose. However, if your eyes are good, you can see Susan and Jacob's initials carved high up on the beech tree from *The Chimneys of Green Knowe* (renamed *The Treasure of Green Knowe* in the United States).

There is a small shop selling Boston's books and local crafts on the ground floor of the house as well.

Hemingford Grey is located near the town of Huntingdon, which is sixteen miles northwest of Cambridge. If you are traveling by car, it takes about an hour and a quarter from London or twenty minutes from Cambridge. Follow the signs for Hemingford Grey off the A14. Once in the village, follow the small signs to the Manor House. Park on the High Street near the Cock Pub and take the peaceful walk along the river to the garden gate. There is limited parking for the disabled at the house. By train, travel from Kings Cross station in London to Huntingdon and then take a taxi for the four-mile trip to Hemingford Grey. The No. 5 bus from Cambridge also stops in Hemingford Grey.

Diana Boston, Lucy's daughter-in-law, continues to live in the house and schedules and guides the tours. It is necessary to make an appointment to visit by calling (01480)-463134 or by faxing (01480) 465026. Admission: £4.00 per person.

LONDON ZOO

The fourth book in the Green Knowe series, *A Stranger at Green Knowe*, won the Carnegie Medal. The story revolves around a young refugee boy from southern China (also a character in *The River at Green Knowe*) who comes to stay at Green Knowe one summer and his involvement in the life of a gorilla he "meets" at the London Zoo. The gorilla is named Hanno, but he is based on a real gorilla named Guy who lived in the London Zoo for many years. Guy was a star attraction at the zoo from

1947 to 1978 and a great favorite of Lucy Boston. She visited him often, and her attitude toward his captivity is clear in the story she wrote. When visiting the London Zoo today, you can't miss the big bronze statue of Guy, erected in 1982, that stands near the primate area. It's an irresistible place to climb for young children, but it has an added poignancy once you've read Boston's story. See the *Winnie-the-Pooh* chapter, page 81, for practical information about the London Zoo.

Other Activities for Children Who Love Boston's Stories

JORVIK VIKING CENTRE, YORK

Lucy Boston's *The Stones of Green Knowe* tells the story of the beginnings of the house in Norman times. It provides a picture of what life was like for a young boy nine hundred years ago in Britain. That picture comes to life at the Jorvik Viking Centre in York, where a ride takes you back in time, century by century, to a re-created Norman village that has been excavated on that site. This is a particularly child-friendly museum, with docents dressed in period clothing walking throughout the exhibits of Norman games, clothing, and everyday items. Even the smells of life back then are re-created, like it or not!

Jorvik Viking Centre is located in the Coppergate shopping area in the center of York. It is accessible by foot from several nearby public parking lots. Hours: 9:00–5:30 P.M., April through October, and 9:00–3:30 P.M., November through March. Admission: £4.99/adults, £3.99/children five–fifteen, free for children under five.

Telephone: (01904) 643-211. Web site: www.jorvik-viking-centre.co.uk.

THE POSTMAN PAT STORIES

by John Cunliffe

$\mathcal{P}$OSTMAN PAT, POSTMAN PAT, POSTMAN PAT AND HIS BLACK and white cat . . ." The Postman Pat jingle has been a fixture on British television since the 1980s. The *Postman Pat* TV series, featuring puppets designed by Ivor Wood, has aired in over sixty-five countries during the last twenty years. The young Prince William even carried a Postman Pat lunchbox on his first day at school. Although Pat has now been retired by the BBC, he and his faithful cat, Jess, still drive the verdant lanes of Greendale in their red Royal Mail van on cable TV reruns and on video. The TV shows themselves and over forty books about Postman Pat were written by John Cunliffe, a former teacher and librarian who lived in the Lake District area he writes about. Once you become familiar with Greendale and its citizens, including Peter Fogg, the local shepherd; Mrs. Goggins, the elderly lady who runs the post office/shop; and the Reverend Timms, local vicar, you'll spot their counterparts all over rural Britain.

The bright red post boxes and pint-size vans used by the Royal Mail can be of great interest to very young visitors to Britain. The Postman Pat stories provide a wonderful way of keeping that enthusiasm alive and of adding interest to a trip to the British countryside. A visit to the two villages that inspired Greendale adds a lovely and nontouristy dimension to a visit to the Lake District. For the postally inclined, it's great fun to see the underground train system run by the Royal Mail or to visit the spot from which the world's first postage stamp was sent. Pat was honored with a special stamp and set of four postmarks (one of which shows Pat wondering, "Now where's that letter?") at the London International Stamp Exhibition in 2000.

A Brief Biography of John Cunliffe

John Cunliffe was born in 1933 in Colne, Lancashire. His career as a librarian and teacher began in Yorkshire at the age of eighteen. After working as a mobile librarian in the very north of England, he earned his library science degrees in Leeds and in London. Several years as a children's librarian in Reading and other points south followed. After marrying Sylvia Thompson, a musician, in 1960, he spent two years in Belgrade, Yugoslavia, as librarian for the British Council. He published his first children's book, *Farmer Barnes Buys a Pig,* in 1964. Eventually, he completed nine Farmer Barnes books and numerous other stories for children.

The first Postman Pat story, *Postman Pat and the Mystery Thief,* emerged during the period when Cunliffe was trying his hand at teaching. He and his family, which now included his son, Julian, spent four years in **Kendal, Cumbria,** in the late seventies while Cunliffe taught at Castle Park School. The stories were published in conjunction with a TV series that Cunliffe was writing for the BBC, *Postman Pat.* Three or four Postman Pat books came out each year throughout the 1980s and on through the nineties. Between the books and the TV series, Postman Pat, the gentle and dedicated civil servant, was soon Britain's most popular "costume character."

After several years teaching in Manchester, Cunliffe became a full-time writer in 1985. He continues to write for children; the newest set of Postman Pat books was introduced in 2001.

Places Connected with the Postman Pat Stories

LONGSLEDDALE AND KENTMERE, LAKE DISTRICT, CUMBRIA

The villages of Longsleddale (pronounced "Long-**sled** -el" with the emphasis on the "sled") and Kentmere are the inspiration for Postman Pat's Greendale, each sitting in its own valley surrounded by farms

and fell country. As you drive along the winding lanes between and through the two villages, you know you are in Greendale: narrow lanes, cottages tucked into hillsides, a tiny village nestled into the steep valley, and if you're lucky, a spunky red postal van twisting and turning its way from farm to farm. Fictional Lake Berkmere is the only part of Greendale that is missing from this area; it was modeled on neighboring Grasmere. A drive to the end of the road in either valley will bring you to hiking trails up and over the fells.

Longsleddale is only four miles up the road from Kendal, but it feels like the heart of rural England. Take the A6 north from Kendal and exit at Watchgate, then head up the road toward Longsleddale and Sadgill Bridge (the end of the road). Alternately, take the A591 from Windermere/Bowness and exit at Stavely. Follow the road through town to Kentmere or head east through beautiful farm country toward Longsleddale.

Mount Pleasant Sorting Office and Postal Railway, Farringdon Road, London

In *Postman Pat Goes to Town*, Pat gets a taste of postal work in urban London, helping out Val, a postwoman who grew up in Jamaica and immigrated to England. Val just about wears Pat out carrying parcels up and down the hills of Hampstead.

Since the closure of the National Postal Museum, the best place to get a look at the real-life workings of the Royal Mail is at the Mount Pleasant sorting office in Clerkenwell, London. This is the center of the underground postal railway that transports mail throughout the various postal stations in London. The public may take a two-hour guided tour of the giant sorting office and the railway by booking three weeks in advance at (0207) 239-2312. The tour is free and includes tea and biscuits, which Pat would certainly approve of. It's not recommended for children under the age of nine.

The postal archives for Britain, the Post Office Heritage, can also be found in back of the Mount Pleasant facility. The office preserves 360 years of mail-related artifacts, including letter boxes, uniforms, and, of course, stamps. It seems the entire collection is on hold, waiting for something to be done about finding a new museum in which to display it all. Until then, only the stamps and archives are available to the public by appointment. Telephone: (0207) 239-2570.

The Mount Pleasant sorting office is located east of the British Museum on Farringdon Road. The closest tube stop is Farringdon. When you exit the tube stop, cross Farringdon Road and head toward Clerkenwell Road. The sorting office will be on your left just after you cross Roseberry Avenue.

Other Activities for Children Who Love the Postman Pat Stories

BATH POSTAL MUSEUM, 8 BROAD STREET, BATH

In 1840, someone at this post office got his instructions confused, put one of the newfangled postage stamps on a letter, and popped it in the mail. The stamps weren't supposed to go into use until several days later, but this misunderstanding caused 8 Broad Street, Bath, to be the first place in the world from which a postage stamp was sent. The Bath

Postal Museum now occupies this historic spot with none other than a larger-than-life Postman Pat waving at passersby from the front window. Jess and the van are there, too, and it's worth stopping in at this small, friendly museum as you wander the impressive streets of Bath.

The museum is self-supporting and offers some modest displays about the history of letter writing over the past four thousand years. The children's room in the back offers puzzles, animal hunts, a computer quiz, and sample stamps for the kids to take home. A low-key tearoom offers snacks and beverages. The gift shop is housed in the actual old post office and features our man Pat.

The museum is open from Monday to Saturday, 11:00–5:00 P.M.; Sundays, 2:00–5:00 P.M. It's located on Broad Street just after it splits off from the High Street, north of Great Pulteney Street. Telephone (01225) 460333.

MUSEUM OF LAKELAND LIFE, ABBOT HALL, KENDAL

Alas, for Postman Pat enthusiasts, his special room at the Museum of Lakeland Life has been dismantled. However, it is still possible to send a letter or message directly to Pat by putting it in the special post box in the gift shop. Incidentally, there is a variety of Postman Pat mementos on the shelves surrounding that post box.

The Museum of Lakeland Life and the Abbot Hall Art Gallery occupy the same set of buildings alongside a lovely bend in the river Kent near the center of Kendal. The museum is open daily from early February until the beginning of the Christmas holidays, 10:30–5:00 P.M. (4:00 P.M. in the winter months). Admission is £3/adults, £1.50/children, £7.50/family. Parking is free (entrance off Kirkland Road), and there is a very good coffee shop. Telephone: (01539) 722464. Web site: www.lakelandmuseum.org.uk.

Kendal is a short drive from junction 36 on the M6.

See the *Swallows and Amazons* chapter, page 260, for more information about the Museum of Lakeland Life.

*C*IDER WITH ROSIE *or* THE EDGE OF DAY

by *Laurie Lee*

♣ The village to which our family had come was a scattering of some twenty to thirty houses down the south-east slope of a valley. The valley was narrow, steep, and almost entirely cut off; it was also a funnel for winds, a channel for the floods and a jungly, bird-crammed, insect-hopping sun-trap whenever there happened to be any sun. . . . Living down there was like living in a bean-pod; one could see nothing but the bed one lay in. Our horizon of woods was the limit of our world.

Cider with Rosie or *The Edge of Day*, 1959

$\mathcal{I}$N ITS 1997 OBITUARY FOR LAURIE LEE, THE *TIMES* (LONDON) stated that no author since Thomas Hardy had claimed a geographical area of Britain so clearly for himself as did Laurie Lee the Slad valley in Gloucestershire. Lee's warm description of life in a Cotswold cottage with five siblings, a lively and erratic mother, and very little money is a classic of British literature. *Cider with Rosie* (renamed *The Edge of Day* for American publication) lies somewhere between autobiography and fiction, and the writing often verges on poetry. When Lee looked back on his childhood and adolescence in Slad, he realized that he "belonged to that generation which saw, by chance, the end of a thousand years' life." He captured the twilight of British rural village life between the world wars with humor and honesty. The book is written on a teenage or adult level and contains some passages about the violence and sexual behavior that were a part of village life. Some parental editing might be needed in reading it aloud to younger children.

The village of Slad, in the South Cotswolds, holds onto remnants of its *Cider with Rosie* days, including the picturesque local pub that Laurie Lee knew as a child and frequented as an adult. The natural beauty of the area remains as vivid, if not as untrammeled, as Lee knew it in his youth and captured in his writing. Some of the people in the book live on in Slad as well, and it's possible to tour the area with one of Laurie Lee's boyhood chums.

A Brief Biography of Laurie Lee

At first they wouldn't touch them with tongs.
—Laurie Lee in 1975, talking about the
reaction of his fellow villagers to his books
about village life

Laurie Lee was born in 1914 in Stroud, Gloucestershire. Laurie's mother was the second wife to his father; she had been his housekeeper, and they had married after the death of his first wife. When Laurie was three, his father went off to fight in World War I. Laurie's mother moved with her children to the nearby village of **Slad**. *Cider with Rosie* (1958), the first book in Lee's autobiographical trilogy of his younger years, begins at the moment of arrival in Slad and describes Lee's childhood in this tiny Gloucestershire village. When the war was over, Laurie's father moved to London to become a civil servant. Laurie's mother was left in the countryside raising, not only her own three boys, but also Laurie's three half sisters, offspring of Laurie's father's earlier marriage. The three half sisters are warmly portrayed in *Cider with Rosie* and described as "the good fortune of our lives," helping Laurie's vibrant, but distracted, mother to raise the younger three boys. *Cider with Rosie* is dedicated "to my brothers and sisters—the half and the whole." Although Lee's father continued to help the family financially, he had all but disappeared from their lives. Decades went by before Laurie's mother gave up her belief that he would return to them someday.

At age nineteen, Laurie left home, walking to London with his fiddle to make a place for himself in the world. He played his fiddle for pennies on his way to London and then supported himself as a construction worker. Wanderlust overcame him, and he was off to Spain, traveling on foot throughout a country on the brink of civil war. *As I Walked Out One Midsummer Morning* (1969), the second book in Lee's autobiographical trilogy, chronicles these adventurous years. The war finally broke out, and Lee was rescued by the British navy and returned to safety in England. He soon realized the import of the war that he had stumbled onto, and he headed back to Spain, slipping into the country on foot over the Pyrenees to join the Republican forces.

Lee went on to work as a scriptwriter of documentary films for the British government in Cyprus, India, and Vietnam during World War II. He became a publications editor for the Ministry of Information after the war. His work for the Festival of Britain in 1950 earned him an MBE. He married a woman from Provence, Catherine Polge, in 1950, and their only child, daughter Jessye, was born soon after. During these years, Lee wrote books of poetry and accounts of his travels around the world, including *A Rose for Winter: Travels in Andalusia. Cider with Rosie* was published in 1959 in Britain and then renamed for American publication in 1960 as *The Edge of Day: A Boyhood in the West of England.* The book's poetic description of village life between the wars was very well received. It has sold over six million copies and was made into a movie for British television in 1998. Laurie Lee recorded the book on audiotape as well. After *Cider with Rosie* was a success, Lee returned to Slad and bought a cottage just behind **The Woolpack,** the village pub. According to the *London Times,* there was "some vexation when the villagers recognized themselves in the book," but in time Lee became a village fixture, often greeting admirers at The Woolpack. Lee continued to write, with *As I Walked Out One Midsummer Morning* coming out in 1969. Other books of poetry and a collection of essays followed. In 1991, Lee completed his autobiographical trilogy with *A Moment of War,* describing his return to Spain in the late 1930s. His account met with some controversy, still unresolved, about the extent of Lee's actual involvement in the war.

Lee died in 1997 at the age of eighty-three. His funeral was held in the Slad village church, and he is buried in the churchyard just across the road from the cottages of his youth and his later years. His gravestone reads: "He lies in the valley he loved."

Places Connected with Cider with Rosie

SLAD, GLOUCESTERSHIRE

The Slad Laurie Lee describes in *Cider with Rosie* was an isolated hamlet, a world unto itself. The radical changes of the last sixty years are evident in the ease with which a visitor can reach Slad these days. The Slad Road (B4070) winds its way north from Stroud, the nearest large town, for about five miles along the narrow Slad valley. The tiny village of Slad stretches out along both sides of the road, with the Woolpack Inn's colorful

sign as its most recognizable landmark. Park near the Woolpack or get off the bus at the nearby bus stop and continue along the road a short way. A small sign for "Rosebank" is the modest marker for Lee's childhood home. The seventeenth-century house sits toward the bottom of the steep slope down from the road. In such a setting, it's no wonder that the threat of flooding turned Lee's mother into a raving fury. Lee claimed that no matter where he lived for the rest of his life, a heavy rainfall sent him scurrying for a broom. Rosebank is a private home and not open to the public. However, from the roadside it is possible to get a good look at the surprisingly large cottage. It's almost possible to imagine the two grannies who shared the "top stroke" of the T-shaped house with Lee's family, never speaking a word to each other but grumbling away about "Er-Down-Under" or "Er-Up-Atop—the Varmint" and pounding on the floorboards at each other as the final years of their lives wound down.

Just across the street is the church and cemetery where Laurie Lee is buried. His grave is at the top of the path, quite near the church door.

THE WOOLPACK INN, SLAD

When Lee returned to Slad after his success, he lived in the pink cottage behind the pub, and he made the most of this proximity. The tiny pub still serves up excellent pints of cider in cozy rooms by a crackling fire. It fits the sterotype of an ancient local pub right down to the two large dogs taking up every inch of space in front of the fire while a few "regulars" grumble about the state of the world. Dinner is offered after 7:00 P.M., and the chips are first-rate. In good weather, there is seating on an outside deck with views of the lovely valley. There is often live acoustic music on the weekends. Telephone: (01452) 813429.

Jim Fern grew up in Slad, a few years behind Laurie Lee. Jim is mentioned in *Cider with Rosie* as "the little Jim Fern" who sits next to the older Laurie at the village school, giving him "a sad, adoring look," which cheers Laurie when he's feeling low. Now well into his eighth decade, Jim leads personal tours of *Cider with Rosie* country. He knew all the people in the book, and he can fill you in on what has happened to many of them over the years, including Rosie herself.

Jim is happy to provide a half-day or full-day guided walk for individuals or groups by appointment. Fees are determined on an individual basis. He can be reached at (01453) 753104.

Other Places Connected with Laurie Lee's Life

The Museum in the Park, Stroud

It's taken seven years and lots of grant money from the national lottery to refurbish this museum (reopened in 2001), and the good citizens of Stroud are justifiably proud of the results. Visitors enter the new wing through a striking courtyard/amphitheater hung with an enormous banner. Laurie Lee is well represented in a display that features recordings of his voice reading passages from *Cider with Rosie.* Visitors can sit in a quaint rocking chair while they listen. A small loft overhead re-creates his cozy cottage bed.

It's a delightful museum to wander through, with a good mammoth exhibit and a playful giant mural of mastadons negotiating a traffic circle. A small playroom upstairs salutes the area's connection with The Reverend W. Awdry, who wrote the Thomas the Tank Engine stories. He spent his retirement nearby.

The museum is located in Stratford Park on the northwest side of town. Stroud is a tangle of one-way streets around a large pedestrian area at the town center. Find your way to the roundabout where Merrywalks, Beeches Green, and the Slad Road all come together. Follow

Beeches Green to Stratford Road (A4171) and take a left. Follow signs to the car park for the Stratford Park. The museum is beyond the leisure center overlooking a small lake. Opening hours are 12:00–5:00 weekdays, and 11:00–5:00 weekends, closed Mondays. Admission is £2.50/adults, £1/children. Telephone: (01453) 763394. Web site: www.stroud.gov.uk.

Other Activities for Children Who Love Cider with Rosie

SEE THE SLAD VALLEY BY BICYCLE

Laurie Lee describes how different life was before cars and planes widened our horizons and speeded up our days. A great way to get a feel for the slower, quieter pace of life in the Slad Valley in the early twentieth century is to get around for a day by bicycle. However, do keep in mind that one reason the area is so scenic is that there are plenty of hills! Bikes are available for rent at Stonehouse Accessories in Stonehouse, a small town just west of Stroud on the A419. The ride from Stonehouse to Slad will be hilly, but it is possible to avoid heavily traveled roads. It's also possible to ride on canal paths all the way to Gloucester or Bristol if you are very ambitious.

Stonehouse Accessories is located at 18 High Street in Stonehouse. Rentals cost £12.50/day per bike. They also rent baby/child seats and "tag-alongs," where a metal bar attaches a single-wheeled bike to an adult bike. The tag-alongs cost £10/day; the baby seats are £5/day. The shop is open from 8:30 to 5:30 P.M. Telephone: (01453) 822-881.

The Railway Children *and* Other Stories
By E. Nesbit

♣ They all climbed to the top of the fence, and then suddenly there was a rumbling sound that made them look along the line to the right, where the dark mouth of a tunnel opened itself in the face of a rocky cliff; next moment a train had rushed out of the tunnel with a shriek and a snort, and had slid noisily past them. They felt the rush of its passing, and the pebbles on the line jumped and rattled under it as it went by. "Oh!" said Roberta, drawing a long breath; "it was like a great dragon tearing by. Did you feel it fan us with its hot wings?"

—*The Railway Children*, 1906

$\mathcal{T}$HE TRANQUIL LIVES OF THREE CHILDREN ARE TURNED UPSIDE down when their father is taken away in the middle of the night. Although their mother keeps his plight a secret, he has been imprisoned under false espionage charges. The children and their mother are forced to move to a small cottage in the country to economize. Suddenly their circumstances are poorer but much freer as they roam the surrounding countryside and become fascinated with the local railway. *The Railway Children* is both a dramatic story of a family coping with a terrible situation and an idyllic depiction of rural life at the turn of the century. The book has never been out of print since it was first published in 1906, and several TV and movie versions have been made, including a BBC version in 1998, shown on PBS in the United States.

If you are visiting London, it's an easy day's journey down into bucolic Kent for a visit to the area that most inspired E. Nesbit, followed by a ride on a wonderful old steam train. If your travels take you northward to Yorkshire, you can relive the entire story through the charming locations used to film *The Railway Children* in 1970, followed by a ride on yet another wonderful old steam train!

A Brief Biography of E. Nesbit

> When I was a little child I used to pray fervently, tearfully, that when I should be grown up I might never forget what I thought and felt and suffered then.
>
> —E. Nesbit, *My School Days*, 1896

E. Nesbit (the pen name of Edith Nesbit Bland) was born in 1858 in Kennington, part of South London, the youngest of six children. Her father was the head of an agricultural chemistry college. He died when Edith was three years old. Her mother struggled to keep the school going after his death. The poor health of an older sister led her mother to give

up the school and take the family first to Brighton and then to France in an effort to find a healthier climate. Edith was sent to a series of boarding schools in England and France, all of which she loathed. Her sister died in 1871, and the family returned to England and settled in the village of **Halstead,** south of London in Kent.

Edith always remembered the three years her family spent in Halstead as the happiest in her life. The family lived in **Halstead Hall,** which still stands today on Station Road in Halstead. In her late teens, Edith's poems began to be published sporadically in magazines. She married Hubert Bland when she was twenty-two and already seven months pregnant. Hubert's failed attempt at starting his own business, coupled with a bout of smallpox, soon put Edith in the role of chief breadwinner for the growing family. In addition to writing novels, poems, and stories for magazines, Edith decorated greeting cards to bring in money.

The Blands were politically active and helped to found the Fabian Society, the earliest organized socialist group in Britain, in 1884. After Hubert recovered, he took up writing and became a successful newspaper columnist and editor. The couple had four children, and a good friend of Edith's, Alice Hoatson, moved in with the Blands to care for the children and keep house. When the unmarried Alice became pregnant, Edith agreed to adopt the child. Months after baby Rosamund was born, Edith learned that Hubert Bland was the father. This scenario was played out again ten years later when Alice gave birth to a boy, John. Both children were unaware of their unorthodox parentage until they were in their teens. Their unusual domestic situation was only the tip of the iceberg, with both Hubert and Edith becoming involved with numerous people over the years. At one time Edith was deeply in love with George Bernard Shaw, another member of the Fabian Society. When Rosamund was just eighteen, she continued the family proclivity for scandal by attempting to run away with H. G. Wells, who was married at the time.

In the late 1890s, Edith began to find some real success in writing serialized children's stories for magazines. *The Story of the Treasure Seekers, The Wouldbegoods,* and *New Treasure Seekers,* three books about the fictional Bastable family, were hugely successful. These were followed by several fantasy stories involving time travel: *The Five Children and It, The Phoenix and the Carpet,* and *The Story of the Amulet.*

In 1906, she wrote *The Railway Children,* which has probably had the most lasting popularity. Nesbit's strong political beliefs are evident in the story of three children whose writer-mother supports them while their father is wrongly imprisoned. When a refugee from Czarist Russia comes to live at their house, the mother explains to the children:

> "He's a writer; he's written beautiful books. But you know in Russia you mustn't say anything about the rich people doing wrong, or about the things that ought to be done to make poor people better and happier. If you do, they send you to prison . . . he was three years in a horrible dungeon, with hardly any light, and all damp and dreadful."

Despite the success of her children's books, Edith Nesbit's final years were financially insecure. After Hubert's death in 1914, she sold the family home and was dependent on a government pension. She began a happy second marriage in 1917 to Thomas Terry Tucker, a retired sea captain known as "Skipper." They moved to Kent soon after their marriage. Edith died there of cancer in 1924 at the age of sixty-six. She is buried in the churchyard at **St. Mary-in-the Marsh.**

Her books continued to be popular throughout the twentieth century. Noel Coward was a great admirer of her work and wrote in 1956:

> [Nesbit's] writing is so light and unforced, her humour is so sure and her narrative quality so strong that the stories, which I know backwards, rivet me as much now as they did when I was a little boy.

Coward had a copy of *The Enchanted Castle* by E. Nesbit next to his bed when he died.

Places Connected with The Railway Children

HALSTEAD HALL, HALSTEAD, KENT

Edith's family lived here from 1872 to '75 when Edith was fourteen to seventeen years old. She remembered these as the golden years of her youth. *The Railway Children* was based in part on her memories of those years. She and her brothers loved to run down to the nearby railroad tracks and watch the trains go by. They occasionally walked the tracks to Chelsfield station, quite a long trek. The closer station at Knockholt was not built until after Edith's family had moved back to London.

The house stands today at the crossroads of Knockholt Road and Otford Lane. Its name is scrolled in the ironwork on the front gate. It is a private home and not open to the public.

To get to Halstead, turn off at junction 4 of the M25 (which rings London). Follow the signs to Halstead. At the T-junction, turn left. Halstead Hall is on the right at the crossroads just beyond the Cock pub.

HAWORTH, NEAR BRADFORD, YORKSHIRE

Lionel Jeffries's 1970 movie version of *The Railway Children* is considered a classic and is much loved in Britain. It was filmed in and around Haworth, Yorkshire, a particularly attractive village, famous as the home of the Brontë sisters. The historic Keighley & Worth Valley Railway (KWVR) runs through the village, its locomotives sending up great white clouds of steam as they pass.

In the movie the children walk up and down the steep village main street collecting birthday presents for their friend, Perks, the station porter. A pamphlet titled "The Railway Children Walk" describes this and other key locations in the filming. It is available for 30 pence at the Tourist Information Centre at the top of the cobbled Marsh Lane or at the KWVR station on Station Road at the bottom of the hill. The six-mile walk can be done in shorter pieces and is fairly level, although boots are desirable if the ground is damp. Bents House, which became

Three Chimneys, the children's home, is located about a mile outside of Haworth off of Marsh Lane. The Railway Cottage across the tracks from Oakworth station played the part of Mr. Perks's home. It's now a bed and breakfast. Even the Brontë parsonage was used as the doctor's house.

After walking some or all of the Railway Children Walk, a ride on the KWVR itself is delightful. As you sit back and enjoy a cup of hot chocolate, the steam billows up through the passing trees, and the old engine chugs its way past several beautifully restored old train stations before entering a more industrial area. Oakworth station, a fully re-created late-Victorian station, was featured in the film. The train also passes through Mytholmes Tunnel, which was used as the tunnel where the children rescue the injured runner. The round-trip takes about an hour and costs £6/adults, £3/children. A family ticket costs £16, and children under five and dogs travel free. Telephone: (01535) 647-777. Web site: www.kwvr.co.uk.

BLUEBELL RAILWAY, KINGSCOTE, SUSSEX

The trains and stations of the Bluebell Railway were used in another production of *The Railway Children* by Edith Nesbit produced by Carlton TV in 1999. The show aired in the United States on public television in 2000. The railway is another volunteer-run preserved steam railway that will take you through the countryside in true *Railway Children* style.

The Bluebell Railway runs between Kingscote and Sheffield Park in Sussex. The closest large town is Crawley. Trains operate daily from April 7 through the end of September each year. Take a regular train to East Grinstead and then transfer to the No. 473 bus to Kingscote station. By car, the easiest access is at the Sheffield Park station on the

A275, two miles north of the junction with the A272. The way is signposted from the A23. Telephone: (01825) 722370.

Other Places Connected with Edith Nesbit's Life

ST. MARY-IN-THE-MARSH, KENT

Edith spent the last years of her life in this village, where she and her second husband, Skipper, converted two brick air force huts into a house, which has since been demolished. Edith loved this part of Kent and spent holidays in the Romney Marsh area throughout her adult life. She loved to ride around the country lanes in a small donkey cart. She is buried in the village churchyard at the south end under an elm tree. Skipper built her grave marker, which simply says POET AND AUTHOR and is inscribed with the clover-leaf symbol she used to sign her initials.

St. Mary-in-the-Marsh can be reached by following the A2070 from Ashford (junction 10 on the M20). Turn left onto the A259 toward New Romney and follow the signs.

Other Activities for Children Who Love The Railway Children

NATIONAL RAILWAY MUSEUM, YORK

As E. Nesbit tells it, "They were not railway children to begin with." The transformation occurs when they have a chance to take a look at real trains whizzing past:

> Here in the deep silence of the sleeping country the only things that went by were the trains. They seemed to be all that was left to link the children to the old life that had once been theirs. . . . They began to know the hours when certain trains passed, and they gave names to

them. The 9:15 up was called the Green Dragon. The 10:07 down was the Worm of Wantley. The midnight town express, whose shrieking rush they sometimes woke from their dreams to hear, was the Fearsome Fly-by-night.

—*The Railway Children,* chapter 3

For those of us who are "railway children" no matter our age, the National Railway Museum in York is a delight. From Stephenson's historic "Rocket" to the "palace on wheels" of the royal family to a ride on the miniature train out back, this museum will fascinate train lovers. There are several huge, gleaming steam locomotives (polished weekly) and a working turntable that is demonstrated at 3:30 P.M. daily.

The museum is extremely kid-friendly, with a picnic area and an Interactive Learning Centre. You can ride a "road train" from York Minster (York's magnificent cathedral) to the National Railway Museum and back. It costs £1 for adults and 50 pence for children. The tram runs every thirty minutes from April to October, less frequently in the off-season. The National Railway Museum is open from 10:00 to 6:00 P.M. daily. Admission is £6.90/adults; children sixteen and under are free.

The museum is located on Leeman Road about a half mile across the river from the museum gardens. Pedestrians can follow the posted signs from anywhere in the center of York. If you are arriving by train, it is an easy walk from the York train station. Although it is best to avoid driving into the center of York if possible, there is long-term parking (fee) at the museum. Follow the signs from the ring road. Telephone: (01904) 621621.

BEKONSCOT MODEL VILLAGE, BEACONSFIELD, BUCKINGHAMSHIRE

Bekonscot, the world's oldest model village, gives visitors a chance to step back in time into 1930s rural England in miniature. Although the actual Railway Children would have been grown up and raising their own families by the 1930s, Bekonscot does portray a time period when village life was the norm, and the railways were the primary means of traveling about. Covering an area of over forty thousand square feet, Bekonscot includes six tiny villages that encompass every feature of British life of that era: a circus, a racecourse, a cricket pitch, a fishing port, an airfield, a coal mine, and a wonderful model steam railway running throughout. The model trains travel to seven stations all controlled by illuminated track diagrams and levers that are operated from a signal house visible to the public. The gift shop by the entrance is even housed in an old railway carriage.

Visitors to Bekonscot walk among all this activity on over two thousand feet of pathways. It's a delightful feeling to stand in the midst of this extensive and amazingly detailed landscape. Even the trees and landscaping have been scaled down to fit the tiny buildings.

There is a full-sized play area for young children, a picnic area, and a refreshments stand. Admission is £3.60/adults, £1.80/children, under three free. The excess profits from Bekonscot are given to charity, with over a million pounds raised since its beginning in 1929. Bekonscot is open from 10:00 to 5:00 P.M. every day from February 14 through November 1. Telephone: (01494) 675284.

Beaconsfield is located just west of London at junction 2 on the M40. Follow the A355 and signs for the model village. It's a short train ride from London and an easy walk from the station to Bekonscot.

THE KENT & EAST SUSSEX RAILWAY, TENTERDEN, KENT

Edith Nesbit and Frances Hodgson Burnett, who wrote *The Secret Garden,* lived for several years within twenty miles of each other in Kent. Both women lived unconventional lives that were considered somewhat scandalous at the time, and both wrote books about gardens that were published in 1911 (Nesbit's being *The Wonderful Garden*). There is no evidence that they ever met, however. If you are planning to visit St. Mary-on-the-Marsh, you might want to drive up the road to Rolvenden and visit the setting that inspired Frances Hodgson Burnett's *The Secret Garden* (see that chapter, page 19 for details). That would take you directly past a lovely preserved steam railway, the Kent East Sussex

Railway, which originates in Tenterden. The Railway Children themselves would certainly not miss the opportunity.

To get from St. Mary-on-the-Marsh to Rolvenden, join the A259 at New Romney. It becomes the B2080, which goes directly to Tenterden.

Follow the signs for the Kent & East Sussex Railway from the High Street in Tenterden. Trains run every weekend from April through October, every day in July and August. The line passes through seven miles of beautiful, rolling countryside. Parking is free. Telephone: (01580) 765155. Web site: www.kesrail.fsnet.co.uk.

After a train ride, take the A28 to Rolvenden to see the Secret Garden.

Swallows *and* AMAZONS
by Arthur Ransome

❧ The island had come to seem one of those places seen from the train that belong to a life in which we shall never take part. And now, suddenly, it was real. It was to be their island after all. They were to be allowed to use the sailing boat by themselves. They were to be allowed to sail out from the little sheltered bay, and round the point, and down the lake to the island. They were to be allowed to land on the island, and to live there until it was time to pack up again and go home to town and school and lessons. The news was so good it made them solemn. They ate their bread and marmalade in silence. The prospect before them was too vast for chatter.

—*Swallows and Amazons*, 1930

THE FOUR WALKER CHILDREN SAIL THEIR SAILBOAT, *SWALLOW,* to Wild Cat Island, where they camp out for a week with no parents or adults to bother them. A mysterious boat circles the island, flying the skull and crossbones, and the war with the Amazons begins. Their enemies soon become allies, and together they take on the mysterious pirate who lives in a nearby bay with a parrot and cannon on board. Arthur Ransome's *Swallows and Amazons* weaves the imaginative adventures of two groups of children with outdoor lore into a plausible and exciting summer vacation story. Set in the Lake District in northern England, the story and the eleven others Ransome wrote between 1930 and 1947 remain extremely popular around the world, although less well-known in the United States.

Ransome based the children's adventures on very specific local places. Searching them out provides a wonderful excuse for exploring this beautiful area by boat, by car, or on foot. The key boats in the stories have been lovingly restored by enthusiasts over the years and are on display. You can have your own adventure by renting a sailboat and setting out for Wild Cat Island under wind power or join a special *Swallows and Amazons* cruise around Coniston Water. For the full *Swallow* experience, stay at the farm where the Walker children began their story on the banks of the lake, now a B and B.

A Brief Biography of Arthur Ransome

We adored the place. Coming to it, we used to run down to the lake, dip our hands in and wish, as if we had just seen the new moon. Going away from it, we were half drowned in tears. While away from it, as children and as grown-ups, we dreamt about it. No matter where I was, wandering about the world, I used at night to look for the North Star and, in my mind's eye, could see the beloved skyline of great hills beneath it. *Swallows and Amazons* grew out of those old memories. I could not help writing it. It almost wrote itself.

> —Arthur Ransome, addressing the question of how he
> came to write the book in the Author's Note to the
> 1958 edition of *Swallows and Amazons*

Arthur Ransome was born in 1884 in Leeds, Yorkshire, the oldest boy in a family of two boys and two girls. His father taught history at the University of Leeds and took his family to Coniston Water in the Lake District each year for their summer holiday. Young Arthur treasured these weeks of freedom, fishing, and sailing. At the age of nine, Arthur was sent to study at a Lake District preparatory school, Old College, Windermere. He was bullied a great deal and quite miserable most of the time. Ransome's father died when Arthur was thirteen, the same year he was sent on to **Rugby School**. After Rugby, Arthur studied chemistry for a short period at the University of Leeds but soon realized that his true calling was writing.

Ransome spent the next several years living a bohemian life in London while working for a publishing house. During these years he also spent many holidays in the Lake District, often staying near **Coniston Water** with the Collingswood family. W. G. Collingswood was a writer, artist, and scholar and something of a hero to Ransome. Arthur eventually proposed marriage to two of the Collingswood daughters. Both refused him, but they remained friends for many years.

In 1909, Ransome married Ivy Walker, a woman he knew in London, and Ransome's only child, Tabitha, was born in 1910. His first real success came with two works of literary criticism, *Edgar Allan Poe* (1910) and *Oscar Wilde* (1912). The latter brought on a libel suit filed by Lord Alfred Douglas, which Ransome eventually won.

His increasingly unhappy marriage, combined with the strain of fighting the lawsuit, led Ransome to take off for Russia for an extended stay. He studied the language and folklore of the country and produced a book of Russian folktales. World War I had broken out, and Ransome found work as a foreign correspondent for the *Daily News* and the *Manchester Guardian.* He knew the Bolshevik leaders well, had free access to the Kremlin, and even played chess with Lenin. Moved and inspired by the Russian Revolution, Ransome wrote in 1918: "Let the revolution fail. No matter. If only in America, in England, in France, in Germany people know why it has failed, and how it failed, who betrayed it, who murdered it. Man does not live by his deeds so much as the purpose of his deeds. We have seen the flight of the young eagles. Nothing can destroy that fact, even if, later in the day the eagles fall to earth one by one, with broken wings."

Ransome had fallen in love with Trotsky's secretary, Evgenia, a Russian woman from a privileged background. He remained in Russia until 1920 and then moved with Evgenia to Estonia and Latvia. It was during these years that Ransome bought his first sailing boat and cruised the Baltic with Evgenia each summer. When his divorce from Ivy became final in 1924, Arthur and Evgenia were married and returned to England. They settled at Low Ludderburn in the Winster valley near Windermere in an isolated cottage. Ransome was sent to Egypt and China as he continued his foreign correspondence work for the *Manchester Guardian.*

In 1929, he gave up journalism and began writing a children's book, *Swallows and Amazons.* Dora Collingswood, her husband, Ernest Altounyan, and their four children, who lived in Syria, had been home on leave and stayed at **Bank Ground Farm** on Coniston Water. Ransome and Ernest had taught the children to sail on the lake in two small boats, one named *Swallow.* Ransome named the four children in his book after the Altounyan children and dedicated the first edition to them. Years later their friendship cooled, and Ransome denied their influence on the book.

Whatever its inspiration, *Swallows and Amazons* told of four children camping and sailing on their own during a summer vacation, combining details of outdoor life (how to put up a tent, how to keep a fire burning, etc.) with fantasy play (pirate battles, buried treasure, etc.). Published in 1930 with no illustrations, it and Ransome's second book, *Swallowdale* (1931), went largely unnoticed. The third book in the series, *Peter Duck* (1932), caught the critics' attention, and from then on the entire series became extremely popular. Ransome won the first Carnegie Medal for Best Children's Book of the Year for the sixth book in the series, *Pigeon Post* (1935). He went on to write twelve books in all, the last being *Great Northern* in 1947. He is credited with inventing the modern holiday adventure story for children, and his books have been translated into twelve languages. An Internet search for *Swallows and Amazons* in 2001 came up with more than fifty web sites in Czech,

Japanese, Russian, and English dedicated to the books, evidence of the series' lasting appeal around the world.

Arthur and Evgenia moved to Suffolk in 1935, where they were able once again to have a seagoing boat. Two of Ransome's books, *Coot Club* and *The Big Six,* are set in the Norfolk Broads, an area where Ransome sailed frequently. In 1940, the Ransomes returned to the relative safety of the Lake District when the violence of World War II threatened the east coast of England. They lived at The Heald on Coniston Water's eastern shore for five years, but failing health and age were taking their toll. They eventually settled into a flat in London for the winters and spent summers at Hill Top (not the same Hill Top as Beatrix Potter) not far from the southern tip of Windermere. Ransome was made a CBE in 1953.

In 1965, after Evgenia's second heart attack and Arthur's second stroke, Arthur entered a hospital in Manchester, where he died in June of 1967. Evgenia survived him by eight years. They are both buried in Rusland Churchyard in a valley between Coniston Water and Windermere.

Places Connected with Swallows and Amazons

Arthur Ransome had a standard reply for children who wrote him asking where various places in *Swallows and Amazons* really were: "All the places in the books are to be found, but not arranged quite as in the ordnance maps." The consensus seems to be that the lake where the four Walker children (the Swallows) and the two Blackett girls (the Amazons) had their adventures is a combination of locations on Coniston Water and Windermere, both in the southern Lake District, situated about seven miles apart.

The Lake District is one of the most popular holiday destinations in Britain. Its dramatic scenery is stunning any time of the year, but be prepared to enjoy it with crowds of people if you visit during the summer months. As with any place on the western side of Britain, the weather is highly changeable, and a sprinkle or a downpour is almost always a possibility. (See the Beatrix Potter chapter, page 98, for more information about the area.)

The Coniston Water Area

BANK GROUND FARM

Known in the book as Holly Howe Farm, this is where the story begins with the four Walker children yearning to sail to the mysterious island they have spotted down the lake. Today the farm offers either B and B or self-catering accommodations. Guests can sail from the farm's jetty in search of the pirate life. Telephone: (01539) 441264.

Bank Ground Farm is located on the eastern shore of Coniston Water, about two miles from Coniston village. Lanehead, the home of the Collingswood family, who befriended Arthur Ransome, is nearby and in use as an outdoor education center. Just beyond Lanehead is Brantwood, the home of John Ruskin, artist and philosopher. Open to the public, Brantwood is a fascinating place to visit, and the tearoom is excellent as well.

PEEL ISLAND

To camp on an island in the middle of a large lake with other children and no adults while getting around by sailboat—is it any wonder that *Swallows and Amazons* intrigues generation after generation of children? The island itself is Peel Island, about two-thirds of the way down Coniston Water. The secret harbor and landing place resemble the ones in the story quite precisely. The Arthur Ransome Society has enhanced the scene even more by planting a "lighthouse tree" at the north end of the island.

Peel Island is owned by the National Trust. It's possible to rent a boat at Coniston Boating Centre (see below) to sail to the island for a picnic. However, be aware that times have changed since the kids made their tea each day over an open fire. Today no fires are allowed on the island.

Another option is to take a "Swallows and Amazons" tour on the Coniston launch, which sails around the island. The traditional timber launch was built in 1923 and is named the *M. L. Ransome.* The tours leave every Tuesday at 2:30 P.M. from the end of March through the end of October and Thursdays at 4:30 P.M. during August. The trip lasts ninety minutes and costs £7/adult, £4/child. Children under six are not allowed on the trip. Follow the boat signs from the town of Coniston to the boating center. Parking is free. Telephone: (015394) 36216. Web site: www.lakefell.co.uk.

THE RIVER CRAKE

Arthur Ransome's family spent their summers in tiny Nibthwaite at the southern tip of Coniston. The river Crake, which runs nearby, is thought to be the river Amazon in the story, with Allan's Tarn being the obvious choice for the Octopus Lagoon. Both the Lagoon and the Amazons's boathouse can be seen by walking up the path toward Bethecar from the village, taking the right hand fork after Laurel House (where the Ransome family stayed in Arthur's childhood). Nibthwaite can be reached by the road that runs along the eastern side of Coniston Water. It joins the A5084 at Lowick Bridge a bit farther south.

THE STEAM YACHT *GONDOLA*

The *Gondola* was built in 1859, and she sailed Coniston Water during Arthur Ransome's youth. She is given partial credit as inspiration for Captain Flint's houseboat, although the *Esperance* seems to have been the primary model (see below under "Windermere Steamboat Centre, Windmere"). The *Gondola* has been fully restored by the National Trust, and she provides by far the most elegant sailing experience in the area. Trips depart from Coniston Pier four times daily between March 31 and October 31. Telephone: (015394) 63856. Web site: www.nationaltrust.co.uk.

The Windermere Area

WINDERMERE STEAMBOAT CENTRE, WINDERMERE

Any *Swallows and Amazons* fans with even the slightest interest in boats should make a point of visiting the Windermere Steamboat Centre. The original *Amazon* (whose real name was *Mavis*) has been restored and is on display with other boats typical of the period. There is even an old sign saying, "This is a very old boat in peaceful retirement—do not disturb her," which used to sit on the *Amazon*. It was painted by the real ship's boy Roger—Roger Altounyan. The 1962 BBC movie of *Swallows and Amazons* plays on a monitor nearby.

However, the real delight comes outside in the "wet dock" area, where Captain Flint's houseboat (officially known as *Esperance*) floats in all her uniqueness, complete with cannon, parrot, and a plank to walk. The galley is set up for the postbattle feast. Free guided tours are given on request if a guide is available. No one is permitted on the boat without a guide.

> *Swallow* was sailing very fast and they saw the thing only for a moment. But there could be no doubt about what it was.
>
> "He's got a cannon," said Roger. "Look, look!"
>
> On the foredeck of the houseboat, on the starboard side, its round shiny nose poking out above the blue planking, was a brightly polished little brass cannon. Once upon a time, perhaps, it had been used for starting yacht races. Now there it was, on a wooden gun carriage, ready for action. Even for Captain John it was proof that the houseboat was more than an ordinary houseboat. A brass cannon and a green parrot."
>
> —*Swallows and Amazons*, chapter 6

Ransome isn't the only children's author honored at the center. The boat from which Beatrix Potter sketched Mr. Jeremy Fisher "floats" on the other side of the room from the *Amazon*.

The center is located beside the lake just north of the center of Windermere on the A592 (Rayrigg Road). It's open from the middle of

March through the end of October, 10:00–5:00 P.M. Admission is £3.40/adults, £2/children; a family ticket is £8.50. The gift shop has lots of *Swallows and Amazons*–related books and toys. Telephone: (015394) 48769. Web site: www.steamboat.co.uk.

WINDERMERE LAKE CRUISES, BOWNESS HARBOR

As the Walker children often said, "Sail's the thing," but if a sailboat isn't going to be part of your visit to the lakes, a cruise will get you out on the water, which must be the next best thing. The cruise down to the southern portion of lengthy Windermere has the added appeal of providing a look at Silver Holme, the inspiration for Cormorant Island, where Titty and Roger find their buried treasure.

Cruises leave from charming Bowness Harbor, called "Rio" by the Walker children in the story. A trip to the southern end of the lake takes about forty minutes each way and costs £6.20/adults, £3/children, and £/16.50/family ticket. There are shorter cruises available to other portions of the lake. Telephone: (015394) 43360.

For more-detailed information about the locations used in *Swallows and Amazons* and in some of Arthur Ransome's other books, the following books are highly recommended:

In Search of Swallows and Amazons by Roger Wardale, Sigma Press, Cheshire, England, 1996.

Arthur Ransome and Captain Flint's Trunk by Christina Hardyment, Jonathan Cape, UK, 1984.

Other Places Connected with Arthur Ransome's Life

NIBTHWAITE, CONISTON WATER

(See the river Crake entry, page 257.)

MUSEUM OF LAKELAND LIFE, ABBOT HALL, KENDAL

The Museum of Lakeland Life and the Abbot Hall Art Gallery occupy the same set of buildings alongside a lovely bend in the river Kent near the center of Kendal. The Museum of Lakeland Life has a wonderful reconstruction of Arthur Ransome's study and a playroom next door called Captain Flint's Locker. Children can learn to tie knots, put on pirate costumes, decode messages, play at fishing, and enjoy the large mural of Wild Cat Island.

Both rooms are upstairs just past the dollhouse display. The museum is open daily from early February through the beginning of the Christmas holidays, 10:30–5:00 P.M. (4:00 P.M. in the winter months). Admission is £3/adults, £1.50/children, £7.50/family. Parking is free, and there is a very good coffee shop and gift shop. Telephone: (01539) 722464. Web site: www.lakelandmuseum.org.uk.

Kendal is a short drive from junction 36 on the M6.

RUSKIN MUSEUM, CONISTON

The Ruskin Museum's brochure has this quote for its heading: "Life without industry is guilt, and industry without art is brutality." Founded by W. G. Collingswood, Arthur Ransome's good friend and mentor, this small museum offers an impressive and sophisticated look at the area's natural and cultural history, with the focus on John Ruskin. The entrance hall is a fascinating time line taking the visitor back in time, step by step, to 1819, the year of Ruskin's birth. The Coniston

Gallery includes a case of Arthur Ransome materials, including a description of Ransome's father carrying Arthur up Coniston Old Man (the local peak) as an infant.

The museum is open daily from 10:00 to 5: 30 P.M., Easter through mid-November. Admission is £3. Telephone: (015394) 41164. Coniston is on the northwest side of Coniston Water on the A593. It's a beautiful forty-five-minute drive on very narrow lanes from the Bowness Ferry. Follow the B5285 from Hawkshead. Turn right at the church. The museum will be on your left off the main road.

RUGBY SCHOOL

Arthur Ransome attended Rugby as a teenager, living in the same rooms as Lewis Carroll had decades before. He is included in a group of distinguished alumni in a display case in the Rugby School Museum. See the Lewis Carroll chapter, page 32 for more information.

Other Activities for Children Who Love Swallows and Amazons

CONISTON BOATING CENTRE/CONISTON LAUNCH

Any truly self-respecting Swallow or Amazon won't want to waste any time before getting out onto the lake in a real boat. These can be rented at the Coniston Boating Centre by the hour or the day. Sailing dinghies, rowboats, and "Canadian canoes" are all available. The cozy Bluebird Café at the docks will rent you fishing nets and sell you duck food or very informal people food. Follow the boat signs from the center of Coniston to the waterside. Telephone: (015394) 41366. E-mail at conistonbc@lake-district.gov.uk.

The Arthur Ransome Society (TARS) was formed in 1990 for "those of all ages who have enjoyed the famous Swallows and Amazons books." This enthusiastic group helps support the Arthur Ransome exhibit at Abbot Hall and

sponsors a wide range of activities annually. Younger readers will enjoy the junior magazine, *The Outlaw,* which features information on charcoal making, compass reading, and the like. For more information, contact TARS, Abbot Hall Gallery, Abbot Hall, Kendal, Cumbria, UK, LA9 5AL

Hikes and rambles

"Walking the fells" is the thing to do in this part of Britain, if age and weather permit! If you want the *Swallows and Amazons* experience on foot rather than on the water, there is no better source than *In the Footsteps of the Swallows and Amazons* by Claire Kendall-Price. It can be purchased at the Abbot Hall gift shop in Kendal for £8 and features nineteen illustrated walks up and down Arthur Ransome country.

$\mathcal{B}$IBLIOGRAPHY

$\mathcal{G}$eneral

Contemporary Authors. Detroit: Gale Research, 1984.

Foster, Allan. *The Movie Traveller.* Edinburgh: Polygon (Edinburgh University Press), 2000.

Hettinga and Smith. *Dictionary of Literary Biography.* Detroit: Gale Research, 1996.

Hunt, Peter, ed. *Children's Literature: An Illustrated History.* Oxford: Oxford University Press, 1995.

Junior Book of Authors, The, New York: H. W. Wilson, 1951.

Something About the Author. Detroit: Gale Research, 2001.

Varlow, Sally. *A Reader's Guide to Writers' Britain.* London: Prion, 1996.

Yesterday's Authors of Books for Children. Detroit: Gale Research, 1977.

$\mathcal{I}$ndividual $\mathcal{A}$uthors

Adams, Richard. *The Day Gone By.* New York: Alfred: Alfred A. Knopf, 1990.

Birkin, Andrew. *J. M. Barrie and the Lost Boys.* N.p.: Clarkson N. Potter, 1979.

Blishen, Edward. *Hugh Lofting.* London: The Bodley Head, 1968.

Briggs, Julia. *A Woman of Passion (Edith Nesbit).* New York: New Amsterdam Books, 1987.

Carpenter, Humphrey. *Tolkien.* London: George Allen and Unwin, 1977.

Fraser, Lindsey. *Conversations with J. K. Rowling.* New York: Scholastic, 2000.

Shapiro, Marc. *J. K. Rowling, the Wizard Behind Harry Potter.* New York: St. Martin's Press, 2000.

Travers, P. L. "Where Did She Come From? Why Did She Go?" *Saturday Evening Post* (November 7, 1964).

Wardale, Roger. *In Search of Swallows and Amazons.* Cheshire, UK: Sigma Press, 1996.

Wilson, A. N. *C. S. Lewis, a Biography.* New York: W. W. Norton, 1990.

Specific Areas

Bounds, David. *Rambling for Pleasure: Kennet Valley and Watership Down.* UK: East Berkshire Ramblers' Association, 1999.

Kendall-Price, Claire. *In the Footsteps of the Swallows and Amazons.* UK: Wild Cat Publishing, 1993.

PERMISSIONS

The illustration by Mary Shepard from *Mary Poppins* by P. L. Travers, copyright © 1934, is used by permission of HarperCollins Publishers UK.

Text from *Ring of Bright Water* by Gavin Maxwell (Penguin Books, 1974), copyright © Gavin Maxwell, 1960, is used by permission of Penguin Books Ltd.

Text and illustrations from *The Otter's Tale* by Gavin Maxwell, © The Estate of Gavin Maxwell, 1962, are used with the kind permission of Gavin Maxwell Enterprises Ltd.

Text from *Charlie and the Chocolate Factory* by Roald Dahl, copyright © 1964 by Roald Dahl. Copyright © renewed 1992 by Felicity Dahl, Tessa Dahl, Theo Dahl, Ophelia Dahl, and Lucy Dahl. Copyright assigned to Roald Dahl Nominee Ltd., 1994. Used by permission of Alfred A. Knopf Children's Books, a division of Random House, Inc.

The illustration from *Charlie and the Chocolate Factory* by Roald Dahl, illustrated by Quentin Blake, is used by permission of A. P. Watt Ltd. on behalf of Quentin Blake.

Text from *The Borrowers* by Mary Norton, copyright © 1952, used by permission of Orion Publishing Group, UK.

Illustration by Diana Stanley from *The Borrowers* by Mary Norton copyright © 1952 by J. M. Dent and Sons Ltd.

Text and illustrations from *The Children of Green Knowe* and *A Stranger at Green Knowe* by Lucy Boston, illustrated by Peter Boston, are used by kind permission of Diana Boston.

Text from *The Hobbit* by J. R. R. Tolkien, copyright © 1966 by J. R. R. Tolkien, is reprinted by permission of Houghton Mifflin Company. All rights reserved.

The Magician's Nephew by C. S. Lewis, copyright © C. S. Lewis Pte. Ltd. 1955. *The Lion, the Witch and the Wardrobe* by C. S. Lewis, copyright © C. S. Lewis Pte Ltd. 1950. Illustration by Pauline Baynes copyright © C. S. Lewis Pte. Ltd. Extracts and illustration reprinted by permission.

ＩNDEX

Adams, Elizabeth Acland (wife), 147, 148
Adams, Juliet (daughter), 147
Adams, Richard, 145, 146, 146–48
Adams, Rosamond (daughter), 147
Admirable Crichton, The (Barrie), 5
AE (George Russell), 135
Aiken, Joan, 175
Alice in Wonderland Centre, The (Llandudno, North Wales), 34
Alice's Adventures in Wonderland (Carroll), 7, 23, 27, 30, 32, 33
Alice's Shop (Oxford), 30
Alnwick Castle (Alnwick, Northumberland), 196–97
Altounyan, Dora Collingswood, 254
Altounyan, Ernest, 254
Altounyan, Roger, 258
America
  and James Barrie, 13
  and Michael Bond, 168
  and J. R. R. Tolkien, 60–61, 61
Anthony, C. L. *See* Smith, Dodie
Appin (Scotland), 124
Arthur Ransome and Captain Flint's Trunk (Hardyment), 259
Arthur Ransome Society, 262
As I Walked Out One Midsummer Morning (Lee), 235, 236
Ashdown Forest (East Sussex), 74, 76, 77, 78–79
Atkinson, Eleanor, 213, 214, 214–15
Atkinson, Francis Blake (husband), 215
Auld Jock's grave, 214, 216
Austin, Jane, 191
Australia House (London), 194
Awdry, Christopher (son), 155, 156
Awdry, Margaret Wale (wife), 155
Awdry, Richard (grandson), 156
Awdry, Reverend W. (Wilbert), 153, 154, 154–56, 238

Babe (King-Smith), 70, 218
badger watching, 45–47
Badger Watch Dorset, 45–46
Ballachulish (Scotland), 124
Bank of England, 37
Bank of England Museum, 42–43, 139
Bank Ground Farm (Coniston Water), 254, 256

Barrie, Alexander (brother), 5, 12
Barrie, David (brother), 5
Barrie, James, 3, 4, 4–6, 9–10, 73
Barrie, Mary Ansell (wife), 5
Barry, Edward Middleman, 12
Bath
  and John Cunliffe, 231–32
Bath Postal Museum (Bath), 231–32
Baynes, Pauline, 61
Bear Called Paddington, A (Bond), 163, 164, 165, 166, 168
Beatrix Potter Gallery (Hawkshead, Lake District), 101
Bed-knob and Broomstick (Norton), 89, 91–92
Bedfordshire
  and Mary Norton, 88, 90–91
Bedknobs and Broomsticks (movie), 89, 91
Beesley, Alec (Dodie Smith's husband), 205
Beinecke Rare Book and Manuscript Library (Yale University), 13
Bekonscot Model Village (Beaconsfield, Buckinghamshire), 93–94, 161–62, 248–49
Berkshire
  and Richard Adams, 146–47, 148–49
  and Kenneth Grahame, 38, 39–40
BFG's, the (Dahl), 172, 174, 177, 180
bicycle trips
  the Slad Valley, 239
Big Six, The (Ransome), 255
Binsey (village near Oxford), 29
Birmingham
  and Roald Dahl, 175–76
Birnam (Scotland), 103–4
Blake, Quentin, 174–75
Bland, Hubert (E. Nesbit's 1st husband), 243, 244
Blidworth Church (Nottinghamshire), 113
Blue Fairy Book, The (Lang), 130
Bluebell Railway (East Sussex), 160–61, 246–47
boarding (public) schools, 199–200
  See also Eton College; Rugby School
Bobby's Bothy gift shop (Edinburgh), 216
Bodleian Library (Oxford University), 61 and J. K. Rowling, 194–95
Bolton Gardens (London), 97, 102–3
Bond, Anthony (son), 165
Bond, Brenda Johnson (wife), 165

Bond, Karen (daughter), 165
Bond, Michael, 163, 164, 166, 168
Bonfires and Broomsticks (Norton). *See Bed-knob and Broomstick*
Bonsey, Lionel (Mary Norton's 2nd husband), 89
Borrowers, The (films & televison), 89
Borrowers, The (Norton), 87, 89, 90–91, 92
Borrowers Afield, The (Norton), 89, 90
Borrowers Afloat, The (Norton), 89
Borrowers Aloft, The (Norton), 89
Borrowers Avenged, The (Norton), 89
Boston, Diana (daughter-in-law), 21
Boston, Harold (husband), 221
Boston, Lucy, 20, 219, 220, 221–22
Boston, Peter (son), 222
Boy: Tales of Childhood (Dahl), 172
Boy David, The (Barrie play), 6
Breck, Alan, 124
Brighton
    and Michael Bond, 167–68
British Airways London Eye, 14, 142
British Library (London)
    and Lewis Carroll, 26, 32
    and Kenneth Grahame, 43
    and Hugh Lofting, 68
    and A. A. Milne, 85
    and Mary Norton, 92
Brodie, William, 128
Buckingham Palace, 82–83, 177
Buckinghamshire
    and Roald Dahl, 174, 178–79, 180
Buckinghamshire County Museum (Aylesbury, Buckinghamshire), 178–79
Burnett, Frances Hodgson, 15, 16–19, 249
Burnett, Lionel (son), 17
Burnett, Swan (husband), 17, 18
Burns, Robert, 128

C. S. Lewis Foundation (Redlands, CA), 55
Cadbury chocolate company, 173
Cadbury World (Birmingham), 175–76
Cambridge
    and Lucy Boston, 220, 221, 222, 223–24
camera obscura (Kirriemuir, Scotland), 9–10
Camusfearna (Scotland), 184, 185–86
Carroll, Lewis, 23–27
Castle Combe (Wiltshire), 67–68
Castle Cottage (Sawrey, Lake District), 97, 99, 104
Castle of Yew, The (Boston), 222
Castle Street (Edinburgh), 42
Cedars House (Leighton Buzzard, Bedfordshire), 88, 90–91
Chapel of St. Christopher (Great Ormond Street Hospital), 12
Charlie and the Chocolate Factory (Dahl), 171, 172, 174, 174

Child's Garden of Verses, A (Stevenson), 118, 119, 120, 127
Children of Green Knowe, The (Boston), 219
Children of Green Knowe stories, 20, 219, 222
    See also Boston, Lucy
Chimneys of Green Knowe, The (Boston), 222, 224
Chitty Chitty Bang Bang (movie), 174
Christ Church College, Oxford University, 25, 30
    College Hall, 31
Christopher Robin books, 71, 72, 74, 75, 77
    See also Milne, A. A.
Chronicles of Narnia, The (Lewis), 49, 52, 191
Cider with Rosie (Lee), 233, 234, 235–36
Clan Donald Visitor Centre (Isle of Skye), 125
Clown (Blake), 175
Colinton (Scotland), 129–30
Collingswood, W. G., 253
Colvin, Sidney, 120
Coniston Boating Centre/Coniston Launch, 261
Coniston Water (Lake District), 253, 254, 256, 260–61
Contemporary Authors, 164
Coot Club (Ransome), 255
Cornwall
    and Kenneth Grahame, 43
Costner, Kevin, 110
Cotswolds
    and Laurie Lee, 236–39
Covent Garden (London), 141–42
Coward, Noel, 244
Crufts Dog Show (Birmingham), 208, 217
Cunliffe, John, 228, 228–29
Cunningham, Alison, 119

Dahl, Felicity Ann Crosland (2nd wife), 174, 180
Dahl, Roald, 171, 172, 172–74, 179
Danny the Champion of the World (Dahl), 180
Daresbury (Cheshire), 25, 31–32
Darling, How Could You! (movie), 205
Day Gone By, The (Adams), 147–48
Day-Lewis, Cecil, 51
Day-Lewis, Daniel, 51
de Grummond Collection (U. of Southern Mississippi), 168
de Havilland, Olivia, 110
de Vries, Richard, 110
Diana, Princess, 4, 7, 13–14
Diana, Princess of Wales Memorial Playground (Kensington Gardens)
Dickens, Charles, 27
Dictionary of Literary Biography, 88
Disney Studios, 75, 76, 89, 134, 136, 139, 204
Doctor Dolittle (movie), 64, 67
Doctor Dolittle books, 63, 66
    See also Lofting, Hugh
Doctor Dolittle's Return (Lofting), 66 Dodgson, Charles. *See* Carroll, Lewis

"Dormouse and the Doctor, The" (Milne), 74
Douglas, Lord Alfred, 253
Dream Days (Grahame), 37
Drink of Water, A (Yeoman), 175
Duckworth, Robinson, 26

Eagle & Child Pub (Oxford), 57, 59–60
East Sussex
   and A. A. Milne, 78–81, 83–84
Ecchinswell (Hampshire), 149–50
Edgar Allan Poe (Ransome), 253
Edge of Day, The: A Boyhood in the West of England
   (*Cider with Rosie*) (Lee), 233, 234, 235–36
Edinburgh
   and Eleanor Atkinson, 213, 214, 215–16
   and James Barrie, 12–13
   and Kenneth Grahame, 36–37, 42
   and J. K. Rowling, 192, 197
   and Robert Louis Stevenson, 118–19, 120,
     122–23, 127–28, 130–31
Edinburgh, University of, 5
Edinburgh Castle, 213
Edinburgh Zoo, 69, 123
   Penguin Parade, 140
"Edward's Day Out," 155
Edwinstowe (Nottinghamshire), 113
Eilean Ban (Isle of Skye, Scotland), 184, 187
Enchanted Castle, The (Nesbit), 244
Enchanted Places, The (C. R. Milne), 75, 76
Enemy at Green Knowe, An (Boston), 222
English Teddy Bear Company (Piccadilly,
   London), 169
English Literature in the Sixteenth Century (Lewis),
   52
Eton College (Eton, Berkshire), 200
Everything a Lady Should Know, 135

Fairy Caravan, The (Potter), 99
Fairyland Trust, 21–22
Falls of Clyde Wildlife Reserve (New Lanark,
   Scotland), 46
Fantastic Mr. Fox (Dahl), 172, 174
Farmer Barnes Buys a Pig (Cunliffe), 229
Fern, Jim, 238
Firth of Forth (Scotland), boat trips, 130–31
Five Children and It, The (Nesbit), 244
Flynn, Errol, 110
Forester, C. S., 173
Foresters, The (Tennyson), 110, 115
Fort William (Scotland), 130
Fortnum, Peggy, 168

Gill's Gap/Galleon's Lap (Ashdown Forest),
   80–81
Gipsy House (Great Missenden,
   Buckinghamshire), 174, 180
Glamis Castle (Scotland), 10

Glasgow
   and James Barrie, 5, 12
Glasgow Academy (Glasgow, Scotland), 12
Glencoe (Scotland), 124
Glenelg (Scotland), 186–87
Gloucester Cathedral (Gloucester), 102, 196
   and J. K. Rowling, 196
Goff, Helen Lyndon. *See* Travers, P. L
Goff, Margaret (P. L. Travers's mother), 134, 135
Goff, Travers (P. L. Travers's father), 134, 135
Gogarth Abbey Hotel (Llandudno, North Wales),
   34
Going Solo (Dahl), 173
Golden Age, The (Grahame), 37
Gondola steam yacht (Coniston Water), 257
Goodman, John, 89
Gracewell Lane (Sarehole, Birmingham), 58–59
Grahame, Alistair "Mouse" (son), 38
Grahame, Bessie (mother), 36–37
Grahame, Elspeth Thomson (wife), 38
Grahame, Kenneth, 35, 36–38, 39, 74–75
Great Maytham Hall (Rolvenden, Kent), 18,
   19–20
Great Northern (Ransome), 254
Great Ormond Street Hospital for Children
   (London), 6, 11–12
Greenbank Hotel (Falmouth, Cornwall), 43
Gremlins (Dahl), 173
Gresham, Joy, 52
Greyfriars Bobby, 214
Greyfriars Bobby (Atkinson), 213, 214, 215
Greyfriars Bobby's Bar (Edinburgh), 216
Greyfriars Bobby's statue (Edinburgh), 215–16
Greyfriars Kirkyard (Edinburgh), 216
Grimm's Fairy Tales, 7
Guide to the Steam Railways of Great Britain, A
   (Awdry/Cook), 159–60
Gurdjieff, Georges, 135
Guy (gorilla), 224–25

Halstead Hall (Kent), 243, 245
Hampshire
   and Richard Adams, 148–49, 149–51
Hampton Court Palace (Surrey), 199
Hardy, Thomas, 12, 234
Hardyment, Christina, 259
Hargreaves, Reginald, 26
Harpoon Venture (Maxwell), 183
Harrison, Rex, 67
Harry Potter and the Chamber of Secrets
   (Rowling), 192
Harry Potter and the Goblet of Fire (Rowling), 192,
   198
Harry Potter and the Philosopher's Stone (British
   title) (Rowling), 192
Harry Potter and the Prisoner of Azkaban
   (Rowling), 192

Harry Potter and the Sorcerer's Stone (American title) (Rowling), 192

Harry Potter and the Sorcerer's Stone (movie), 193, 194

Hartfield (East Sussex), 74, 75, 83–84

Haunted Man, The (Dickens), 27

Hawes Inn (South Queensferry, Scotland), 122–23

Hawkshead (Lake District), 100–101

Haworth (Yorkshire), 245–46

hedge mazes, 198–99, 208–9

Heelis, William (Beatrix Potter's husband), 97, 99

Hemingford Grey Manor House (Cambridge), 21, 220, 221, 222, 223–24

Henry Stephen–C. S. Lewis Nature Reserve (Oxford), 54

hikes and rambles
  Hampshire, 149
  Lake District, 262
  Pentland Hills, 131

Hill Top Farm (Sawrey, Lake District), 97–98, 99–100

Hoatson, Alice, 243

Hoatson, John (son), 243

Hoatson, Rosamund (daughter), 243

Hoban, Russell, 175

Hobbit, The (Tolkien), 49, 57–58, 60, 61

Hogwarts Express (Severn Valley Railway), 195

Holy Trinity Church (Oxford), 55

Hopkins, Anthony, 52

Horn Book magazine, 96

House at Pooh Corner, The (Milne), 71, 72, 74, 80

House of the Tailor of Gloucester (Gloucester), 101–2

Hunny Pot (Ayr, Scotland), 85–86

Huntly House Museum (Royal Mile, Edinburgh), 216–17

Hyde Park (London), 4, 6, 7–8, 9

Hyde Park Corner, 177

I Capture the Castle (Smith), 205

In Search of Swallows and Amazons (Wardale), 259

In the Footsteps of the Swallows and Amazons (Kendall-Price, Clair), 262

Isis River (Oxford), 26, 28–29 28–29 See also Thames River

It's Too Late Now (A. A. Milne), 74

James and the Giant Peach (Dahl), 172, 174, 174

James and the Giant Peach (movie), 174

James of the Glens, 124

James the Red Engine (Awdry), 155

Jeffries, Lionel, 245

John Ritblat Gallery (British Library), 33

Johnny Appleseed (Atkinson), 215

Jorvik Viking Centre (York), 225

Junior Book of Authors, The, 64

Keighley & Worth Valley Railway (West Yorkshire), 160, 245–46

Kendal (Lake District, Cumbria), 229, 232

Kensington Gardens (London), 4, 5–6, 6, 7–8, 13–14

Kent
  and Frances Hodgson Burnett, 18–19, 19–20
  and E. Nesbit, 243, 244, 245, 247
  and Dodie Smith, 208–9

Kent & East Sussex Railway, 22, 161, 249–50

Kentmere (Lake District, Cumbria), 229–30

Kidnapped (Stevenson), 117, 118, 120, 122–26

Kilns, The (Lewis Close, Oxford), 51, 52, 54–55

King-Smith, Dick, 70

Kings Cross Station (London), 193–94

Kipling, Rudyard, 93

Kirriemuir (Fife, Scotland), 4, 5, 6, 9–11

Kite Store (London), 140–41

Kylerhea Otter Haven (Isle of Skye, Scotland), 188

Lady Stair's House/Writers' Museum (Edinburgh), 128

Lake District
  and John Cunliffe, 229–30
  and Beatrix Potter, 96, 97–98, 98–101, 104, 106–7
  and Arthur Ransome, 252, 253, 255–59

Lake Windermere ferry ride, 106

Lang, Andrew, 130

Lansbury, Angela, 89

Lee, Catherine Polge (wife), 235

Lee, Jessye (daughter), 235

Lee, Laurie, 233, 234, 234–36

Leeds Castle (Maidstone, Kent), 198, 208–9

Leighton Buzzard (Bedfordshire), 88, 90–91

Leinster Terrace and Bayswater Road (London), 11

Lewis, C. S. (Clive Staples), 36, 49, 50–53
  friendship with Tolkien, 50, 52, 54, 57, 59–60

Lewis, Warren (brother), 50, 51, 54

Liddell, Alice, 25–26, 30, 33

Liddell, Edith (sister), 26, 30

Liddell, Lorina (sister), 26

Lion, the Witch and the Wardrobe, The (Lewis), 49

Little Lord Fauntleroy (Burnett), 17–18

Little Lord Fauntleroy (various movies), 17–18

Little Princess, A (Burnett), 18

Little White Bird, The (Barrie), 7

Llewelyn Davies, Sir Arthur, 5, 6

Llewelyn Davies, George (son), 5, 6

Llewelyn Davies, Jack (son), 5, 6

Llewelyn Davies, Michael (son), 5, 6, 9

Llewelyn Davies, Nico (son), 5, 6

Llewelyn Davies, Peter (son), 5, 6

Llewelyn Davies, Sylvia, 5, 6

Loch Linnhe (Scotland), boat trips, 130
Lofting, Colin (son), 65, 66
Lofting, Elizabeth (daughter), 65, 66
Lofting, Flora Small (1st wife), 65
Lofting, Hugh, 63, 64, 64–66, 146
Lofting, Josephine Fricker (2nd wife), 65
London
    and the Reverend W. Awdry, 159–61
    and James Barrie, 4, 6–7, 7–9, 11–13, 13–14
    and Michael Bond, 166–67
    and Lucy Boston, 224–25
    and John Cunliffe, 230–31
    and Kenneth Grahame, 42, 43
    and A. A. Milne, 72, 81–83, 84–85
    and Mary Norton, 91–92
    and Beatrix Potter, 97, 102–3
    and J. K. Rowling, 193–94
    and Dodie Smith, 206–7
    and P. L. Travers, 137–42
London Zoo, 69
    and Lucy Boston, 224–25
    and A. A. Milne, 72, 81–82
    and P. L. Travers, 137–38
London's Transport Museum, 162
Longsleddale (Lake District, Cumbria), 229–30
Look Back with Astonishment (Smith), 206
Look Back with Gratitude (Smith), 206
Look Back with Love (Smith), 206
Look Back with Mixed Feelings (Smith), 206
Lord of the Rings (Tolkien), 50, 57, 58, 60, 61
Lutyens, Sir Edwin, 93
"Lytell Geste of Robyn Hode," 110

Magdalen College (Oxford University), 55
Magic Bed-Knob, The. See Bed-knob and Broomstick
Magic Finger, The (Dahl), 172, 174
Magician's Nephew, The (Lewis), 53
Maid Marian (Peacock), 110
Mallord Street (Chelsea, London), 74, 84
Manor House (Hemingford Grey,
    Cambridgeshire), 20–21
Mapledurham House (Berkshire), 40–41
Margaret (child friend of Barrie), 8
Marion E. Wade Center, Wheaton College
    (Wheaton, IL), 61
Mary Poppins (movie), 134, 136
Mary Poppins (Travers), 84, 133, 134, 135–36
Mary Poppins and the House Next Door (Travers), 136
Mary Poppins Comes Back (Travers), 136
Mary Poppins in Cherry Tree Lane (Travers), 136
Mary Poppins in the Park (Travers), 136
Mary Poppins Opens the Door (Travers), 136
Mary Rose (Barrie), 5
Matilda (Dahl), 172, 174, 174
Maugham, Somerset, 93
Maxwell, Gavin, 181, 182, 182–84
mazes, 198–99, 208–9

Memorial Library, Marquette University
    (Milwaukee, WI), 60–61
Memory in a House (Boston), 222
Merry Adventures of Robin Hood, The (Pyle), 109
Midnight Kitten, The (Smith), 205
Milne, A. A. (Alan Alexander), 36, 38, 71, 72,
    73–75
Milne, Christopher Robin (son), 72, 73, 75–76,
    77
Milne, Clare (granddaughter), 76
Milne, Daphne de Selincourt (wife), 73–74, 75,
    76
Milne, Ken (brother), 73
Milne, Lesley de Selincourt, (Christopher Robin's
    wife), 76
Milne House (Mallord Street Chelsea, London),
    84
Mitford, Jessica, 191
Moment of War, A (Lee), 236
Moore, Janie, 51, 52, 54
Morgan, Fr. Francis Xavier, 56, 57
Mount Pleasant Sorting Office and Postal
    Railway (London), 230–31
Mr. Pim Passes By (A. A. Milne), 74
Murray, Neil (J. K. Rowling's husband), 193
Museum in the Park (Stroud, Gloucestershire),
    159, 238–39
Museum of Childhood (Royal Mile, Edinburgh),
    131
Museum of Lakeland Life (Abbot Hall, Kendal),
    232, 260
My School Days (Nesbit), 242

Narnia books, 52
    See also Chronicles of Narnia, The
National Birds of Prey Centre (Newent,
    Gloucestershire), 201
National Museum of the Performing Arts
    (London), 47
National Railway Museum (York), 157–58,
    247–48
Natural History Museum (London), 97, 103
Neal, Patricia (Roald Dahl's 1st wife), 173–74
Nerli, Pier, 130
Nesbit, E. (Edith Nesbit Bland), 18, 161, 191,
    214, 242, 242–44, 247, 247–48
New Forest Badger Watch, 45
New Treasure Seekers (Nesbit), 243
Newbury (Berkshire), 146
Newtown Churchyard (Hampshire), 149–50
Nibthwaite (Coniston Water), 257
Nicolson's Café (Edinburgh), 192, 197
Norton, Mary (Pearson), 87, 88, 88–89
Norton, Robert (1st husband), 89
Norwegian Church (Cardiff Bay, Wales), 172
Norwegian Church Arts Centre (Cardiff, Wales),
    179

Nottingham Castle (Nottingham), 110, 111–12
Nottinghamshire
   and Robin Hood, 110, 111–13, 114
Now We Are Six (Milne), 72, 74
Nuthanger Farm Area (Hampshire), 149–50

Olga Da Polga books, 165
   See also Bond, Michael
On the Trail of Robin Hood (de Vries), 110
"100 Aker Wood" (Ashdown Forest), 78, 81
101 Dalmatians, The (various movies), 204, 205
101 Dalmatians, The (Smith), 203, 204, 205
102 Dalmatians (movie), 204
Oscar Wilde (Ransome), 253
Otter's Tale, The (Maxwell), 181, 182, 184
Outlaw magazine, 262
Overton/river area (Hampshire), 151
Owen, Robert, 46
Owl Centre, Muncaster Castle (Cumbria, Lake
   District), 200–201
Oxford
   and Lewis Carroll, 23–27, 28–29
   and C. S. Lewis, 54–55
   and J. K. Rowling, 194–95
   and J. R. R. Tolkien, 57–58, 59–60, 61
Oxford Tourist Information Centre, 60
Oxford University, 59
   Bodleian Library, 61, 194–95
   Christ Church College, 25, 30, 31
   Magdalen College, 55

Paddington and Friends Shop (Bath, Somerset),
   169
Paddington at Work (Bond), 168
Paddington Bear stories, 163, 164, 166, 168
   See also Bond, Michael
Paddington Station (London), 166
Pagan Papers (Grahame), 37
Pangbourne (Berkshire), 38, 39–40
Parabola magazine, 136
Parrish, Maxfield, 37
Path Through the Tree, The (C. R. Milne), 76
Patricia Neal Therapy Extension Program, 174
Peacock, Thomas Love, 110
Peak District (Rowsley, Derbyshire), 44–45
Peel Island (Coniston Water), 256–57
Pentland Hills (Scotland), 129, 131
Pentland Rising (Stevenson), 129
Perch pub (Binsey), 29
Persephone (Boston), 222
*Perverse and Foolish: A Memoir of Childhood and
   Youth* (Boston), 222
Pet Rescue (TV show), 70
Peter and Wendy (Barrie book), 6
Peter Duck (Ransome), 254
Peter Pan in Kensington Gardens (Barrie book), 6,
   7, 7–8, 8

Peter Pan or the Boy Who Would Not Grow Up
   (Barrie book), 6
Peter Pan or the Boy Who Would Not Grow Up
   (Barrie play), 3, 6–14
Peter Pan statue (Hyde Park), 4, 6, 7–8, 9
Phillimore Place (London), 42
Phoenix and the Carpet, The (Nesbit), 244
Pigeon Post (Ransome), 254
Pittsburgh Press, 146
Plague Dogs, The (Adams), 147–48
Pooh Corner (Hartfield, East Sussex), 83–84
Poohsticks Bridge (Ashdown Forest), 79–80
Poor Stainless (Norton), 89
Porthos (Barrie's Saint Bernard dog), 5
Portobello Market (London), 91–92, 166–67
Postman Pat (TV series), 228, 229
Postman Pat and the Mystery Thief (Cunliffe), 229
Postman Pat Goes to Town (Cunliffe), 229
Postman Pat stories, 228
   See also Cunliffe, John
Potter, Beatrix, 95, 96, 96–98, 99, 107, 258
Primrose Hill (London), 138–39, 206
Punch magazine, 27, 73, 77–78, 175
Pyle, Howard, 109, 110

Queen Mary's Doll House (Windsor Castle,
   Berkshire), 93

Rabbit World (Amesbury, Wiltshire), 107–8,
   151–52
Rackham, Arthur, 7, 8, 38
Railway Children, The (movie & TV versions),
   245 , 246
Railway Children, The (Nesbit), 161, 241, 241,
   242, 244, 245, 247–48
*Rambling for Pleasure: Kennet Valley & Watership
   Down* (guidebook), 149, 150
Rannoch Moor (Scotland), 125–26
Ransome, Arthur, 32, 251, 252, 252–55
Ransome, Evgenia (2nd wife), 254, 255
Ransome, Ivy Walker (1st wife), 253, 254
Ransome, Tabitha (daughter), 253
Raven Seek Thy Brother (Maxwell), 183
Red Fairy Book, The (Lang), 130
Regent's Park (London), 137, 206–7
"Reluctant Dragon, The" (Grahame), 37
Ring of Bright Water (Maxwell), 181, 182,
   183–84, 185
Ring of Bright Water (movie), 184
River at Green Knowe, The (Boston), 222, 224
river Crake (Coniston Water), 257
river Isis (Oxford), 26, 28–29
   See also river Thames
river Thames, 39, 47
Robert the Bruce, 36
Roberts, Cecil, 66
Robin Hood (movie), 110

Robin Hood, Price of Thieves (movie), 110
Robin Hood legend, 109–15
Rocks Remain, The (Maxwell), 183
Roosevelt, Eleanor, 173
Roosevelt, Theodore, 37
Rosen, Martin, 147
Rothschild, Walter, 68–69
Rowling, Di (sister), 190, 192
Rowling, J. K. (Joanne Kathleen), 36, 190, 190–93
Rowling, Jessica (daughter), 191–92, 193
Royal Pavilion (Brighton), 168
Rugby School (Rugby, Warwickshire), 25, 32–33, 199–200, 253, 261
Ruskin Museum (Coniston), 260–61
Russell, George (AE), 135

St. Giles Cathedral (Edinburgh), 128
St. James Park (London), 207
St. Mary-in-the-March (Kent), 244, 247
St. Paul's Cathedral (London), 139–40
Salon magazine, 190, 193
Sandleford Park (Newbury, Berkshire), 149
Sara Crewe, or, What Happened at Miss Minchin's (Burnett), 18
Sarehole (Birmingham), 56, 58–59
Saturday Evening Post, 134, 136, 173
Sawrey (Lake District), 97, 99
Scarlet, Will, 113
School Library Journal, 192
"Scot Abroad, The" (Stevenson), 118
Scotland
    and Eleanor Atkinson, 213, 214, 215–16
    and James Barrie, 4–6, 9–11, 12–13
    and Kenneth Grahame, 42
    and Gavin Maxwell, 184, 185–88
    and Beatrix Potter, 97, 103–4
    and J. K. Rowling, 192, 197
    and Robert Louis Stevenson, 118–19, 120, 122–23, 125–31
    See also Edinburgh
Scott, Robert, 10
Scott, Sir Walter, 128
Scottish National Portrait Gallery (Edinburgh), 12–13, 130
Screwtape Letters, The (Lewis), 52
Sea Egg, The (Boston), 222
Secret Garden, The (Burnett), 15, 16, 18, 249–50
    various movie an stage incarnations of, 17–18, 18–19
Selznick, David O., 17–18
Seuss, Dr., 175
17 Heriot Row (Edinburgh), 119, 127
Severn Valley Railway, 195
Shadowlands (movie), 52
Shardik (Adams), 147
Shaw, George Bernard, 12, 243

sheepdog demonstrations (Kincraug, Scotland), 69–70, 218
Shepard, E. H. (Ernest Howard), 36, 38, 39, 74, 76–78, 80, 85, 207
Shepard, Florence Chaplin (wife), 77
Shepard, Graham (son), 77
Shepard, Mary (daughter), 77, 84, 136, 207
Shepard House (Regent's Park, London), 84
Sherwood Forest (Nottinghamshire), 112–13
Sitwell, Mrs. Frances, 119–20
Slad (Gloucestershire), 235, 236–37, 237, 238
Smith, Dodie (Dorothy Gladys), 203, 204, 204–6
Snowdonia National Park (Wales), 159
Something About the Author, 204
South Yorkshire
    and E. Nesbit, 245–46
Stanley, Diana, 92
Starlight Barking, The (Smith), 205
Stephen, Henry, 54
Stepney the "Bluebell" Engine (Awdry), 160
Stevenson, Frances "Fanny" (wife), 120–21
Stevenson, Robert Louis, 37, 42, 117, 118, 118–21, 128
Stirling (Scotland), 126
Stones of Green Knowe, The (Boston), 222, 225
Story of Doctor Dolittle, The (Lofting), 63, 66, 68, 146
Story of the Amulet, The (Nesbit), 244
Story of the Treasure Seekers, The (Nesbit), 243
Strange Case of Dr. Jekyll and Mr. Hyde, The (Stevenson), 120, 128
Stranger at Green Knowe, A (Boston), 222, 224
Strongholds (Boston), 222
Strupag Café (Glenelg, Scotland), 186–87
Surprised by Joy (Lewis), 52
Swallowdale (Ransome), 254
Swallows and Amazons (BBC movie), 258
Swallows and Amazons (Ransome), 251, 252, 254–55, 255, 258
Swanston (Scotland), 119, 129, 131

Tailor of Gloucester, The (Potter), 101–2
Tale of Jemima Puddle-Duck, The (Potter), 95, 97
Tale of Johnny Town-Mouse, The (Potter), 100
Tale of Mr. Jeremy Fisher, The (Potter), 101
Tale of Mr. Tod, The (Potter), 101
Tale of Peter Rabbit, The (Potter), 95, 97, 99, 102, 104
Tale of Pie and the Patty Pan, The (Potter), 99, 101
Tale of Pigling Bland, The (Potter), 101
Tale of Samuel Whiskers, The (Potter), 97, 100
Tale of Tom Kitten, The (Potter), 97, 99, 100
Tales of Robin Hood Attraction, The (Nottingham), 114–15
Talyllyn Railway (Tywyn, Wales), 156, 158–59

Tenniel, Sir John, 26, 27, 30, 32
Tennyson, Alfred Lord, 110, 115
Thames River, 39, 47
    See also Isis River
Theater Museum (London), 47
Thomas the Tank Engine (Awdry), 153, 154, 155–56
Three Railways Engines, The (Awdry), 155
Through the Looking-Glass (Carroll), 25–27
Time Is Undone (Boston), 222
Toad of Toad Hall (Grahame/A. A. Milne), 74–75
Toad Hall, 40–41
Tolkien, Arthur (father), 56
Tolkien, Edith Bratt (wife), 56–57, 58
Tolkien, Hilary (brother), 56
Tolkien, J. R. R. (John Ronald Reuel), 49, 56–58
    friendship with Lewis, 50, 52, 54, 57, 59–60
Tolkien, John (son), 57
Tolkien, Mabel (mother), 56
Tolkien, Roland (brother), 56
Townsend, Stephen, 18
Trafalgar Square (London), 141
Travers, P. L. (Pamela Lyndon), 133, 134, 134–36
Treacle Well (Binsey), 29
Treasure Island (Stevenson), 120
Treasure of Green Knowe, The. See Chimneys of Green Knowe, The
Trotters & Friends Animal Farm (Lake District), 107
Troutbeck Park Farm (Lake District), 104
Truman, Harry, 173
Tucker, Thomas Terry (E. Nesbit's 2nd husband), 244
20 Northmoor Road (Oxford), 60
Twits, The (Dahl), 172

Uninvited, The (movie), 205

Vailima (Stevenson estate, Samoa), 121
"Vespers" (A. A. Milne), 74, 75
Vicar of Nibbleswicke, The (Dahl), 174
Victoria, Queen, 7, 9
Victoria and Albert Museum (London), 105
Voyages of Doctor Dolittle, The (Lofting), 66

Wales
    and the Reverend W. Awdry, 156, 158–59
    and Lewis Carroll, 34
    and Roald Dahl, 172–73, 179
Walter Rothschild Zoological Museum (Tring, Hertfordshire), 68–69
Wardale, Roger, 259

Watership Down (Adams), 145, 147, 149, 150, 151
Watership Down (film and TV versions), 147
Watership Down (Hampshire), 146, 150
Weber, Andrew Lloyd, 149
Wells, H. G., 243
"Wendy" as a name, 8
West Highland Line (Scotland), 125–26
What the Bee Knows: Reflections on Myth, Symbol & Story (Travers), 136
When We Were Very Young (A. A. Milne), 72, 74, 77, 82, 82–83
Whitchurch Bridge (Pangbourne, Berkshire), 40
Wilde, Oscar, 12
Willie Wonka and the Chocolate Factory (Dahl), 173
Wiltshire
    and Hugh Lofting, 67–68
Wind in the Willows, The (Grahame), 7, 35, 36, 38, 39, 40, 74–75, 77, 190–91
Wind in the Willows Attraction, The (Rowsley, Derbyshire), 44–45
Windermere Lake Cruses (Bowness harbor), 259
Windermere Steamboat Centre (Windermere), 106–7, 258–59
Windsor Castle (Windsor, Berkshire), 93
Winger, Debra, 52
Winnie (bear cub), 81–82
Winnie-the-Pooh (A. A. Milne), 72, 74, 85
Winnie-the-Pooh books, 71, 72, 74, 75, 85
    See also Milne, A. A.
Witches, The (Dahl), 172
Witches, The (movie), 173
Wonderful Garden, The (Burnett). *See Secret Garden, The*
Wonderful Garden, The (Nesbit), 249
Woolpack Inn (Slad, Gloucestershire), 237
World of Beatrix Potter™ Attraction, The (Crag Brow, Bowness-on-Windermere), 106
Wouldbegoods, The (Nesbit), 243
Wovercote (Oxford), 58
Wovercote Cemetery, 60
Wren, Sir Christopher, 30

Yeoman, John, 175
Yew Hall (Boston), 222
Yorkshire
    and the Reverend W. Awdry, 157–58
    and Robin Hood, 113–14
You Only Live Twice (movie), 174
Young Book Trust (London)
    and Mary Norton, 92
    and Beatrix Potter, 105

Zagazoo (Blake), 175
Zwerger, Lisbeth, 30